From Jobs to Careers

SOUTH ASIA DEVELOPMENT FORUM

From Jobs to Careers

Apparel Exports and Career Paths for Women in Developing Countries

STACEY FREDERICK, GLADYS LOPEZ-ACEVEDO, RAYMOND ROBERTSON, AND MEXICO A. VERGARA BAHENA

1818 H Street NW, Washington, DC 20433
Telephone: 202-473-1000; Internet: www.worldbank.org

1 2 3 4 24 23 22 21

ISBN (paper): 978-1-4648-1803-5
ISBN (electronic): 978-1-4648-1804-2
DOI: 10.1596/978-1-4648-1803-5

Cover illustration and design: Alejandro Espinosa, Sonideas. Further permission required for reuse.

Library of Congress Control Number: 2021922094

South Asia Development Forum

Home to a fifth of humankind, and to almost half of the people living in poverty, South Asia is also a region of marked contrasts: from conflict-affected areas to vibrant democracies, from demographic bulges to aging societies, from energy crises to global companies. This series explores the challenges faced by a region whose fate is critical to the success of global development in the early 21st century, and that can also make a difference for global peace. The volumes in it organize in an accessible way findings from recent research and lessons of experience, across a range of development topics. The series is intended to present new ideas and to stimulate debate among practitioners, researchers, and all those interested in public policies. In doing so, it exposes the options faced by decision-makers in the region and highlights the enormous potential of this fast-changing part of the world.

Contents

Boxes

Figures

Acknowledgments

The preparation of this report was led by Stacey Frederick (director, Duke Global Value Chains Center); Gladys Lopez-Acevedo (lead economist, Poverty and Equity Global Practice, World Bank); Raymond Robertson (Helen and Roy Ryu Chair in Economics and Government, Texas A&M University); and Mexico A. Vergara Bahena (consultant, Middle East and North Africa Region [MENA], World Bank). Team members included Deeksha Kokas (consultant, MENA, World Bank); Jaime Roche Rodríguez (consultant, MENA); and Abdel Ra (intern, Texas A&M University). The team is grateful to Laura Wallace for the skillful editing of the report and to Mary Anderson for thorough copyediting. The peer reviewers for the report were Maurizio Bussolo (lead economist, World Bank Office of the Chief Economist, South Asia Region [SARCE]) and Maria Eugenia Genoni (senior economist, Poverty and Equity Global Practice, World Bank). The work greatly benefited from the guidance and encouragement of Hans Timmer (chief economist, SARCE) and economists Maurizio Bussolo and Nayantara Sarma (East South Asia Poverty and Equity [ESAPV]).

Funding by the World Bank's Trust Fund for South Asia Regional Integration (TF0B0701) and UKAid's Program for Asia Connectivity and Trade (TF0B5220); administrative support by Neelam Chowdhry (program assistant, SARCE); and production support by Mark McClure (publishing associate) are gratefully acknowledged. The cover illustration for this report was conceptualized and executed by Alejandro Espinosa (https://sonideas.com/).

About the Authors

Stacey Frederick is the director and a research scientist at the Duke Global Value Chains Center. Her research uses global value chain (GVC) analysis to identify economic, social, and environmental upgrading opportunities for countries and firms in a variety of industries, including textiles and apparel; electronics, digital, and information and communication technology; medical and pharmaceutical; automotive; and several other manufacturing and technology-based sectors. She has used the GVC analysis framework to analyze issues ranging from employment generation to trade policy impacts for global organizations, including the World Bank, the International Labour Organization, the UN Statistics Division, and the United Nations Industrial Development Organization (UNIDO); regional organizations, including the Islamic Development Bank and the Inter-American Development Bank; and the national governments of Bahrain, Costa Rica, the Republic of Korea, Nicaragua, the Philippines, and the United States. One of her primary interests is developing new research methods that combine qualitative and quantitative approaches to evaluate country and firm participation in GVCs. She holds a bachelor's degree in textile management and a doctorate in textile technology management from North Carolina State University.

Gladys Lopez-Acevedo is a lead economist and a program lead in the World Bank's Poverty and Equity Global Practice, working primarily in the Middle East and North Africa Region. Her areas of analytical and operational interest include trade, welfare, gender, conflict, and jobs. Previously, she was a lead economist in the World Bank Office of the Chief Economist, South Asia Region (SARCE), and a senior economist in the Poverty Reduction and Economic Management (PREM) unit of the Central Vice Presidency, as well as in the Latin America and the Caribbean Region. She is a research fellow at the Institute of Labor Economics, the Mexican National Research System, and the Economic Research Forum. Before joining the World Bank, she held high-level positions in the government of Mexico and was a professor at the

Instituto Tecnológico Autónomo de México (ITAM). She holds a bachelor's degree in economics from ITAM and a doctorate in economics from the University of Virginia.

Raymond Robertson is the Helen and Roy Ryu Chair in Economics and Government in the Department of International Affairs, Bush School of Government and Public Service, Texas A&M University. He also serves as the director of the Mosbacher Institute for Trade, Economics, and Public Policy at Texas A&M University. He is a research fellow at the Institute of Labor Economics in Bonn and a senior research fellow at the Mission Foods Texas-Mexico Center at Southern Methodist University. He has taught at Syracuse University and the Monterrey Institute of Technology's Mexico City campus. Widely published in the field of labor economics and international economics, he previously chaired the US Department of Labor's National Advisory Committee for Labor Provisions of US Free Trade Agreements; he served on both the State Department's Advisory Committee on International Economic Policy and the Center for Global Development's Advisory Board. He holds a doctorate in economics from the University of Texas at Austin.

Mexico A. Vergara Bahena is a consultant in the World Bank's Poverty and Equity Global Practice. He has been working on female labor participation and distributional effects of trade in the Middle East and North Africa and South Asia Regions. Previously, he worked as an economist in the Bank of Mexico's International Economy Division. He holds bachelor's degrees in economics and political science, as well as a master's degree in applied economics from the ITAM.

Overview

Key Messages

- Apparel exporting creates many jobs—which tend to be more formal and higher paying than other opportunities available to women with less than secondary education—but few careers.
- Lower-middle-income countries must address three barriers to expand female career opportunities: (a) low demand for career-related occupations in the service sector due to insufficient national income (low gross domestic product per capita); (b) low education levels; and (c) societal and cultural norms that inhibit or dissuade women from working.
- Low- and middle-income countries can help women transition from jobs to careers by using the apparel industry as an indirect launching pad to overcome the fixed costs of introducing more women into the labor markets.
- But this strategy will only work if countries also adopt complementary policies to boost human capital as well as labor market and family policies that define a gender-equal structure of work.

Why Jobs versus Careers?

By now, it is well established that bringing more women into the formal labor force is critical for economic development. Yet 60 percent of women in low- and middle-income countries (LMICs) remain in the informal sector (ILO 2018), lacking basic social protection largely because of exclusion from the legal and contractual protections that formal workers enjoy. Moreover, as the COVID-19 (coronavirus) pandemic continues to unfold, informal workers are especially vulnerable to job loss, increased poverty, and greater food insecurity—all of which can exacerbate social tensions and undercut progress for women and girls on economic and social fronts.

As a result of the COVID-19 outbreak and the response to its rapid spread, women have experienced significant added burdens on their time owing to their multiple care responsibilities, such as being largely responsible for informal household care (De Paz et al. 2020). Further, school closures may lead many girls—who are already under pressure to drop out—to never resume their education. A 2015 United Nations Development Group (UNDG) report notes that this often occurred after the 2014–16 Ebola crisis in West Africa, widening the gender gaps in access to education (UNDG–Western and Central Africa 2015). Also worrisome is that the combination of lower family incomes and the inadequate safety nets may force households to engage in negative coping mechanisms, such as lower food consumption by girls and women or early marriage.

One strategy often cited for turning this situation around is to further integrate LMICs into global trade, particularly global value chains (GVCs). International trade can contribute to female labor market outcomes through the (a) expansion of female-intensive industries; (b) establishment of exporting firms that tend to employ more women and pay higher wages; and (c) introduction of innovations, such as new digital platforms, that help women expand entrepreneurial skills and develop the flexibility to manage both work and household responsibilities (World Bank and WTO 2020).

CAN AN APPAREL-LED EXPORT STRATEGY BOOST WOMEN'S CAREERS?

A big question, frequently debated, is whether the apparel industry—the most female-intensive and globally engaged of manufacturing industries—can be a key player in this regard. In recent decades, the apparel industry has shifted its production to low-wage LMICs, in turn increasing the demand for women, closing male-female wage gaps, and bringing women into the formal labor force from agricultural and informal work (Artuc et al. 2019; Lopez-Acevedo and Robertson 2012). Indeed, the benefits of apparel exports have reached the female population, but is an apparel-led export strategy sufficient to induce women's transitions from jobs to careers?

Here, we should note that "jobs" are most often considered to be remunerated activities that people do to survive. They often require relatively little education and training and provide the income necessary to maintain a given standard of living irrespective of inherent satisfaction. In contrast, "careers" are remunerated activities associated with a long-run view of labor market experience and identity. As such, they often are associated with occupations that require time investments (such as in education), entail a long-term commitment to the labor market, and include advancement opportunities. Although jobs and careers are not synonymous with occupation, jobs tend to be associated with low-skill occupations and careers with high-skill occupations (HSOs).

Moreover, between the extremes of working because they have to and because they want to, people also experience a transition in which their employment, whether because of wages or skills, provides a greater sense of self-worth from being able to contribute to the family, the workplace, or society. There is a significant shift in mindset within the home regarding a woman's contribution to work outside the household. Both jobs and careers represent different manifestations of women's economic and social empowerment because they represent distinct emancipatory benefits and decision-making power.

This report contributes to the apparel and female empowerment debate by asking, How does exporting apparel contribute to the jobs-to-careers transition? And is an apparel-led export strategy sufficient to induce this transition? It focuses on seven countries where the apparel industry plays an important role in their export baskets: Bangladesh, Cambodia, the Arab Republic of Egypt, Pakistan, Sri Lanka, Turkey, and Vietnam. Apparel has been an important export for them all at some point over the past three decades, and except for Egypt, they have all been top apparel exporters to the global market.

The report is structured around the path from jobs to careers, which is filled with both opportunities and obstacles and thus in need of targeted policies (figure O.1). Previous literature has found the positive employment effects of apparel exports, particularly on jobs. A hope is to shift the paradigm of how we think of women's participation in the labor force by demonstrating the importance of the distinction between jobs and careers.

One novel feature of this unfolding story line is an initial look at the US path from jobs to careers for women over the 20th century—a path periodically used as a point of comparison for the seven case countries. Following a seminal study by Claudia Goldin (2006) and her new book, *Career and Family: Women's Century-Long Journey toward Equity* (Goldin 2021), the report represents the path from jobs to careers as one in which women move from informal and agricultural work to factory work and then slowly switch to mid- and high-skill occupations, thanks to postponing entry into the workforce and marriage while pursuing higher levels of education. Women may achieve their career aspirations in various ways, but understanding *how* each country makes progress toward a more equitable life between men and women will pave the way for a better route forward.

FIGURE O.1 **The Jobs-to-Careers Pathway for Women in the Apparel Industry**

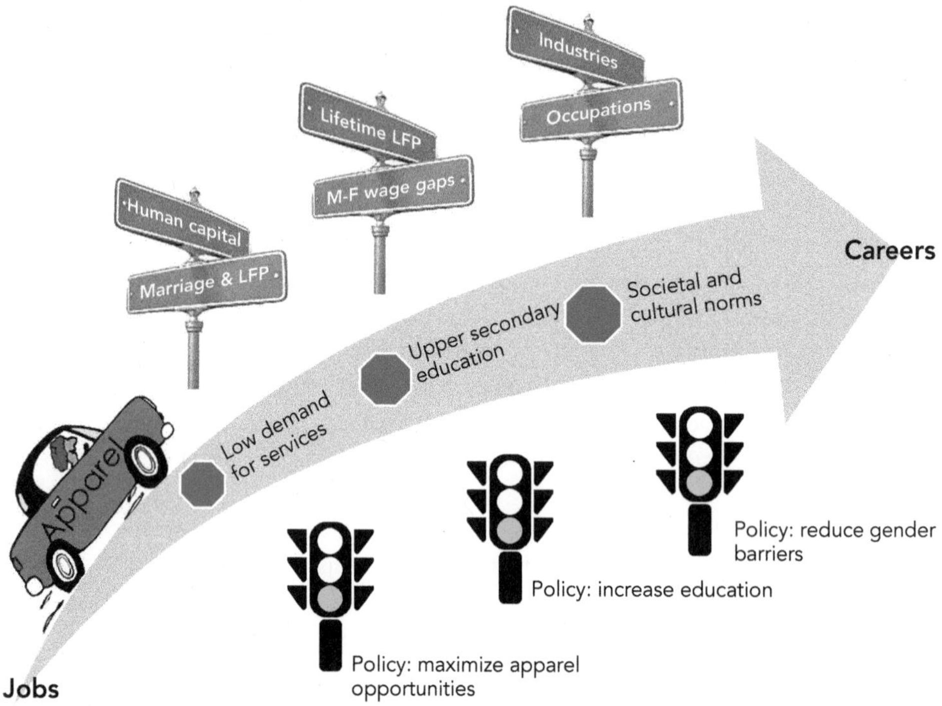

Source: World Bank.
Note: LFP = labor force participation; M-F = male-female.

HOW DOES HOUSEHOLD DECISION-MAKING AFFECT WOMEN'S EMPLOYMENT?

The report draws on two models for how households make decisions about labor supply—that is, about whether women will enter the labor force and then whether they will stay or leave the labor force. The first model assumes that for exports to contribute to rising female wages, they must increase the demand for women more than the demand for men (figure O.2). An increase in female wages is associated with an increase in female labor force participation (FLFP); however, female-intensive exports must account for most of a country's exports for there to be a statistically significant correlation, as shown in chapter 1.

Even so, as apparel exports provide job opportunities that bring women into the labor force, they also enable women to economically contribute to their families and increase family wealth. The latter is highly associated with higher upper-secondary graduation rates—a vital driver of career development, which in turn reduces the need for young adults to enter the labor market to support their families before completing their education.

A second model centers on the contribution of apparel employment to female career development by providing an intergenerational pathway (figure O.3). Traditional female

FIGURE O.2 **Model of FLFP Variation in Relation to Female and Male Contributions to Higher Family Income**

Source: World Bank elaboration.
Note: In this model, as family income rises in relative value, the spouse whose home production is valued more highly will work less in the labor market (holding wages constant). As demand for women's labor for apparel exports rises relative to men (left section), their wages rise, and women are more likely to enter the labor force and work more hours. But as men transition to industrial jobs with even higher wages (center section), those rising incomes are associated with less formal labor market work by women in the same household. A country's transition to a more services-led economy (right section) again increases both demand and wages for women, resulting in a higher female labor supply. FLFP = female labor force participation.

jobs—such as those held by apparel workers—are essential to the development process. In the absence of export-oriented manufacturing and services, women in many lower-middle-income countries have few formal employment opportunities. Without such jobs, there is low demand to increase female education, few ways to increase family income, and ultimately fewer opportunities to support women transitioning to careers.

These models support the report's key findings: (a) that countries should take advantage of the apparel industry as a launching platform to overcome the fixed costs of introducing more women into the labor market; and (b) that apparel exports do contribute to the jobs-to-careers transition, albeit indirectly. However, for this approach to work, complementary policies must be in place that tackle the barriers that hinder women in their pursuit of long-term participation in the labor force and better-paid occupations—policies that achieve the following:

- Increase the participation of female production workers in export-oriented apparel manufacturing and related industries
- Increase the number of female supervisors and upgrading jobs within apparel to manufacturing-related services
- Increase access to education to promote female participation in careers
- Break glass ceilings.

FIGURE O.3 **Model of an Intergenerational Female Pathway from Apparel Jobs to Careers**

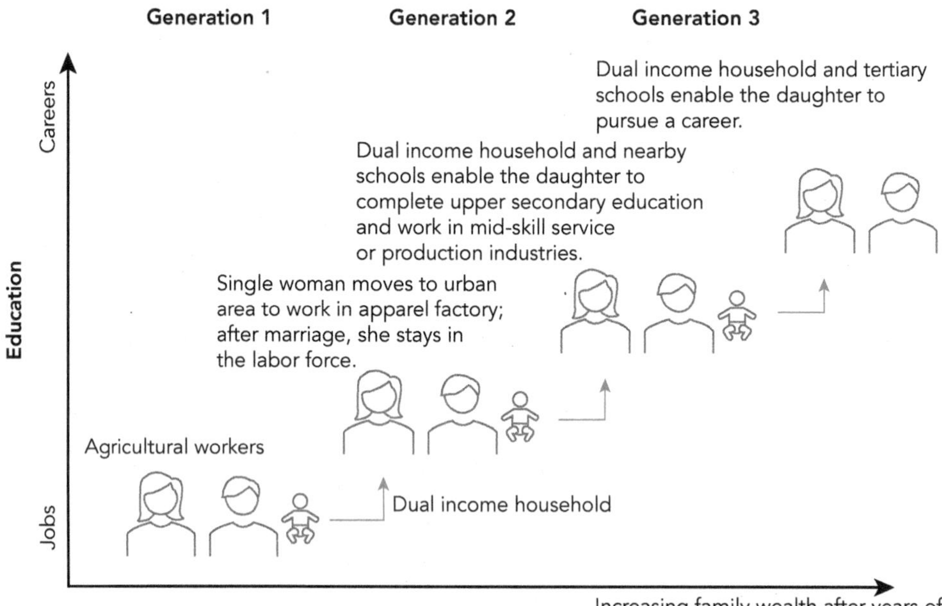

Source: World Bank.

The Transition from Jobs to Careers: A "Quiet Revolution"

A first step in evaluating whether exports, especially in apparel, can lead to better employment opportunities for women is to assess how women are progressing in apparel-exporting countries. During the twentieth century in the United States, several fundamental changes in women's employment and family relationships have characterized what Goldin (2006) calls a "quiet revolution," such as the sense of identity that emerges when a woman finds individuality in her occupation and a longer horizon of work.

But how can women's progress in this regard be measured in low- and middle-income countries? Since the transition from jobs to careers for women is multidimensional, several indicators help demonstrate how apparel exports support the transition and identify barriers that directed policies might address (as further discussed in chapter 2). Labor force surveys can capture five such performance indicators (Goldin 2006):

- *Investment in human capital* focuses on the extent of investment in people through formal education, especially secondary educational attainment.
- *Marriage and labor force participation* evaluates how households make labor supply decisions—such as whether a woman will decide to stay in the labor market after marriage.
- *Lifetime labor force participation* looks at the average age of women in apparel compared with those in other industries to assess whether women working in apparel tend to stay in the workforce.
- *The earnings gap between men and women* focuses on the gender wage gap—which, on average worldwide, favors men over women.
- *Employment across industries and occupations* examines the segregation of men and women into different sectors and occupations.

Our findings show that although our case countries have made progress in the jobs-to-careers transition, none of them has yet reached the goalpost (table O.1). The apparel industry alone cannot enable women to make this transition, but it may well help them indirectly. Apparel jobs provide opportunities for women with primary and lower-secondary education but offer little incentive to attain the higher education needed for careers.

However, the findings also suggest that significant returns to education can incentivize women to invest in their education, which is a prerequisite for careers that require higher human capital. The good news is that all the country cases show great returns in the labor market for women with lower- and upper-secondary education (figure O.4). Yet although significant educational wage premiums for women offer grounds for optimism, labor demand is still too low to absorb women, even in countries where they have acquired the necessary human capital to shift to careers.

Three Barriers to Career Development

So, what is stopping women from making the full shift? There must be barriers strewn along the pathway. Our research reveals that LMICs face three barriers to expanding female career opportunities (further discussed in chapter 3).

Low service sector demand. Insufficient national income (low gross domestic product per capita) limits demand for career-related occupations in the service sector. Although HSOs account for 15 percent of female employment in lower-middle-income countries, they make up 32 percent in upper-middle-income countries and 43 percent in high-income countries (figure O.5). Similarly, certain industries that have been traditionally important for females—like social work and residential care activities—are only prominent in high-income countries.

TABLE O.1 **Findings on Female Apparel Workers' Jobs-to-Careers Transition in Seven Case Countries, by Performance Indicator**

Country	Education of female workers	Marriage and FLFP	Lifetime FLFP	Gender earnings gap	Occupational distribution
Bangladesh	Education increased but is lower than the level required for careers.	Income effect suggests the prevalence of jobs. Most working women are married, but most married women do not work. Female married workforce and FLFP increased.	Average age of female apparel workers increased, but most are still 21–30 years old.	Female wages increased, and gap decreased.	Low share of women in clerical occupations
Cambodia	Education increased but is lower than level required for careers.	Substitution and income effects are at odds. Most working women are married, and most married women work. Female married workforce and FLFP greatly increased.	Average age of female apparel workers increased, but most are still 21–30 years old.	Female wages increased, and gap decreased.	Low share of women in clerical occupations
Egypt, Arab Rep.	Education increased and is higher than the level required for careers.	Substitution effect dominates, suggesting attractive employment opportunities. Most working women are married, but most married women do not work. Female married workforce and FLFP decreased.	Average age of female apparel workers increased, but the average age of female workers in all industries decreased.	Female wages increased, but gap increased.	Neither clerical occupations nor manufacturing are important female employment sources
Pakistan	Education increased but is lower than the level required for careers.	Income effect suggests the prevalence of jobs. Most working women are married, but most married women do not work. Female married workforce and FLFP increased.	Average age of female apparel workers increased, but most are still 21–30 years old.	Female wages increased, but gap increased.	Low share of women in clerical occupations

(Table continues next page)

TABLE O.1 **Findings on Female Apparel Workers' Jobs-to-Careers Transition in Seven Case Countries, by Performance Indicator** *(continued)*

Country	Education of female workers	Marriage and FLFP	Lifetime FLFP	Gender earnings gap	Occupational distribution
Sri Lanka	Education increased and is higher than level required for careers.	Substitution and income effects are at odds. Most working women are married, but most married women do not work. Female married workforce increased, and married FLFP was stable or slightly decreased.	Average age of female apparel workers increased, and most are 31–45 years old.	Female wages increased, and gap decreased.	Low share of women in clerical occupations
Turkey	Education increased and is on par with income level.	Substitution effect dominates, suggesting attractive employment opportunities. Most working women are married, but most married women do not work. Female married workforce is stable, and married FLFP increased.	Average age of female apparel workers increased, and most are 31–45 years old.	Female wages increased, but gap increased.	Low share of women in clerical occupations
Vietnam	Education increased and is on par with income level.	Substitution and income effects are at odds. Most working women are married, and most married women work. Female married workforce increased, and married FLFP is stable.	Average age of female apparel workers increased, and most are 31–45 years old.	Female wages increased, but gap increased.	Low share of women in clerical occupations

Source: World Bank.
Note: Green shading indicates a positive relationship with the transition from jobs to careers; orange shading, a negative relationship; and gray shading, no specific relation. FLFP = female labor force participation. For the full discussion of these findings in each country, by indicator, see chapter 3.

FIGURE O.4 **Returns to Education for Females in Selected Countries, 2007–15**

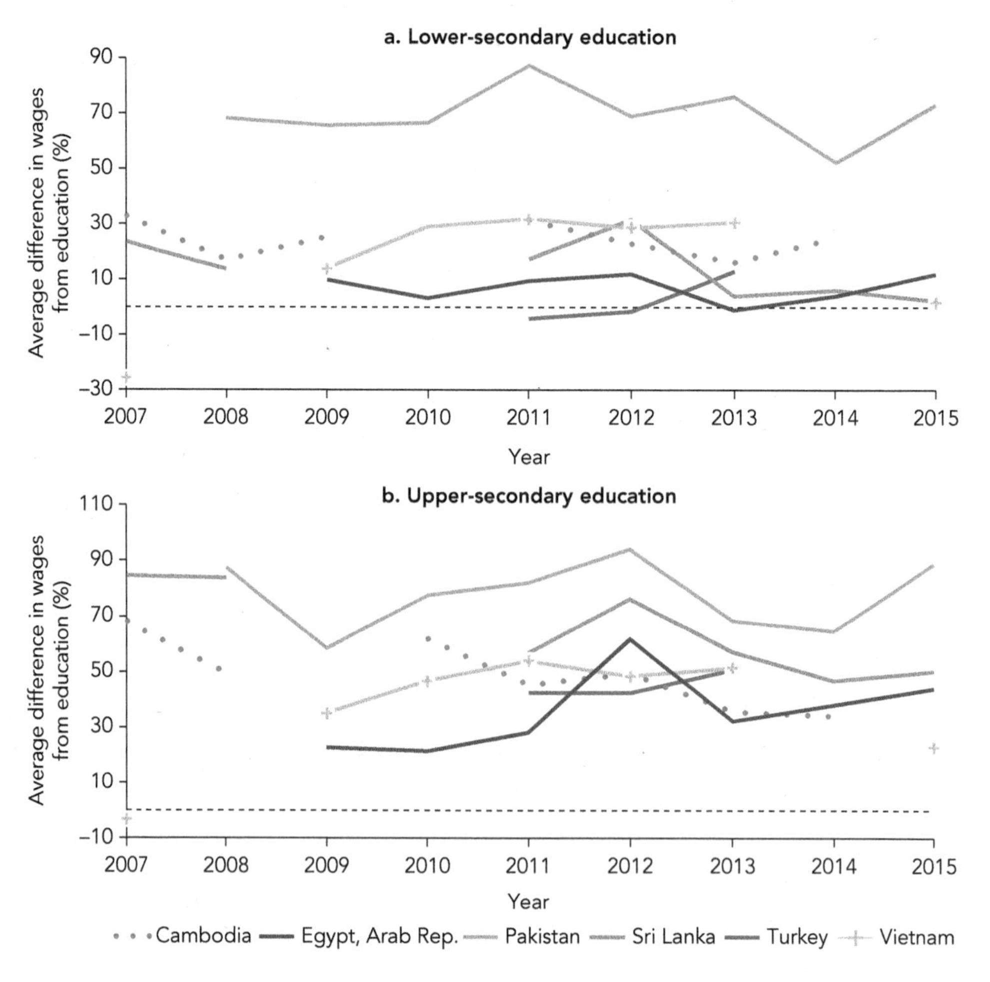

Source: Estimates using countries' labor force survey (LFS) data.
Note: A comparison of panels a and b shows that women gain the most if they continue past lower-secondary education. The elaboration uses Mincerian equations and LFS data. Some lines are discontinuous owing to missing rounds of data. For the full set of Mincerian regression results, see chapter 2, annex 2A. Bangladesh is omitted due to data comparability issues for the education variable, as explained in appendix A.

Our results suggest that returns from employment in the occupations available in lower-middle-income countries are perhaps not sufficient to draw women into the workforce, especially given the number of hours worked relative to wages received.

Low education. As noted earlier, "careers" are more associated with HSOs because they require more education, imply a long-run vision for labor market participation, and provide opportunities for leadership and advancement, whereas "jobs" are more associated with low-skill occupations. Our findings suggest that the education levels in three sample countries (Bangladesh, Cambodia, and Pakistan) are insufficient to meet

FIGURE O.5 **Decomposition of Occupations in Women's and Total Employment Worldwide, by Broad Category and Country Income Level, 2017**

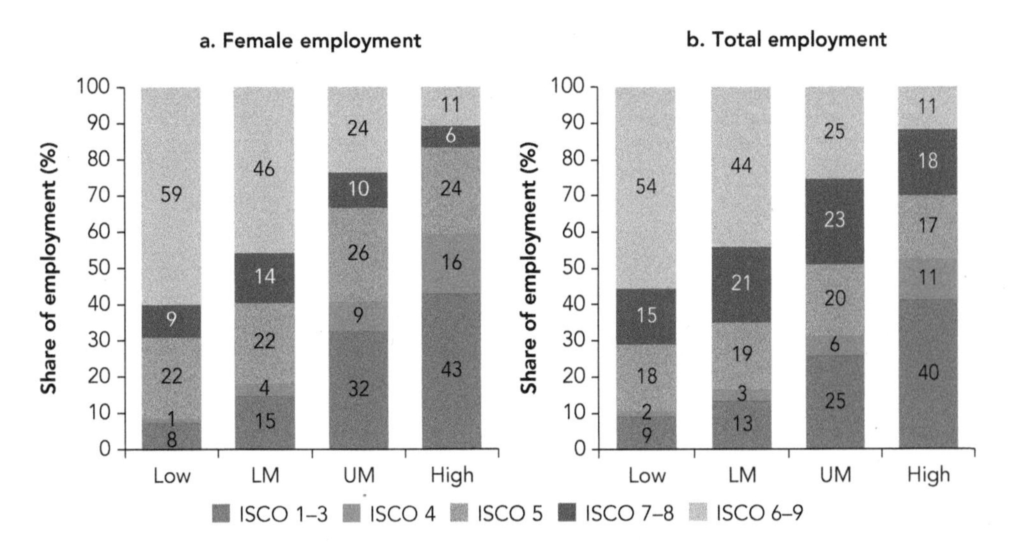

Source: Based on ILOSTAT data, International Labour Organization.
Note: Data cover 102 countries, using the International Standard Classification of Occupations ISCO-08 Index of Occupational Titles. (All countries' data are from 2017 ILOSTAT, except Pakistan's, which are from 2018. The sample excludes India because its use of the earlier ISCO-88 Index raised comparability issues.) By broad category, ISCO groups 1 to 3 include managers, professionals, and technicians and associate professionals; ISCO 4, clerical support workers; ISCO 5, services and sales workers; ISCO 7 and 8, craft and related trades workers as well as plant and machine operators and assemblers; and ISCO 6 and 9, skilled agricultural, forestry, and fishery workers as well as elementary occupations. Country income categories are by World Bank classifications. LM = lower-middle income; UM = upper-middle income.

the education requirements of career-oriented occupations, particularly for women. But in the other countries (Egypt, Sri Lanka, Turkey, and Vietnam), women's education levels are not only sufficient but also equal or exceed men's education levels. Thus, the problem in those countries is more likely to be low demand for workers in select industries and misalignment between education and workforce development.

Societal and cultural norms. In most of our case countries, certain laws either limit women's ability to undertake certain occupations, to earn or move between occupations equally to men, or lack limitations on discrimination in the workplace (table O.2). Moreover, prevailing gender norms further limit women's involvement in the labor force or diminish the workplace environment, deterring them from staying.

Women in middle-income countries mainly work in a select number of industries, but men outnumber women in these same industries in most of our sample countries. For example, looking at the occupational breakdown within manufacturing industries in chapter 3, in most cases, men outnumber women in HSOs—except in apparel, where the number of women equals or exceeds that of men in HSOs (as in Cambodia, Sri Lanka, and Vietnam).

TABLE O.2 Summary of Laws Limiting Gender-Based Employment Discrimination in Seven Case Study Countries, 2020

Country	Equal remuneration by law	Dismissing pregnant women is prohibited	Discrimination in employment based on gender is prohibited	Women can do the same night work as men	No mobility restrictions for women	Women can work in the same industrial jobs as men
Bangladesh	X	X	X	✓	✓	X
Cambodia	X	✓	✓	✓	✓	✓
Egypt, Arab Rep.	X	✓	✓	X	X	X
Pakistan	X	X	✓	X	X	X
Sri Lanka	X	✓	X	X	✓	X
Turkey	✓	✓	✓	✓	✓	X
Vietnam	✓	✓	✓	✓	✓	X

Source: World Bank's Women, Business and the Law 2020 database.
Note: A checkmark designates the existence of the specified legal provision, and an X the lack of it.

How an Apparel Export Strategy Fits into the Transition

The era of GVCs took off in the 2000s, part of a process that began in the 1980s as global manufacturing expanded significantly and as multinationals in high-income countries moved production to LMICs. This shift in production generated formal sector jobs, particularly for females in LMICs to engage in lower-skill, lower-value-adding activities, while high-income countries continued to generate higher-skill, career-oriented activities and occupations (figure O.6). That said, participation in labor-intensive GVCs—such as apparel manufacturing—has limits in terms of supporting a transition to careers (discussed in chapter 4).

Despite being the top employer of women, the apparel industry's limitations stem mostly from its structure and governance. Apparel GVCs are characterized by an asymmetry of decision-making power and profit margins between apparel brand owners in high-income countries and suppliers in LMICs. Brand owners control the most profitable activities (like research and development and marketing) and set the price of the final product. This leaves LMICs locked into low-value-added activities—that is, manufacturing—because there is little room to move into the high-skill activities, and these countries must keep labor costs low to remain globally competitive. Thus, although GVC integration can lead to large-scale job creation, technical knowledge, and supervisor and middle-management experience, it can also lead to sustained low wages and inequalities for low-skilled female workers with few career opportunities (Farole 2016).

FIGURE O.6 **Relationships of GVC Activities and Country Roles to Occupational Skill and Country Income Levels**

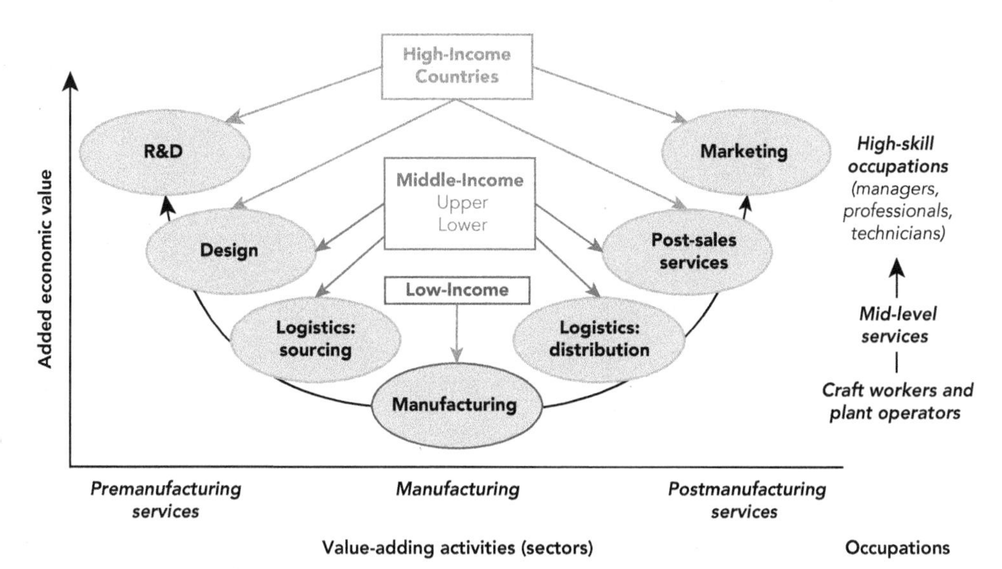

Sources: Updated from Fernandez-Stark, Frederick, and Gereffi 2011 and Frederick 2010. Further permission required for reuse.
Note: Yellow ovals represent service sector industry and high-skill or sales or service occupations. Red outlines designate manufacturing and craft or production workers. (In some countries, elementary occupations are also used as helpers.) GVC = global value chain; R&D = research and development.

The apparel industry employs two types of workers: (a) production workers and (b) knowledge-intensive service occupations (table O.3). Over 75 percent of workers are involved in production, with little opportunity for advancement and only small wage returns. The opportunities for functional upgrading and associated careers are limited and require postsecondary training or tertiary education and associated computer and interpersonal (soft) business skills. HSO occupations—managers, professionals, and technicians—are more educated and higher paying than craft and plant operators, but they account for less than 25 percent of the apparel manufacturing workforce.

Further, despite generating jobs, evidence in chapter 4 suggests that unless the country's exports are heavily concentrated in apparel—above 81 percent of total exports—a positive impact on FLFP is unlikely to appear. However, such a concentrated export basket makes the country vulnerable to external negative demand shocks.

TABLE O.3 **Employee and Wage Profile for the Apparel Value Chain, Global Estimates, 2017–19**

Stage	Position	Share of workforce (%)	Education	Tasks or skills	Wages
Production	Sewing machine operators (55%)	75	Primary education or on-the-job training	Knowledge of sewing machine operation	Low
	Other assembly-related (15%)		Primary or technical	Cutters, packers, spreaders, helpers	Low-Medium
	Supervisors and inspectors (5%)		Secondary education, technical	Communication skills	Medium
Services[a]	Sourcing and logistics (backward links)	15	Tertiary; university degree in business	Purchasing, organizational, computer, communication	Medium
	Sales, merchandising (forward links)		Tertiary; university degree in business	Customer service, order taking, finding buyers	Medium-High
	Design		Tertiary; university or apparel-specific degree	Creativity, computer-aided design (CAD)	Medium-High
	Administrative	10	Upper secondary or tertiary; university degree in business	Sales, finance, customer service	Medium
	Top management (general manager, factory manager, department manager, quality manager)		Tertiary; university degree in business, industrial engineering	Business, interpersonal, communication	High

Wage Levels	Low	Low-Medium	Medium	Medium-High	High
	Hourly; Minimum wage or piece rate	Hourly	Hourly or salary; approximately twice wages of an operator	Salary	Highest-paid employees; salary

Source: Frederick 2017, 2019.
a. Services account for approximately 10–30 percent of the workforce depending on the business model of the firm. The sector accounts for a larger share of the workforce in companies that sell their own brands, because workers are needed for brand development, market research, retailing, and creative design.

Another factor that affects female labor market outcomes and occupational upgrading in the export-oriented apparel industry is firm ownership and strategy. In some countries, apparel investment from foreign investors has helped governments (like Sri Lanka) to invest in human capital, engage in more upgrading, and retain skilled workers. But in other countries (like Cambodia), apparel manufacturers based their headquarters in other countries, reserved career occupations for expats, and kept wages low as part of their overall internationalization strategy. On the other hand, domestic firm ownership provides more local decision-making power, but in countries with stringent social norms against female employment, it has led to a male-dominated labor force.

In sum, countries can reap the most benefits by engaging with an eye toward workforce investment and using apparel manufacturing as a springboard to other sectors. Apparel can help raise a country's human capital, enable movement to other industries, and increase wages to promote domestic services. Countries that stay in apparel without upgrading can continue to remain competitive at the low end, but this does not advance a country along the jobs-to-careers trajectory. It is important for countries to be aware of these caveats and to develop a longer-term strategy to achieve professional development; otherwise, countries may become stuck in the "middle-income trap"—gaining a higher income status from increased exports but becoming stuck there after losing a competitive edge.

How to Speed Up the Jobs-to-Careers Transition

How can apparel-exporting countries, development institutions, and other stakeholders reenergize and speed up the jobs-to-careers transition in LMICs? This report suggests four policy recommendations—all of which apply to our seven sample countries, depending on how far along they are in the transition—with a focus on designing policies to target specific types of workers in the apparel industry (table O.4).

Broadly, the recommendations suggest that countries take advantage of the apparel industry as a launching platform to overcome the fixed costs of introducing more women into the labor market. But for this strategy to work, there will need to be complementary policies that tackle the barriers that hinder women in their pursuit of long-term participation in the labor force and better-paid occupations (as further discussed in chapter 5).

Recommendation 1: Increase the participation of female production workers in export-oriented apparel manufacturing and related industries

This means adopting measures to attract and retain female workers in these industries—such as easing concerns about mobility and safety issues (whether by reserving spaces for women in public transportation or providing bicycles as an alternative means of transportation). There is also room to expand production and job opportunities in

TABLE O.4 Policy Recommendations to Increase FLFP and Women's Transition from Jobs to Careers in Seven Case Study Countries

Policy recommendation	Implementation considerations	Countries[a]
Increase participation of female production workers in export-oriented apparel manufacturing and related industries	Implement programs to attract and retain female workers to export-oriented manufacturing	Bangladesh; Egypt, Arab Rep.; Pakistan; Turkey
Increase the number of female supervisors, and upgrade jobs within apparel to manufacturing-related services	Implement internships and skill-specific training programs to upskill female production workers and include more women in mid-skill occupations	Sri Lanka, Turkey, Vietnam
	Focus programs on supplying graduates who are employable and aligned with industrial policy development	Egypt, Arab Rep.; Sri Lanka; Turkey
Increase access to education to promote female participation in careers	Increase upper-secondary enrollment and entry points to the industry	Bangladesh, Cambodia, Pakistan
	Reduce information gaps on available career paths	All
Break glass ceilings	Reform legal barriers that reduce women's access to and permanence in employment opportunities	Bangladesh; Egypt, Arab Rep.; Pakistan; Sri Lanka
	Promote inclusive workplace practices	All
	Engage foreign support and involvement	All

Source: World Bank.
Note: FLFP = female labor force participation.
a. Policies can be addressed by all seven countries studied in this report; however, some are more relevant to specific countries based on our results.

rural areas, especially in countries like Sri Lanka, where distances are relatively short, and in countries like Vietnam, where there are multiple apparel and manufacturing clusters.

Recommendation 2: Increase the number of female supervisors, and upgrade jobs within apparel to manufacturing-related services

One way to do this is with internships and skill-specific training programs to upskill female production workers and include more women in mid-skill occupations. To address cost concerns, the government can provide direct subsidies to incentivize employers to hire and train women. In addition, training programs should focus on supplying graduates who are employable and aligned with industrial policy development. Vocational and short-term training can be particularly effective for filling industry gaps when employers and training providers work together.

Recommendation 3: Increase access to education to promote female participation in careers

Here the emphasis is on increasing access to upper-secondary education—a level that is typically necessary to meet the basic requirements for clerical and supervisory roles or for managerial and professional jobs. Stipend programs for girls at the primary, secondary, and upper-secondary levels can be an effective way to increase female enrollment and achieve better gender balance. There is also a need to reduce information gaps on available career paths. Certainly, sharing information that breaks down occupational characteristics (such as average hours, education, and salary) would help job seekers to make informed decisions.

Recommendation 4: Break glass ceilings

For women to pursue career paths—either through long-term investments in education or through job experience and permanence—policy makers have a responsibility to define a gender-equal structure of work in terms of labor market and family policies. One way to do this is by reforming legal barriers that reduce women's access to and permanence in employment opportunities. A second is by promoting inclusive workplace practices. And a third is by engaging foreign support and involvement. For example, the Better Work program, an initiative of the International Labour Organization and the International Finance Corporation (of the World Bank Group), aims to improve working conditions in garment factories and promote private sector competitiveness in GVCs.

Conclusion

This report's four recommendations seek to increase the probability of women entering the labor market and of creating an environment that supports female career development. However, pursuing them in a postpandemic world will add to the challenge, especially in lower-income countries—such as Bangladesh, Cambodia, and Pakistan—where women are largely engaged in forms of work that lack social protection (such as informal employment or domestic work) and that heighten their vulnerability to poverty in times of crisis. For example, the decrease in income and livelihoods and the scarcity of jobs due to the pandemic may force households to engage in negative coping mechanisms (such as reductions in food consumption by girls and women and early marriage) and will also increase the burden of all informal care in the household, often asymmetrically assigned to women (De Paz et al. 2020).

Although beyond the scope of this report, understanding how the COVID-19 pandemic affected women in our seven sample countries would shed light on whether the transition toward careers was halted, momentarily reversed, or given an unexpected added boost. For example, flexible work arrangements due to the pandemic might also persist, supporting women's inclusion and permanence in the labor market. Another area for future research might be to conduct an evaluation similar to ours but, for comparison, of countries that are *not* apparel exporters. Also helpful would be (a) field research or surveys to better understand barriers to women in career occupations across different countries, (b) evaluations of gendered perceptions of women's skills and abilities, and (c) surveys of former or current female apparel workers to evaluate intergenerational benefits and employment transitions throughout their lifetimes.

In sum, industrial alignment and diversification, education expansion and skill training, and action to counter conservative norms have intertwined synergies. For example, more jobs or careers in an industry will not secure women positions if their human capital is too low or if cultural barriers limit their hiring. Nor can educated women increase their labor participation if their skills are not aligned with available occupations or if childcare responsibilities reduce their available working time. Fortunately, today, the "quiet revolution" need not take the 100 years that it took in the United States.

References

Artuc, E., G. Lopez-Acevedo, R. Robertson, and D. Samaan. 2019. *Exports to Jobs: Boosting the Gains from Trade in South Asia*. South Asia Development Forum Series. Washington, DC: World Bank.

De Paz, C., M. Muller, A. M. Munoz Boudet, and I. Gaddis. 2020. "Gender Dimensions of the COVID-19 Pandemic." Policy Note, World Bank, Washington, DC.

Farole, T. 2016. "Do Global Value Chains Create Jobs? Impacts of GVCs Depend on Lead Firms, Specialization, Skills, and Institutions." *IZA World of Labor* (291): 1–11.

Fernandez-Stark, K., S. Frederick, and G. Gereffi. 2011. "The Apparel Global Value Chain: Economic Upgrading and Workforce Development." Report, Duke Center on Globalization, Governance & Competitiveness (Duke CGGC), Durham, NC.

Frederick, S. 2010. "Development and Application of a Value Chain Research Approach to Understand and Evaluate Internal and External Factors and Relationships Affecting Economic Competitiveness in the Textile Value Chain." Dissertation, North Carolina State University, Raleigh, NC.

Frederick, S. 2017. "Apparel Skills Mapping and Functional Upgrading in Vietnam: Jobs Diagnostic." Unpublished manuscript, World Bank, Washington, DC.

Frederick, S. 2019. "Apparel Skills Mapping and Functional Upgrading in Cambodia: Jobs Diagnostic." Unpublished manuscript, World Bank, Washington, DC.

Goldin, C. 2006. "The Quiet Revolution That Transformed Women's Employment, Education, and Family." *American Economic Review* 96 (2): 1–21.

Goldin, C. 2021. *Career and Family: Women's Century-Long Journey toward Equity*. Princeton, NJ: Princeton University Press.

ILO (International Labour Organization). 2018. *Women and Men in the Informal Economy: A Statistical Picture*. Geneva: ILO.

Lopez-Acevedo, G., and R. Robertson, eds. 2012. *Sewing Success? Employment, Wages, and Poverty Following the End of the Multi-Fibre Arrangement*. Directions in Development Series. Washington, DC: World Bank. doi:10.1596/978-0-8213-8778-8.

UNDG (United Nations Development Group) – Western and Central Africa. 2015. "Socio-Economic Impact of Ebola Virus Disease in West African Countries: A Call for National and Regional Containment, Recovery and Prevention." UNDP Africa Reports 267635, UNDG, New York. doi:10.22004/ag.econ.267635.

World Bank and WTO (World Trade Organization). 2020. *Women and Trade: The Role of Trade in Promoting Gender Equality*. Washington, DC: World Bank.

Abbreviations

AUW	Asian University for Women
FDI	foreign direct investment
FLFP	female labor force participation
GDP	gross domestic product
GVC	global value chain
GEAR	Gender Equality and Returns (Bangladesh)
HSO	high-skill occupation
IFC	International Finance Corporation (World Bank Group)
ILO	International Labour Organization
ISCO	International Standard Classification of Occupations
ISIC	International Standard Industrial Classification of All Economic Activities
LFP	labor force participation
LFS	labor force survey
LMICs	low- and middle-income countries
MFA	Multifiber Arrangement
SAR	special administrative region (China)
SMAM	singulate mean age at marriage

CHAPTER 1

Why Jobs versus Careers?

Key Messages

- Given that exports, especially in apparel, create job opportunities for women, the big question is whether they can lead to better employment opportunities—particularly careers—and if so, how.
- The way the United States accomplished a gradual jobs-to-careers transition for women in the twentieth century offers insights on how low- and middle-income countries can boost women's contributions.
- This report evaluates the experiences of seven middle-income apparel exporting countries: Bangladesh, Cambodia, the Arab Republic of Egypt, Pakistan, Sri Lanka, Turkey, and Vietnam. In all of them, apparel is the largest employer of females among manufacturing industries, although the share of women in manufacturing is lower than in services.
- Our results show that apparel exports can contribute to the job-to-career transition, but only indirectly, and there must be complementary measures to help empower women.

Introduction

Incorporating women into the formal labor force is critical for economic development. Women's contributions—both actual and potential—in all levels of the economy are now well established and widely accepted. Closing the gender labor participation gap, for example, would increase gross domestic product (GDP) by an average of 35 percent (Ostry et al. 2018). The question of how to fully incorporate women into the formal economy, however, is still being debated at a time when 60 percent of women in low- and middle-income countries (LMICs) remain in the informal sector (ILO 2018). These women must cope with insecure working conditions, unstable revenues, and lack of access to social safety nets.

One strategy that has been heralded in several recent publications by major intergovernmental organizations is globalization (Korinek, Moïsé, and Tange 2021; World Bank and WTO 2020). These reports argue that exports tend to favor women, whether by reducing firms' ability to discriminate against women, by increasing the demand for women through the expansion of female-intensive industries, or by spreading learning and norms of equal treatment. Mounting empirical evidence supports these theories. The World Bank and WTO (2020) report, *Women and Trade: The Role of Trade in Promoting Gender Equality*, outlines several ways that trade can improve female labor market outcomes:

- Exporting firms tend to employ more women, pay higher wages, and increase the likelihood of formal employment.
- Moving women out of informal employment (including household and agricultural production) can reduce birth rates, increase agency, foster investment in children's education, and increase the talent pool.
- The changing global economy offers new opportunities for women through services, global value chains (GVCs), and digital platforms. For example, digital technology and new online platforms create new ways for women to bypass traditional trade barriers, expand entrepreneurial skills, and develop flexible careers that help them to balance work and household responsibilities.

The goal of this report is to shift the paradigm of how we think of women's participation in the labor force by demonstrating the importance of the distinction between jobs and careers. This is a distinction with a difference: Workers take "jobs" when feeling the demand to generate income and do not necessarily consider the job to be a long-term commitment. On the other hand, "careers" require more investment in both education and time in the workforce to gain experience—in return, offering opportunities for advancement and leadership.

For women, the transition from a job to a career also involves an important shift in mindset within the home. It changes the weight the household places on a woman's contribution to work at home relative to work outside the home while also changing how the household adapts to changing wages in the labor market.

This report focuses on the most female-intensive and globally engaged manufacturing industry: apparel. The apparel industry has fundamentally changed over the past quarter century in terms of production and the opportunities created for women in the poorest countries. Shifts in production to low-wage LMICs have increased the demand for women, narrowed male-female wage gaps, and brought women into the formal labor force from agricultural and informal work (Artuc et al. 2019; Lopez-Acevedo and Robertson 2012).

But how does exporting apparel contribute to the jobs-to-careers transition? And is an apparel-led export strategy sufficient to induce this transition? To answer these questions, the report focuses on seven countries where the apparel industry plays an important role in the export basket—Bangladesh, Cambodia, the Arab Republic of Egypt, Pakistan, Sri Lanka, Turkey, and Vietnam—to see how they are faring on the building blocks needed for women to move from jobs to careers. Apparel has been a primary export for all of them at some point over the past three decades, and except for Egypt, they have all been top apparel suppliers to the global market. We include Egypt as a reference country that did not pursue an apparel export–oriented development strategy although apparel makes up an important share of its exports.

Throughout the report, we define "jobs" as remunerated activities that people do to survive. In other words, they offer little inherent satisfaction but do generate the income necessary to maintain a given standard of living. On the other hand, "careers" are remunerated activities that provide both income and purpose, even an identity. Here we should note that the difference between jobs and careers is associated with, but goes beyond, occupational classification and educational attainment. Although jobs and careers are not synonymous with occupation, jobs tend to be associated with low-skill occupations, and careers are more often associated with high-skill occupations (HSOs).

The report's key findings are that although apparel exports–contribute to the transition from jobs to careers, they are far from sufficient to fully realize women's potential in the economy. Complementary policies must accompany apparel exports—policies that target increased access to education, reduced gender segregation in occupations and industries, and development of a post-apparel strategy. Few countries combine such policies with an apparel-led growth strategy, possibly missing the chance that apparel exports could help women more fully realize their long-run economic potential.

This chapter begins with a review of the literature on women's empowerment to motivate the focus on the jobs-to-careers transition and to suggest that the time is ripe for reframing how we think about promoting women's economic participation. It then presents a simple, forward-looking intertemporal household labor supply decision model to illustrate the transformative effects of shifting from a jobs mindset to a career orientation. This is followed by the story of the US path from jobs to careers for women, starting at the end of the nineteenth century; a snapshot of the classification systems being used to determine sectors and skill levels in various occupations; and a road map for the structure of the report.

The Case for Empowering Women

One reason the jobs versus careers distinction is important is that each represents different manifestations of women's economic and social empowerment. Although the distinction is difficult to quantify, numerous studies, particularly on the apparel industry, associate formal employment with improvements in females' views of their roles in society and the household as well as in males' perceptions of women (Lopez-Acevedo and Robertson 2012; Safa 1994; Tokatli, Kızılgün, and Cho 2011).

Paid employment, particularly, provides emancipatory benefits and social and economic freedoms for women, contributing to United Nations Sustainable Development Goal 5: "Achieve gender equality and empower all women and girls."[1] Our emphasis is on increasing female participation and decision-making power by raising awareness of the need to transform the structures and institutions that may inhibit women's access to resources, education, and opportunities.

The literature is filled with examples of such empowerment:

- *In Egypt,* a survey of 925 women across industries found that formal employment, compared with other explanatory variables, was most consistently associated with a range of empowerment indicators (Kabeer 2013).
- *In India,* a study suggests that feminization of labor brought greater recognition and remuneration for women's work, improved women's bargaining power relative to men within households, and increased self-worth (Ghosh 2002).
- *In Turkey,* a study finds that manufacturing jobs contributed to women's empowerment in Istanbul and increased their capacity to control their own lives (Tokatli, Kızılgün, and Cho 2011).
- *In the Dominican Republic,* a study finds that working women gained greater authority over household budgetary and other decisions as a result of larger economic contributions (Safa 1994). In addition, more egalitarian relationships exist when both spouses are employed. For example, if the gains weaken the man's role as principal breadwinner, it could contribute to higher rates of marital instability and female-headed households.

Moreover, both jobs and careers contribute to economic growth, although the benefits are different. When working in jobs that increase earned incomes, women are more likely than men to support household welfare and children's education (World Bank 2011). Promoting pro-poor development can open doors to new life opportunities, especially for daughters. And working in GVCs provides millions of women with jobs and incomes—which can bring greater economic independence, social connections, and voice (Christian, Evers, and Barrientos 2013).

One Bangladesh study finds that employment in the apparel industry contributed to female empowerment because earnings raised women's value within the family and strengthened their capacity to negotiate with family members (Rahman and Islam 2013). Another suggests that because apparel employment required females to move away from their natal homes, it enabled them to better negotiate their position in society (Feldman 2009). The opportunity to live independently enabled women to separate themselves and reframe family obligations such as pressure to marry early or give money to their families.

In addition, as the proportion of women who work rises—as usually happens when available jobs increase and reach a certain threshold—beliefs about work become more positive. Fernández (2013) explains that when few women work in the labor market, the negative prior beliefs about working reinforce the restraint from entering the labor market. With more women moving into formal sector jobs, a cultural shift occurs and the inclusion of women in the labor market accelerates. Further, several studies suggest that the expansion of jobs eventually leads to better employment opportunities for women. A study on the apparel industry in Bangladesh finds that when male operators are exposed to female supervisors, it improves their view of females in supervisory positions (Macchiavello et al. 2020).

The Path of US Women from Jobs to Careers

Given that the growth in apparel exports in these low-wage countries is creating job opportunities for women, the story of US women who moved increasingly from jobs to careers over the twentieth century—a story involving the expansion of industrial jobs, especially in apparel—might hold some insights and lessons for how to increase women's economic contributions to the labor force in LMICs today.

FOUR PHASES OF THE JOBS-TO-CAREERS TRANSITION

A seminal study on this topic mapped out this path using the framework of a transition from jobs to careers (Goldin 2006). It consists of four distinct phases (as further described below), starting with informal and agricultural work and proceeding from there (figure 1.1).

Phase I. In the late 1800s, US women were mainly involved in agricultural or factory work. As the Industrial Revolution took hold, women increasingly took jobs in factories. The rapid expansion in demand for labor brought women both out of agriculture and into the formal labor force. However, these jobs were often characterized by long hours, poor conditions, and low pay (Levine 1924). Because these jobs were often taken out of necessity to support family income, subsequent increases in spousal (husbands') income were associated with falling female labor force participation (FLFP). As husbands earned more, wives did not need to work as much outside the home, and their work in the home was substituted for work in the labor market.

FIGURE 1.1 **The Path from Jobs to Careers for US Women in the Twentieth Century**

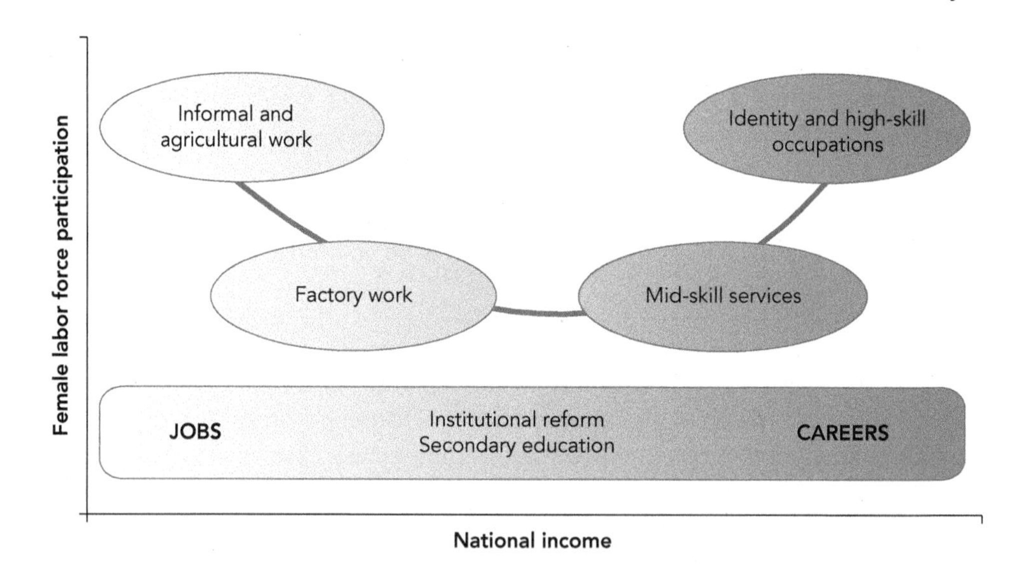

Sources: Based roughly on Goldin (1995, 2006).
Note: The shading of the stages represents the gradual transition, in a probabilistic sense, from jobs (lighter) to careers (darker).

Phase II. In the early 1900s, the expansion of clerical jobs offered a more pleasant alternative to factory work. Goldin (2006) argues that these working environments helped to ease the social stigma that had discouraged women from working in the formal labor market. At the same time, educational opportunities expanded, and women gained what economists call "general" skills that could be applied to a wide range of industries.

The shift from Phase I to Phase II (1890–1950) was associated with a significant shift across several indicators related to education, marriage, and the composition of women's employment in specific industries. Specifically, there was a decline in the share of employed (nonfarm) females in manufacturing, accompanied by a rise in both the share of services workers who were female and the share of females who worked in services. In the United States, this trend was related to the increased availability of clerical work. When women started working in clerical occupations, single women led the way, but later in the 1900s, it became the norm to find married women in these positions.

As secondary education expanded between 1910 and 1930, clerical workers earned higher wages, and more women could enter the workforce. In 1890, 32 percent of (nonfarm) employed females had worked in manufacturing and 4 percent as clerical workers; by 1920, these shares were 26 percent and 22 percent, respectively. By 1950, the share of women in manufacturing dipped to 22 percent and those in clerical work rose to nearly 28 percent (Goldin 1984). Similarly, between 1890 and 1920, females' share of total manufacturing employment dropped from 20 percent to 15 percent, and their share of all clerical workers increased from 15 percent to 48 percent. By 1950, females made up 62 percent of all clerical employment.

Phase III. The next phase (1950–70) included rising education levels and falling legal and other barriers to women's long-run attachment to the labor force. Throughout these years, the reduction of formal barriers to work and the expansion of opportunities in higher (postsecondary) education helped women shift from clerical positions into mid-skill services (such as teaching, nursing, social work, and library services) that required more investment in human capital. Even so, these occupations were characterized by intermittent interruptions in labor force participation (such as for child-rearing). Women could leave and return to the labor force without losing too much human capital because their general skills were not specific to a particular employer. These changes laid the foundation for what Goldin (2006) termed a "quiet revolution" in women's employment during Phase IV.

Phase IV. Starting in the late 1970s and extending into the twenty-first century, several fundamental changes occurred in women's employment and family relationships that characterize the "quiet revolution." One of the most important was the emergence of a sense of identity that came with work. Women invested in human capital with the expectation of long-term, consistent participation in the labor market. Another key change was that increases in their spouses' income were no longer associated with lower labor force participation. On the contrary, women's labor force participation became positively associated with their mates' income. In addition, women acquired a greater sense of identity within their occupations. Although career aspirations are achieved in different ways (Goldin 2021), a rising sense of identity tied to work increasingly motivated women to enter the labor force. Their income became less of a substitute for spousal income and more of a complement to it.

What Goldin describes as "identity" is related to a large and growing body of literature on female empowerment. Being formally employed as a single woman, or delaying entry into the workforce and marriage while pursuing a university education, offers a woman the opportunity to develop an identity apart from her parents and before marriage. Between the extremes of working because they have to and working because they want to, people experience a transition in mindset that employment, whether because of wages or skills, creates a greater sense of self-worth from being able to contribute to family, the workplace, or society.

Overall, these four phases represent a gradual transition from jobs to careers for the American woman, Goldin contends. The shading of figure 1.1 represents that transition, whereby factory work can include careers, and even occupations that some people associate with "careers" might be considered by others as "jobs." Importantly, the movement along the horizontal axis is also associated with rising education levels. That is, as women move from jobs to careers, they invest more in education. This is not to say that women in occupations that do not require much education do not consider their work to be a career, but rather that occupations requiring less education are less likely to be considered careers by most people.

That said, significant evidence is emerging that suggests that apparel employment can be associated with female empowerment. But whether it represents a transition from jobs to careers has not been explored.

THE "FEMINIZATION U HYPOTHESIS"

Economic development is closely related to female empowerment and specifically to labor participation. Since the 1960s, numerous researchers have stylized the "U-shaped" pattern found between female labor force participation (FLFP) and development (as evidenced by GDP per capita). Figure 1.2 illustrates what is now often called the "feminization U hypothesis"—that is, that FLFP first declines and then rises with the socioeconomic development process (Sinha 1967; Goldin 1995).

FLFP rates are high in poor countries because of the share of women engaging in subsistence activities, especially certain types of agriculture, as paid or unpaid workers on family farms. As countries industrialize, FLFP rates fall in middle-income countries, and the upward slope is characterized by growth in services, which opens opportunities for women and is accompanied by declining fertility rates and expansion of education for women.

FIGURE 1.2 Incidence of the U-Shaped Relationship between FLFP and National Income, 2017

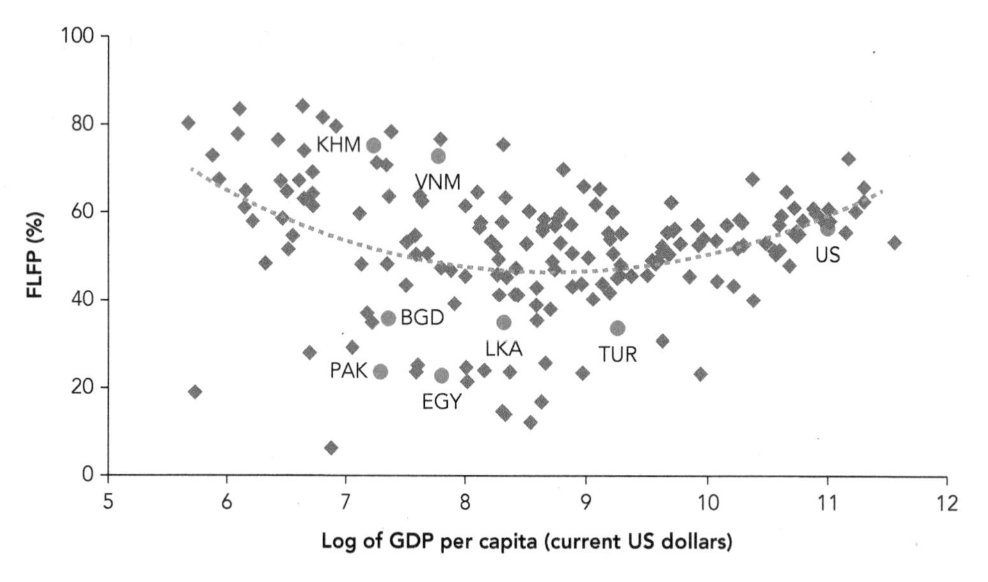

Sources: International Labour Organization model estimates and World Development Indicators data.

Note: The data cover 176 countries across all regions and income groups. The polynomial trend is not the best trend, because of outliers. ISO alpha-3 codes designate the seven case study countries: Bangladesh (BGD), Cambodia (KHM), the Arab Republic of Egypt (EGY), Pakistan (PAK), Sri Lanka (LKA), Turkey (TUR), and Vietnam (VNM). FLFP = female labor force participation; ISO = International Standards Organization; US = United States.

The history of women's employment in early-developing economies, such as the United States, follows the same pattern (Goldin 1995). Whereas the downward portion of the curve is related to an *income effect* suppressing women's formal labor market participation, the rising portion is explained by a predominant *substitution effect.*

Directly related to rising GDP per capita, Goldin argues that the expansion of education—specifically secondary education—was one of the most important triggers of sustained female labor inclusion and the occupational changes that later allowed women to transition from jobs to careers. The significant increase in secondary education during the first decades of the 1900s explains the upward portion of the curve, because it allowed women to have better-paid jobs, increased the cost of staying at home (substitution effect), and opened the doors to clerical occupations. In other words, the transition from jobs to careers seems to parallel the evolution of FLFP, according to the feminization U hypothesis.

However, the existence of this U-curve is increasingly debated. Many studies emphasize data issues with labor force surveys that make measurements of FLFP difficult and inaccurate (Gaddis and Klasen 2014); identify many countries that do not follow this pattern (Verick 2018); and suggest other significant factors that affect FLFP (Klasen 2019).

Moreover, a recent study points out that the relevance of the U-shape varies with country income, being (a) greater in high-income countries; (b) somewhat weaker in upper-middle-income countries; (c) not consistently found in lower-middle-income countries; and (d) not found at all in low-income countries, which have a reverse U-shape (Lechman and Kaur 2015). The study also points to high variability in the FLFP rate across countries in the same income groups or regions—which might reflect not only economic growth but also a wide array of legal, cultural, and social factors or the complexity of structural changes. This finding suggests that the U-shape was a more common development trajectory for countries moving from low to high income in the early twentieth century and may no longer be the norm. Several other explanatory factors are discussed in box 1.1.

What is relevant for this report is that although the U-shape mainly portrays a relationship between FLFP and national income, it is also closely related to the jobs-to-careers trajectory. Chapter 3 shows how, on a global scale, the distribution of female employment by sector follows the same U-shaped pattern, and thus the availability of low-, mid-, and high-skill occupations varies as country income rises. In fact, the distribution of employment across industries and occupations is one of the indicators that Goldin (2006) analyzes to explain the transition from women seeking jobs to women seeking careers in the United States. We take a similar approach to analyze whether the growth in apparel exports a decade (or more) ago is associated with the transition from jobs to careers, using four additional indicators: (a) investment in human capital, (b) marriage and FLFP, (c) lifetime FLFP, and (d) gender earnings gap.

BOX 1.1 Alternative Explanations for the Much-Debated Feminization U-Shaped Curve

The literature has put forward several factors as explanations for countries not showing a U-shaped pattern of FLFP and income.

Institutional and Cultural Factors

Restrictions associated with religion appear to have a strong relationship with FLFP in the Middle East and North Africa Region, where Verme (2015) finds no clear evidence of a U-shape—although it does exist in southern Mediterranean countries (Tsani et al. 2013; Verme 2015). Outside that region, countries sharing the same religion have contrasting results. There is evidence of a U-shaped link between FLFP and economic growth in Pakistan (Mujahid and Zafar 2012) but not in Turkey, which has a reverse U-shaped link (Dogan and Akyüz 2017).

Socialism has also had a strong and lasting impact on FLFP rates, as seen in countries in Eastern Europe and Central Asia (Klasen 2019). Socialism strongly promoted an ideology of gender equality, reflected by legal changes toward equality, universal schooling, and policies to promote the compatibility of employment with having small children (Klasen 1993). In addition, the persistent labor shortages associated with inefficient state-owned enterprises and collective farms necessitated more workers, and drawing more women into the labor force was essential for growth (Kornai 1992). Thus, cultural norms play an important but not a deterministic role.

The Education Factor

LMICs do not necessarily experience a decline in FLFP as national incomes increase, because economic growth is often accompanied by planned expansions in education. Education is an important enabler for women to obtain high-skill jobs as the economy develops (Lincove 2008).

Education is particularly seen as a potential booster for incorporating women into the labor force. In Latin America and the Caribbean and in East Asia, education policy has strongly increased the numbers of female university graduates (Gasparini and Marchionni 2017). More-educated women are usually paid higher wages, reinforcing the importance of education in FLFP (Lam and Duryea 1999). In Bangladesh, Brazil, and South Africa, the FLFP rate is rising uniformly with education (Klasen et al. 2020; Rahman and Islam 2013).

Trade-Related Factors

Women play an integral role in industrial employment and export production in LMICs (Lincove 2008). In Bangladesh, with the boom of the apparel industry and rise of livestock rearing (linked to access to microcredits), FLFP rates experienced a rapid increase after a low initial condition—without exhibiting the U-shaped path of development (Verick 2018). In the Middle East and North Africa, female participation is somewhat stronger in countries where export-oriented manufacturing and tourism play an important role (such as Egypt, Morocco, and Tunisia) than in the rest of the region (World Bank 2004).

Further, firms may invest more in technology in response to imported competition (Bloom, Draca, and Van Reenen 2016) or to export market expansion (Bustos 2011). This helps the FLFP rate because computerization and technology upgrading reduces the demand for strength-intensive skills, which are often the comparative advantage of male workers (Juhn, Ujhelyi, and Villegas-Sanchez 2014).

Note: FLFP = female labor force participation; LMICs = low- and middle-income countries.

Conceptual Framework: Household Labor Supply Decisions

How should we think about the many factors that affect female engagement in the labor market in the context of trade? One way to formalize these relationships is with a simple model of female labor supply—such as a simplified family-level standard labor supply model—that illustrates how many factors, including trade, can shape labor supply decisions (box 1.2).

BOX 1.2 A Model for Household Labor Supply Decisions

Consider a model of household labor supply that assumes that labor supply decisions are forward looking. One possible starting point is the seminal Stephens (2002) intertemporal household labor supply model. The model begins with a representative family's multiperiod utility optimization problem. Consider a representative family in which two spouses (represented by m and f) choose a level of consumption (C) and time spent in household production (including childcare, housework, and possibly leisure) of each spouse (L^m and L^f) to maximize the period t expected value of the discounted utility stream over the relevant time horizon (denoted as T, which might be the expected date of retirement). Defining p as the household's subjective discount rate, this maximization problem can be represented as

$$\max U_t = E_t\left[\sum_{k=t}^{T}\left(\frac{1}{1+\rho}\right)^{k-t} U(C_k, L_k^m, L_k^f)\right]. \tag{1.1}$$

Assuming the price of consumption goods is equal to one, households can consume up to the sum of labor income and current wealth. Households optimize according to equation (1.1) in every period by updating their information set. Defining current period wealth as A_t and exogenous market wages for each W_t^m and W_t^f, we can define the wealth accumulation to be a function of income, consumption, and a (real) interest rate r as

$$A_{t+1} = (1+r)\left[A_t + W_t^m(\bar{L} - L_t^m) + W_t^f(\bar{L} - L_t^f) - C_t\right]. \tag{1.2}$$

The total time available for work and leisure combined is $\bar{L}$. The utility function U is assumed to be strictly concave.

Optimization generates the key results that guide both our intuition and our empirical approach. Defining λ_t as the marginal utility of consumption (wealth), the optimal conditions are

$$\partial U / \partial C = \lambda_t = \left(\frac{1+r}{1+\rho}\right) E_t(\lambda_{t+1}), \tag{1.3}$$

$$\partial U / \partial L^m \geq \lambda_t W_t^m, \text{ and} \tag{1.4}$$

$$\partial U / \partial L^f \geq \lambda_t W_t^f. \tag{1.5}$$

(Box continues next page)

BOX 1.2 A Model for Household Labor Supply Decisions *(continued)*

Equations (1.3)–(1.5) can be used to express the conditions necessary for FLFP (the extensive margin) and the number of hours worked (the intensive margin). Since the utility function is strictly concave, we can show that

$$L_t^f = \begin{cases} L^f\left(\lambda_t, W_t^m, W_t^f\right) \text{ if } \partial U / \partial L^f = \lambda_t W_t^f \\ \bar{L} \text{ if } \partial U / \partial L^f > \lambda_t W_t^f \end{cases} . \quad (1.6)$$

The upper expression shows that the amount that women work (the intensive margin) is determined by the point at which the marginal utility of home production (possibly including leisure) is equal to the product of the marginal utility of wealth and the wage. Notably, this result is directly analogous to papers that explicitly model household production by equating the marginal value of the spouse's contribution to household production (the marginal revenue product) with the market wage (for example, Donni and Matteazzi 2018) but retains the intertemporal optimization that Stephens (2002) shows drives labor supply decisions.

The lower expression describes the decision to participate in the labor market (the extensive margin). If the marginal utility of leisure is greater than the marginal utility of wealth (consumption) times the labor market wage, then the woman would not participate in the labor market. As the market wage for women rises, participation is more likely. Given that female wages are generally lower than male wages in the labor market, lower FLFP rates are consistent with this model.

A LABOR SUPPLY-SIDE MODEL

The decision to work can depend on whether an individual is part of a household that includes other potential workers. Unmarried people living on their own in LMICs rarely have an option. Without unemployment insurance or other income support, single people are much more likely to work. Within a household, however, the decision to work can depend on whether other household members are working and what they earn. Work within the home also has value to the family. As a result, much of the labor supply literature focuses on household labor supply decisions that compare the value of working at home with the value of working in the market.

Although simple, this model generates a rich set of predictions. In many LMICs, social norms and pressures often result in the belief that women are more valued at home. This model shows that as the perceived relative value of household production rises, the spouse with the higher household value of home production will work less in the labor market (holding wages constant). If this ratio changes over the life cycle (such as over the ages of children), then the labor supply would vary appropriately (Attanasio, Low, and Sánchez-Marcos 2005). In addition, as women's wages rise, women are more likely to enter the labor force and work more hours. Therefore, to understand the link between trade and female labor market outcomes, we now turn to a simple model of the demand side of the labor market.

A LABOR DEMAND-SIDE MODEL

Consider a two-sector model in which both sectors use a combination of women and men to produce final output. If men and women are imperfect substitutes in production (for whatever reason) and the two sectors use different ratios of men and women, we can describe one as "female intensive" and the other as "male intensive." Many trade models—including recent models with heterogeneous firms (for example, Melitz 2003) with two sectors that differ in factor intensity—conclude that exports of one sector (holding the other constant) will increase demand for the workers intensively employed in that sector. Bernard, Redding, and Schott (2007) demonstrate this for skilled and less-skilled workers.

Traded goods have significant overlap with manufacturing industries. Within manufacturing, apparel is usually considered female intensive and other industries (as a group) as male intensive. Among export-oriented industries, the apparel industry employs a high number of females (labor intensive) and is the most female-intensive manufacturing industry. This is supported by our analysis and country studies (Klasen 2019; Kucera and Tejani 2014). As such, the apparel industry is not only the logical choice to explore in more depth but also has historically been among the only options for employing large numbers of female workers.

Given that we can describe traded industries as female intensive in apparel and male intensive in other manufacturing, consider figure 1.3. It follows directly from

FIGURE 1.3 **Model of FLFP Variation in Relation to Female and Male Contributions to Higher Family Income**

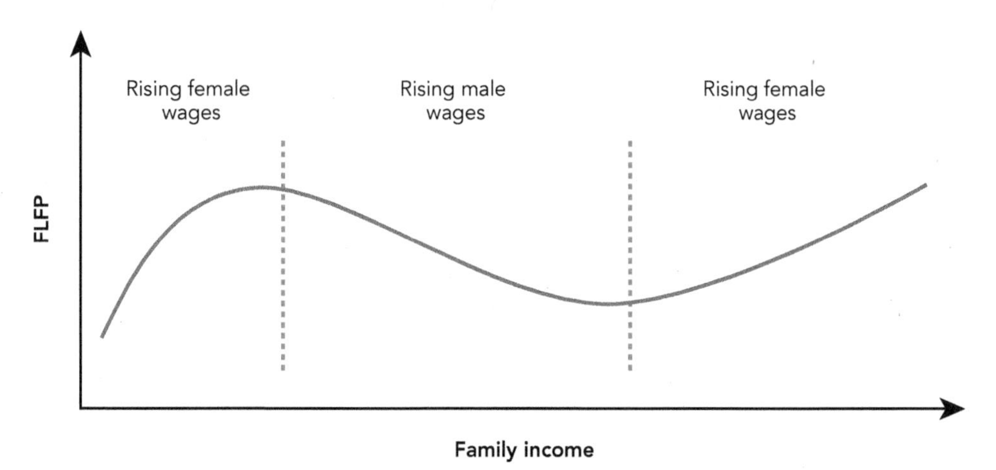

Source: World Bank elaboration.

Note: In this model, as demand for women's labor for apparel exports rises relative to men's (left section), women's wages rise, and women are more likely to enter the labor force and work more hours. But as men transition to industrial jobs with even higher wages (center section), those rising incomes are associated with less formal sector work by women in the same household. A country's transition to a more services-led economy (right section) again increases both demand and wages for women, increasing the female labor supply. FLFP = female labor force participation.

equations (1.3)–(1.6) and demonstrates how female engagement in the labor market, along either the extensive or intensive margin, increases as (family) income increases. It is divided into three areas, depending on whose income is driving the increase in family income:

- *In the leftmost section,* a rise in apparel exports increases the demand for women relative to men, so the relative wages of women increase. As a result, women work more on either the intensive margin or the extensive margin.
- *In the middle section,* male wages are rising relative to female wages. Within the household, equations (1.3)–(1.6) show that the rise in male wages induces a fall in the female labor supply. As the country diversifies and the share of male-intensive exports increases, the relative wages of males increase. For example, the move from female-intensive apparel toward automobiles and machinery is often associated with a transition from female to male employment because, for whatever reason, those industries hire more men. FLFP rates fall because of the transition of men to industrial jobs with higher wages than agriculture—in turn having a strong income effect for women living with men. The rise in husbands' incomes is hence associated with less formal sector work by wives.
- *In the rightmost section,* the economy transitions toward services, causing demand for women to increase again, and the higher wages in services result in a higher female labor supply. Over time, the change in one spouse's labor supply in response to changes in the other's earnings (and their own) can also change dramatically (Blau and Kahn 2007). The upward slope is explained by a strong substitution effect in which the rise in women's wages is associated with more time spent in the formal labor market owing to a larger labor demand.

The point of this model is that exports can either increase or decrease female employment, consistent with the varied results for the feminization U hypothesis in the literature. For exports to contribute to rising female employment, they must increase the demand for females more than the demand for males, which implies that exports of female-intensive goods will only increase FLFP if the exports are a significant fraction of exports and economic activity. The model also shows that FLFP could rise if the relative weights of female and male contributions within the home move toward equality, which might be the case as women move from jobs to careers.

Of course, there are numerous paths to boosting family income besides the departure from the labor market of one spouse, often the female. Another is a dual income household where neither spouse exits the labor market—assuming there are adequate employment opportunities for both men and women. In this scenario, apparel exports provide job opportunities that bring women into the labor force and raise family income because there are two wage earners. Importantly, this scenario can also contribute to female empowerment because it enables women to contribute economically to their family and provides a sense of identity outside the home.

Following the US findings of Goldin (2006), the transition from jobs to careers is associated with higher rates of upper-secondary graduation, which is highly associated with greater family wealth. The latter is an important driver of career development because it reduces the need for young adults to enter the labor market to support their families before completing secondary education. Goldin also found an increasing share of married women in the US workforce, indicating not only that women are staying in the labor market longer but also that dual income households are increasing.

Goldin's description of the US experience spans 100 years, roughly four to five generations. Pulling these pieces together provides an intergenerational pathway of how apparel employment contributes to female career development. In this model, we follow the case of a lower-middle-income country with an apparel industry. After primary or perhaps lower-secondary education, a daughter will likely leave school to work on the farm or assist with household activities. In fact, the few jobs that exist in such a rural area would require only low levels of education and tend to be filled by men. We can summarize an example of this process as follows (figure 1.4):

FIGURE 1.4 Model of an Intergenerational Female Pathway from Apparel Jobs to Careers

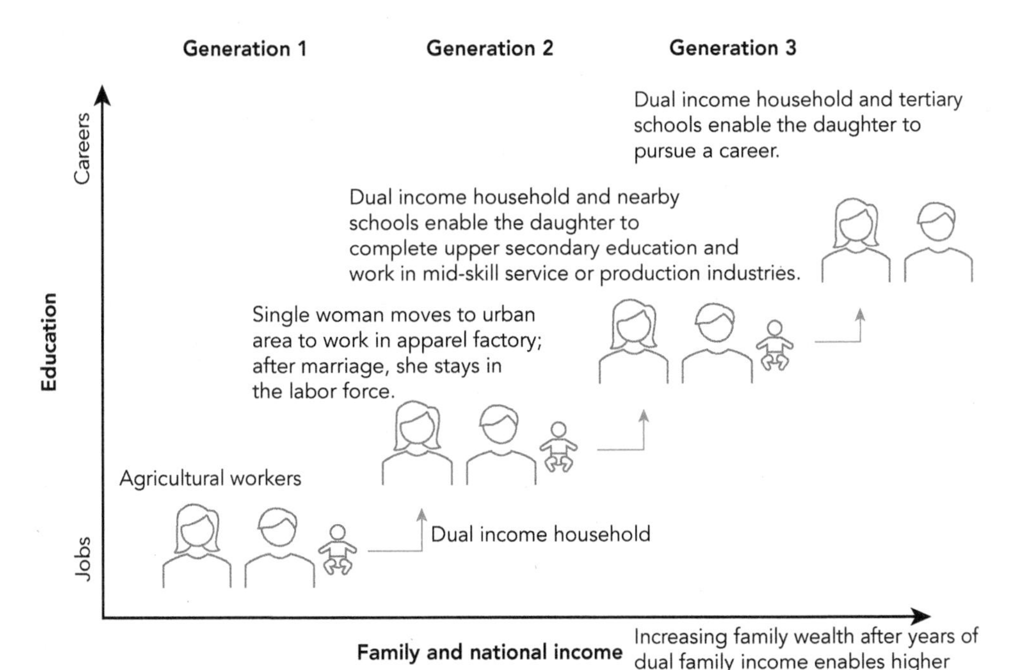

Source: World Bank.

- *First generation.* Consider a married couple that engage in agricultural work on a family farm and have a daughter. Since they live in a country with an export-oriented apparel industry, they can encourage their daughter to move to more-urban areas to work in an apparel factory. The daughter takes a job in an apparel factory and sends most of her earnings home to her parents to support the family, which also increases the average income of families in that rural area.
- *Second generation.* While this woman is working in the apparel factory, she gets married, and she and her husband have a daughter. Her income supports her husband and children, and she stays employed in the apparel factory. With the extra income earned through her job and the availability of secondary schools in the area, her daughter can complete upper-secondary education, giving her the credentials as a young woman to pursue a more career-like opportunity in a mid-skill service industry as a clerk or as a sales or service associate. Or perhaps a new apparel factory opens that pays higher wages and requires workers to have upper-secondary education, and the young woman chooses to continue in the industry.
- *Third generation.* If this woman then marries and continues to work, her daughter, in turn, could continue her studies through tertiary education and enter the labor market as a career professional—thanks to greater family wealth, access to tertiary education, and availability of career opportunities in urban areas.

This exact pattern may be unlikely in many cases. The intergenerational jumps in education and occupations may be smaller, a young woman may have multiple children and leave the workforce, or she may return to her hometown to raise a family. But the example does illustrate the importance of female jobs, such as apparel work, to the development process. In the absence of export-oriented manufacturing and services, women in lower-middle-income countries often have few formal employment opportunities. Without female jobs, there is low demand to increase female education and few ways to increase family income.

Country Cases and Labor Market Classifications

We naturally select countries important to the global apparel industry to identify labor market characteristics, opportunities, and challenges that the industry represents for the jobs-to-careers transition. Our apparel country cases represent a variety of circumstances and geographic areas. Other LMICs with important apparel industries (such as Costa Rica, the Dominican Republic, and Jordan) were considered but were not selected because of data limitations.

CASE COUNTRY CHARACTERISTICS

All the case countries except Egypt have been among the top 10 global apparel exporters at some point in the past three decades, and all have a higher apparel export value than the global average. Another commonality is their dependence on apparel exports. Among our case countries, Bangladesh, Cambodia, and Sri Lanka have the highest shares of total exports from apparel (with textile and apparel products being their main national exports), and Bangladesh and Cambodia have been dependent on apparel exports for over two decades.

Yet the apparel industry is also at varying stages of importance among these countries. The apparel share of exports peaked and is now declining in Cambodia, Egypt, Turkey, and Vietnam; is still increasing in Bangladesh and Pakistan; and remains flat in Sri Lanka.

Moreover, our case countries entered apparel exporting in different ways and advanced in income status during different periods. Cambodia, Sri Lanka, and Vietnam began in apparel manufacturing, whereas Bangladesh, Egypt, Pakistan, and Turkey focused on fibers and textiles before moving into apparel exporting. Bangladesh, Cambodia, Pakistan, and Vietnam transitioned from low-income to lower-middle-income countries between 2005 and 2015, while Egypt and Sri Lanka transitioned between 1994 and 1997, and Turkey transitioned from lower-middle- to upper-middle-income status in 2004.

In all the countries, however, apparel is the largest employer of females among manufacturing industries, and the number of female and male apparel workers increased over the periods of the labor force surveys analyzed. But while females account for 80 percent of apparel employment in Vietnam, 79 percent in Cambodia, and 72 percent in Sri Lanka, they represent less than half (46 percent) in both Bangladesh and Pakistan and 31 percent in Egypt (table 1.1). Turkey stands exactly at the halfway point.

Strikingly, consistent with the U-shape found in the cross-section of FLFP statistics and GDP per capita (shown earlier in figure 1.2), our case countries show that women are highly employed in either the agriculture or services sector, depending on each country's stage of industrialization. And wherever there is high female concentration in either of those sectors, the overall share of women in manufacturing is low. Yet the apparel manufacturing industries (often combined with textiles and leather manufacturing) are the major employers of women in manufacturing in all the case countries (box 1.3).

LABOR MARKET CLASSIFICATIONS

Note that the International Standard Industrial Classification of All Economic Activities (ISIC) system is the basis for describing economic activities. It can be used to group economic activities into three sectors: agriculture (which includes forestry, fishing, and

TABLE 1.1 Data Points on Female Labor in the Apparel Industry of Sample Middle-Income Countries

Country	Year of peak apparel export share	Peak share of apparel in total exports (%)	Share of apparel in total exports, 2018 (%)	Apparel share of all female labor (%)[a]	Female share of all apparel employment (%)[a]	FLFP rate, 1995–2015 (%)
Bangladesh	2018	88	88	8 (2016)	46 (2017)	26–32
Cambodia	2003	84	66	17 (2014)	79 (2017)	77–74
Egypt, Arab Rep.	1998	13	7	2 (2015)	31 (2017)	21–22
Pakistan	2017	39	37	9 (2015)	46 (2018)	13–24
Sri Lanka	2000	55	47	12 (2015)	72 (2017)	36–36
Turkey	1992	30	15	5 (2013)	50 (2017)	31–31
Vietnam	2003	19	11	6 (2015)	80 (2017)	72–73
Avg. all countries	2002	9	4	3 (2017)	57 (2017)	51–48

Sources: United Nations Comtrade database, representing Standard Industrial Trade Classification (SITC) 1-digit code 84 (articles of apparel and clothing accessories); International Labour Organization ILOSTAT data (1990–2030).

Note: FLFP = female labor force participation.

a. Data year is indicated within parentheses.

mining); manufacturing/industry; and services. This report uses "industry" to refer to a given 2-digit ISIC code.

We also define jobs and careers by occupational code using the International Standard Classification of Occupations (ISCO), comprising 10 major groups. The ISCO system associates occupational groups with skill levels, which are associated with education levels (table 1.2). ISCO skill levels traditionally have been based on typical educational attainment, but they now also emphasize the nature of the work performed—for example, the tools and machinery used and the amount of in-job training or experience needed for competent performance.

For our purposes, we focus on formal education at each skill level and occupation because of data availability. HSOs require more education, imply longer-term commitment to the labor market, and provide advancement opportunities; therefore, we often equate them with careers. However, we also recognize that career paths include long-term labor participation associated with in-job experience and permanence in the labor market. HSOs fall within ISCO codes 1–3, which include managerial, professional, and technician occupations. The occupations most likely to be associated with careers require workers to have upper-secondary and tertiary education.

BOX 1.3 Apparel: The Most Important Manufacturing Industry for Female Jobs

International Labour Organization data from the seven sample countries confirm that apparel is the most important manufacturing employer of women (table B1.3.1).

Agriculture Sector

Agriculture is the leading employer of women in Bangladesh and Pakistan, accounting for 60 and 66 percent of female employment, respectively. However, this is much less so in the other sample countries, where the agriculture sector's share of total female employment ranges from a low of 28 percent in Turkey to a high of 42 percent in Vietnam.

Manufacturing Sector

As with the global results across country income levels (later shown in chapter 3), the manufacturing sector overall accounts for the lowest share of female employment across the country cases. It accounts for the highest share in Sri Lanka (26 percent) and is insignificant in Egypt (6 percent). Within manufacturing, female employment is primarily in apparel (including textiles and leather) in Bangladesh, Cambodia, and Pakistan, whereas females work in a wider range of manufacturing industries in Sri Lanka, Turkey, and Vietnam.

Among apparel, textiles, and leather, apparel is the most important employer of women across the case countries—ranging from 2 percent of all female employment in Egypt to 16 percent in Cambodia. Textiles come second but are especially significant in Bangladesh, Pakistan, and Turkey, as are leather products (including footwear) in Vietnam. Apart from these segments, food product manufacturing matters in Sri Lanka, where it accounts for 5 percent of female employment.

Services Sector

Services account for a significant share of female employment in Egypt (57 percent), Turkey (57 percent), and Sri Lanka (45 percent). Across these countries, higher-skill, domestic-serving industries (such as education, human health services, and public administration) account for the largest shares, particularly in Egypt.

In Cambodia and Vietnam, high-skill industries are not yet important employers of females, but the mid-level service industries of retail trade and food and beverage services, combined, employ a share of females similar to the manufacturing sector. In Bangladesh, female employment is primarily in low-skill industries. In Pakistan, women work in a mix of high- and low-skill services, driven by the education industry and households as employers of domestic personnel.

(Box continues next page)

BOX 1.3 Apparel: The Most Important Manufacturing Industry for Female Jobs *(continued)*

TABLE B1.3.1 Share of Total Female Employment, by Sector and Selected Industries, in Sample Middle-Income Countries, 2017

Percent

Industry (ISIC4[a] code)	Turkey	Egypt, Arab Rep.	Bangladesh	Pakistan	Sri Lanka	Vietnam	Cambodia
Agriculture, forestry, mining (01–09)	28	37	60	66	30	42	41
Crop production (01)	28	37	59	66	29	39	38
Manufacturing (10–33)	14	6	15	16	26	20	22
Textiles, apparel, leather (13–15)	8	3	12	14	15	11	19
Textiles (13)	3	1	3	4	2	1	2
Apparel (14)	5	2	8	10	12	7	16
Leather (15)	0	0	0	0	1	4	1
Other manufacturing (10–12, 16–33)	6	3	4	2	11	9	3
Services (35–99)	57	57	25	17	45	39	38
High-skill services (84–86)	19	36	7	10	19	9	4
Mid-skill services (47, 56)	12	10	4	2	12	19	22
Low-skill services (96–97)	3	2	10	4	4	2	2
Residential care, social work (87–88)	4	1	0	0	0	0	0
Financial (64–69)	3	2	1	0	3	1	1
Other services	16	7	4	1	7	8	9

Source: International Labour Organization, ILOSTAT database.

Note: Table links aggregate data from International Labour Organization labor force surveys to International Industrial Standard Classification (ISIC) data to decompose female employment shares, by industry, in the seven case countries. (All ILOSTAT data are for 2017 except for 2018 data from Pakistan.) Shares are based on the sum of female employment available at the 2-digit ISIC level. In some cases, this provides different shares than data aggregated by economic activity; however, differences are 1 percentage point or less. Shares may not sum to sector and total shares because of rounding.

a. ISIC4 = *International Standard Industrial Classification of All Economic Activities (ISIC), Rev. 4* (UN DESA 2008).

TABLE 1.2 Job Classification by ISCO Code, Skill Level, and Education Level

ISCO major group	ISCO-88[a] major group	ISCO-08[b] major group	ISCO skill level	Education level	Aggregate group (ISCO codes): other terms used[c]
1	Legislators, senior officials, and managers	Managers	High (Levels 3 and 4)	Tertiary and upper secondary	Managers, professionals, and technicians (1–3): high-skill occupations (HSOs), careers
2	Professionals	Professionals			
3	Technicians and associate professionals	Technicians and associate professionals			
4	Clerks	Clerical support workers	Medium (Level 2)		Clerical workers (4): clerks
5	Service workers and shop and market sales workers	Services and sales workers		Secondary	Service and sales (5)
7	Craft and related trades workers	Craft and related trades workers			Craft trade and plant operators (7–8): production workers
8	Plant and machine operators and assemblers	Plant and machine operators and assemblers			
6	Skilled agricultural and fishery workers	Skilled agricultural, forestry, and fishery workers		Primary	Agricultural workers (6)
9	Elementary occupations	Elementary occupations	Low (Level 1)		Elementary occupations (9)
0	Armed forces[d]	Armed forces	Low, Medium, or High (Levels 1, 2, or 4)	Primary, secondary, or tertiary	n.a.

Source: Based on ILO 2012.

Note: ISCO skill levels are partially based on typical education levels attained, but since the 2008 adoption of ISCO-08, more emphasis has been placed on the nature of work performed. Hence, the education level associated with a particular ISCO major group (1–10) does not always align directly with that of other groups within the same skill level (high, medium, or low). For example, although ILO (2012) associates skilled agricultural and fishery workers (ISCO code 6) with Level 2 skill (generally associated with secondary education), our analysis finds that this occupation should instead be associated with primary education and is most appropriately grouped with elementary occupations (ISCO code 9). Similarly, we find that clerical occupations (ISCO code 4)—also associated with Level 2 skill, usually requiring secondary education—require upper-secondary education on average, and workers often have some tertiary education as well. ISCO = International Standard Classification of Occupations; n.a. = not applicable (not represented in this report).

a. ISCO-88, adopted in 1988, used the same 10 major groups as in the subsequent ISCO-08 but had named some of them slightly differently. In addition, its conceptual model placed more emphasis than ISCO-08 on formal education and training requirements in determining an occupation's skill level.

b. ISCO-08, adopted in 2008, reflects occupational changes (largely because of technological advancement) in the 20-year period since the development of ISCO-88. It also increased the emphasis on the nature of the work performed in determining an occupation's skill level.

c. "Aggregate group" represents the occupations as grouped in this report.

d. In ISCO-08, within ISCO major group 0—armed forces (military occupations)—occupations in submajor group 01 (commissioned officers) are at Skill Level 4, associated with tertiary education; those in submajor group 02 (noncommissioned officers) are at Skill Level 2, associated with secondary education; and all other occupations in major group 0 are at Skill Level 1, associated with primary education.

Road Map for the Report

As noted earlier, this report is structured around the path from jobs to careers and explores the relationship between apparel exports and the jobs-to-careers transition for women. The remaining chapters present the findings as follows:

- *Chapter 2: Do Apparel Exports Support a "Quiet Revolution"?* We ask how our sample countries fare on five performance indicators of this transition: (a) investment in human capital; (b) marriage and FLFP; (c) lifetime FLFP; (d) gender earnings gaps; and (e) distribution of employment across industries and occupations. The results show that, for most women, the transition from jobs to careers is still quite limited, suggesting the presence of significant barriers.
- *Chapter 3: What Are the Barriers to Career Development?* We identify and explore three barriers to the transition: (a) low demand for professional service industries (due to low GDP); (b) low education levels; and (c) societal and cultural norms that inhibit or dissuade women from working. The main results show that in some LMICs, limited demand for HSOs, combined with below-average female participation in mid-skill industries, are profound constraints that limit the opportunities for women beyond apparel production.
- *Chapter 4: How Does an Apparel Export Strategy Fit into the Jobs-to-Careers Transition?* We examine how apparel exports can contribute to the jobs-to-careers transition, focusing on how exporting apparel intersects with the three barriers. The main results are that the HSOs associated with careers are limited in manufacturing and that it is difficult for female apparel workers to move into other HSOs. Apparel offers opportunities beyond those in other manufacturing industries, but without a post-apparel economic development plan, apparel exports are not sufficient to drive a successful transition.
- *Chapter 5: How Can Countries Speed Up the Jobs-to-Careers Transition?* We pull these results together to offer policy recommendations to help countries better navigate the jobs-to-careers transition. The key finding is that the apparel industry can provide a launching pad for women if countries adopt complementary policies to boost human capital and strengthen the economy. These include (a) increasing the participation of female production workers in export-oriented apparel manufacturing and related industries; (b) increasing the number of female supervisors and upgrading jobs within apparel to manufacturing-related services; (c) increasing access to education to promote female participation in careers; and (d) breaking glass ceilings.

Note

1. For more information about Sustainable Development Goal (SDG) 5 on Gender Equality, including its specific targets and indicators, see the UN's SDG 5 Knowledge Base page: https://sdgs.un.org/goals/goal5.

References

Artuc, E., G. Lopez-Acevedo, R. Robertson, and D. Samaan. 2019. *Exports to Jobs: Boosting the Gains from Trade in South Asia*. South Asia Development Forum Series. Washington, DC: World Bank.

Attanasio, O., H. Low, and V. Sánchez-Marcos. 2005. "Female Labor Supply as Insurance against Idiosyncratic Risk." *Journal of the European Economic Association* 3 (2–3): 755–64.

Bernard, A., S. Redding, and P. Schott. 2007. "Comparative Advantage and Heterogeneous Firms." *Review of Economic Studies* 74 (1): 31–66.

Blau, F., and L. Kahn. 2007. "Changes in the Labor Supply Behavior of Married Women: 1980–2000." *Journal of Labor Economics* 25 (3): 393–438.

Bloom, N., M. Draca, and J. Van Reenen. 2016. "Trade Induced Technical Change? The Impact of Chinese Imports on Innovation, IT and Productivity." *Review of Economic Studies* 83 (1): 87–117. doi:10.1093/restud/rdv039.

Bustos, P. 2011. "Trade Liberalization, Exports, and Technology Upgrading: Evidence on the Impact of MERCOSUR on Argentinian Firms." *American Economic Review* 101 (1): 304–40.

Christian, M., B. Evers, and S. Barrientos. 2013. "Women in Value Chains: Making a Difference." Revised Summit Briefing No. 6.3, Capturing the Gains, Manchester, UK. http://www.capturingthegains.org/pdf/ctg_briefing_note_6.3.pdf.

Dogan, B., and M. Akyüz. 2017. "Female Labor Force Participation Rate and Economic Growth in the Framework of Kuznets Curve: Evidence from Turkey." *Review of Economic Business Studies* 10 (1): 33–54.

Donni, O., and E. Matteazzi. 2018. "Collective Decisions, Household Production, and Labor Force Participation." *Journal of Applied Econometrics* 33 (7): 1064–80.

Feldman, S. 2009. "Historicizing Garment Manufacturing in Bangladesh: Gender, Generation, and New Regulatory Regimes." *Journal of International Women's Studies* 11 (1): 268–88.

Fernández, R. 2013. "Cultural Change as Learning: The Evolution of Female Labor Force Participation over a Century." *American Economic Review* 103 (1): 472–500.

Gaddis, I., and S. Klasen. 2014. "Economic Development, Structural Change, and Women's Labor Force Participation: A Reexamination of the Feminization U Hypothesis." *Journal of Population Economics* 27 (3): 639–81.

Gasparini, L., and M. Marchionni, eds. 2017. *Bridging Gender Gaps? The Rise and Deceleration of Female Labor Force Participation in Latin America*. Montevideo, Uruguay: Center for Distributive, Labor and Social Studies (CEDLAS).

Ghosh, J. 2002. "Globalization, Export-Oriented Employment for Women and Social Policy: A Case Study of India." *Social Scientist* 30 (11/12): 17–60.

Goldin, C. 1984. "The Historical Evolution of Female Earnings Functions and Occupations." *Explorations in Economic History* 21 (1): 1–27.

Goldin, C. 1995. "The U-Shaped Female Labor Force Function in Economic Development and Economic History." In *Investment in Women's Human Capital*, edited by T. P. Schultz, 61–90. Chicago: University of Chicago Press.

Goldin, C. 2006. "The Quiet Revolution that Transformed Women's Employment, Education, and Family." *American Economic Review* 96 (2): 1–21.

Goldin, C. 2021. *Career and Family: Women's Century-Long Journey toward Equity*. Princeton, NJ: Princeton University Press.

ILO (International Labour Organization). 2012. *International Standard Classification of Occupations, ISCO-08, Volume I: Structure, Group Definitions and Correspondence Tables.* Geneva: ILO.

ILO (International Labour Organization). 2018. *Women and Men in the Informal Economy: A Statistical Picture.* 3rd ed. Geneva: International Labour Office.

Juhn, C., G. Ujhelyi, and C. Villegas-Sanchez. 2014. "Men, Women, and Machines: How Trade Impacts Gender Inequality." *Journal of Development Economics* 106: 179–93.

Kabeer, N. 2013. *Paid Work, Women's Empowerment and Inclusive Growth: Transforming the Structures of Constraint.* New York: UN Entity for Gender Equality and the Empowerment of Women (UN Women).

Klasen, S. 1993. "Gender Inequality and Development Strategies: Lessons from the Past and Policy Issues for the Future." Working Paper 992987383402676, International Labour Office, Geneva.

Klasen, S. 2019. "What Explains Uneven Female Labor Force Participation Levels and Trends in Developing Countries?" *World Bank Research Observer* 34 (2): 161–97.

Klasen, S., L. Tú Thị Ngọc, J. Pieters, and M. Santos Silva. 2020. "What Drives Female Labour Force Participation? Comparable Micro-Level Evidence from Eight Developing and Emerging Economies." *Journal of Development Studies* 57 (3): 417–42.

Korinek, J., E. Moïsé, and J. Tange. 2021. "Trade and Gender: A Framework of Analysis." OECD Trade Policy Paper No. 246, Organisation for Economic Co-operation and Development Publishing, Paris. doi:10.1787/6db59d80-en.

Kornai, János. 1992. *The Socialist System: The Political Economy of Communism.* Princeton, NJ: Princeton University Press.

Kucera, D., and S. Tejani. 2014. "Feminization, Defeminization, and Structural Change in Manufacturing." *World Development* 64: 569–82.

Lam, D., and S. Duryea. 1999. "Effects of Schooling on Fertility, Labor Supply, and Investments in Children, with Evidence from Brazil." *Journal of Human Resources* 34 (1): 160–92.

Lechman, E., and H. Kaur. 2015. "Economic Growth and Female Labor Force Participation – Verifying the U-Feminization Hypothesis: New Evidence for 162 Countries over the Period 1990–2012." *Economics & Sociology* 8 (1): 246–57.

Levine, L. 1924. *The Women's Garment Workers: A History of the International Ladies' Garment Workers' Union.* New York: B. W. Huebsch.

Lincove, J. 2008. "Growth, Girls' Education, and Female Labor: A Longitudinal Analysis." *Journal of Developing Areas* 41 (2): 45–68.

Lopez-Acevedo, G., and R. Robertson, eds. 2012. *Sewing Success? Employment, Wages, and Poverty Following the End of the Multi-Fibre Arrangement.* Directions in Development Series. Washington, DC: World Bank. doi:10.1596/978-0-8213-8778-8.

Macchiavello, R., A. Menzel, A. Rabbani, and C. Woodruff. 2020. "Challenges of Change: An Experiment Promoting Women to Managerial Roles in the Bangladeshi Garment Sector." Working Paper 27606, National Bureau of Economic Research, Cambridge, MA. doi:10.3386/w27606.

Melitz, M. J. 2003. "The Impact of Trade on Intra-Industry Reallocations and Aggregate Industry Productivity." *Econometrica* 71 (6): 1695–1725.

Mujahid, N., and N. uz Zafar. 2012. "Economic Growth–Female Labour Force Participation Nexus: An Empirical Evidence for Pakistan." *Pakistan Development Review* 51 (4): 565–85.

Ostry, J., J. Alvarez, R. Espinoza, and C. Papageorgiou. 2018. "Economic Gains from Gender Inclusion: New Mechanisms, New Evidence." Staff Discussion Note No. 18/06, International Monetary Fund, Washington, DC.

Rahman, R., and R. Islam. 2013. "Female Labour Force Participation in Bangladesh: Trends, Drivers and Barriers." Asia-Pacific Working Paper Series, International Labour Organization, Geneva.

Safa, H. 1994. "Export Manufacturing, State Policy, and Women Workers in the Dominican Republic." In *Global Production: The Apparel Industry in the Pacific Rim*, edited by E. Bonacich, L. Cheng, N. Chinchilla, N. Hamilton, and P. Ong, 247–67. Philadelphia: Temple University Press.

Sinha, J. N. 1967. "Dynamics of Female Participation in Economic Activity in a Developing Economy." In *Proceedings of the World Population Conference, Belgrade, 30 August–10 September 1965. Volume IV.* New York: United Nations.

Stephens, M., Jr. 2002. "Worker Displacement and the Added Worker Effect." *Journal of Labor Economics* 20 (3): 504–37.

Tokatli, N., Ö. Kızılgün, and J. E. Cho. 2011. "The Clothing Industry in Istanbul in the Era of Globalisation and Fast Fashion." *Urban Studies* 48 (6): 1201–15.

Tsani, S., L. Paroussos, C. Fragiadakis, I. Charalambidis, and P. Capros. 2013. "Female Labour Force Participation and Economic Growth in the South Mediterranean Countries." *Economics Letters* 120 (2): 323–28.

UN DESA (United Nations Department of Economic and Social Affairs). 2008. *International Standard Industrial Classification of All Economic Activities (ISIC), Rev. 4.* New York: United Nations.

Verick, S. 2018. "Female Labor Force Participation and Development." *IZA World of Labor* 87v2: 1–11.

Verme, P. 2015. "Economic Development and Female Labor Participation in the Middle East and North Africa: A Test of the U-Shape Hypothesis." *IZA Journal of Labor & Development* 4: Article 3. doi:10.1186/s40175-014-0025-z.

World Bank. 2004. *Gender and Development in the Middle East and North Africa: Women in the Public Sphere.* Washington, DC: World Bank.

World Bank. 2011. *World Development Report 2012: Gender Equality and Development.* Washington, DC: World Bank.

World Bank and WTO (World Trade Organization). 2020. *Women and Trade: The Role of Trade in Promoting Gender Equality.* Washington, DC: World Bank.

CHAPTER 2

Do Apparel Exports Support a "Quiet Revolution"?

Key Messages

- This report investigates five performance indicators to evaluate whether there are signs of a jobs-to-careers transition for women in seven middle-income apparel exporting countries.
- The five performance indicators are (a) investment in human capital (notably, education); (b) marriage and labor force participation; (c) lifetime labor force participation; (d) earnings gaps between men and women; and (e) distribution of employment across occupations and industries.
- Even though countries such as Sri Lanka and Vietnam provide enough access to education to activate women's career paths in clerical and managerial occupations, the presence of women in such positions does not by itself signal that the transition has occurred.
- A career pathway that rewards labor market experience over education might still be feasible for women in countries with insufficient incentives for—and cultural norms against—continued studying. In Sri Lanka, however, women must have more than lower-secondary education to have better returns than males, although the wage gap is narrowing.

Introduction

A first step in examining whether exports, especially in apparel, can lead to better employment opportunities for women—particularly for "careers" as opposed to "jobs"—is to evaluate how women are doing in their effort to become more empowered in apparel exporting middle-income countries. But how can this be measured?

The transition from jobs to careers for women is multidimensional. Goldin (2006) identifies at least five performance indicators that labor force surveys can capture (figure 2.1):

- Investment in human capital
- Marriage and labor force participation
- Lifetime labor force participation
- Earnings gaps between men and women
- Distribution of employment across occupations and industries

This chapter evaluates these performance indicators in the apparel exporting countries featured in this report: Bangladesh, Cambodia, the Arab Republic of Egypt, Pakistan, Sri Lanka, Turkey, and Vietnam. These indicators help demonstrate how apparel exports support the transition from jobs to careers as well as identify barriers that directed policies might address. Because the indicators have been most thoroughly evaluated in the United States, we informally compare their evolution in the United States with current measures in our focus countries.

Here, we draw on the US experience in the twentieth century. Goldin (2006) divides this transition from jobs to careers into four phases (further described in chapter 1):

I. *In the late 1800s,* many women who had been mainly involved in agricultural work moved into factory work as the Industrial Revolution took hold.

II. *In the early 1900s,* women increasingly moved out of manufacturing and into clerical jobs.

III. *Between 1950 and 1970,* women moved into occupations that required more investment in human capital—changes that laid the foundation for Phase IV.

IV. *Starting in the late 1970s,* women's employment underwent fundamental changes that Goldin (2006) termed a "quiet revolution" in women's employment. A sense of identity emerged that came with work, and women invested in their human capital with the expectation of long-term, consistent participation in the labor force.

Note that we consider "jobs" to be remunerated activities that people do to survive. They offer little inherent satisfaction but provide enough income to maintain a given standard of living. In contrast, "careers" are remunerated activities that provide both income and purpose given the investments (such as in education) necessary to have

FIGURE 2.1 **Five Indicators of Women's Shift from Jobs to Careers, as Captured by Labor Force Surveys**

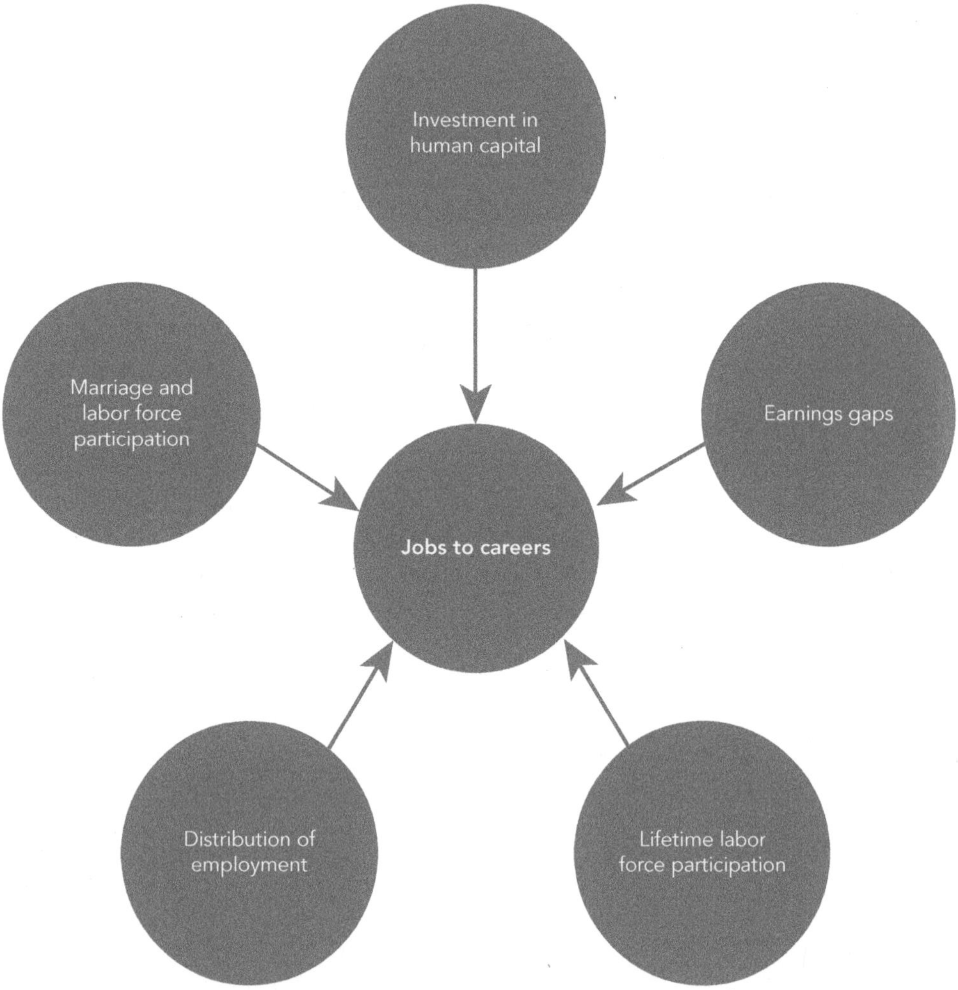

Source: World Bank based on Goldin 2006.

such occupations. The difference also goes beyond occupational classification and educational attainment. Although jobs and careers are not synonymous with occupations, jobs tend to be associated with low-skill occupations and careers with high-skill occupations (HSOs).

This chapter reviews each indicator, using labor force survey data, to illustrate how the indicators differ across our sample countries and then compares them with the same indicators in the United States during its jobs-to-careers transition. A key finding from this study is that apparel does not directly support such a "quiet revolution"—but it does indirectly help lay the groundwork for this to happen.

Indicator One: Investment in Human Capital

By "investment in human capital," this study means investment in people through formal education. At least as far back as Becker (1975), scholars have documented a significant positive relationship between education and earnings. Kabeer and Natali (2013) argue that education plays a critical role in helping to maximize women's contribution to economic growth. Different levels of education matter for accessing either job- or career-oriented pathways. Literacy and completion of primary education are associated with lower fertility levels and positive health-seeking behavior. Completion of upper-secondary and tertiary education is needed to enter many, if not most, occupations associated with careers.

US EDUCATION PATTERNS AND DRIVING FACTORS

Some interesting education patterns emerge from Goldin's work on the United States, focusing on women's attainment of secondary education and the importance of expanding it to facilitate the jobs-to-careers transition (Goldin 2006; Goldin and Katz 2008a, 2008b). In the United States, the shift from Phase I to Phase II—that is, from agriculture and factory work to clerical work—was accompanied by an increase in high school (upper-secondary) graduation rates and the growth of secondary educational institutions from the 1910s to the 1940s (Goldin 2006). US overall high school graduation rates increased from 9 percent in 1910 to 27 percent in 1928. In the states outside the South, the corresponding increase was from 11 percent to 32 percent, and then to 56 percent by 1938.

Education levels result from both *supply-side factors* (the presence, distribution, and quality of public and private schools as well as government requirements for education) and *demand-side factors* (reflecting individuals' or families' decisions to invest in education). Several studies that explore measures of both the supply and demand sides around the world show that both play critical roles in determining educational outcomes (Goldin and Katz 2008a, 2008b). In the United States particularly, state expenditures on public colleges and universities created a powerful incentive for youths to graduate from high school.

Although Goldin and Katz (2008a) suggest that compulsory schooling and stricter child labor laws did not play the most pivotal roles in increasing US secondary school graduation rates, evidence from other countries suggests that such laws have been effective, particularly when accompanied by large increases in education access and spending. The researchers argue that US secondary school enrollment expanded because of factors such as the substantial wage returns to each additional year of school, increased family wealth, and greater school access. Governments can always invest in providing more education, so we focus on the more nuanced demand-side investment decision.

Children's parents affect the decision to stay in school, and family wealth affects whether they encourage children to stay in school after lower-secondary education or to enter the workforce. The decision to send one's children to school or perhaps even to invest in more schooling for oneself depends on both direct costs (such as tuition, fees, and supplies) and indirect costs (such as forgone earnings) as well as on the longer-run benefits that come in the form of higher lifetime earnings. Market factors influence these higher lifetime earnings—referred to as "returns to education" or "returns to human capital."

Market factors can also affect the earnings workers would forgo by choosing to stay in school rather than entering the workforce. For example, Goldin and Katz (2008b) find that the expanding US manufacturing sector was a deterrent to high school graduation, especially in the US South and select industrial states in New England. More recently, Atkin (2016) finds a similar result from the expansion of Mexican manufacturing along the US-Mexico border. Therefore, the expansion of apparel employment in low- and middle-income countries (LMICs) might make working more attractive than staying in school and thus might slow the transition from jobs to careers.

EDUCATION PATTERNS IN THE CASE COUNTRIES

What has happened with education levels in our sample countries in recent years? Although our study has limited time series (generally of only five to seven years), it consistently finds that the share of females with some formal education has increased (table 2.1). In Cambodia, Egypt, and Pakistan, the shares of women who completed primary and lower-secondary education rose. Lower-middle-income Sri Lanka and Vietnam resemble the trends in Turkey, an upper-middle-income country, where the share of Turkish women completing upper-secondary and tertiary education increased.

To the extent that years of education are comparable across countries, it is useful to compare the 7.4 average years of education observed in the United States in 1900 (before US women were transitioning to clerical occupations) with the current education levels in apparel exporting countries. The results show that education policies are clearly much more relevant in some countries than others.

In the first year for which we have data, women in all the case countries except Sri Lanka have lower average education levels than US women did in 1900. In contrast, Sri Lanka shows average years of education similar to the United States in 1940, which was toward the end of its Phase II.

By the latest years of data, women in Egypt and Vietnam and working women in Turkey also have average education levels similar to US women in the early 1900s. In these countries, more than one in every two women have at least completed lower-secondary education, and one in every three women have completed upper-secondary education.

TABLE 2.1 Average Years of Female Education in Sample Middle-Income Countries and the United States, Overall and by Labor Participation Status

	First data year			Last data year		
Country (data years)	Population	Nonworking	Working	Population	Nonworking	Working
Bangladesh (2013)[a]	—	—	—	7.4	7.4	7.2
Cambodia (2007, 2014)	3.4	3.1	3.6	4.8	5.2	4.8
Egypt, Arab Rep. (2009, 2015)	6.1	5.8	7.7	7.1	6.7	9.2
Pakistan (2008, 2015)	4.0	4.3	2.6	4.6	5.2	2.8
Sri Lanka (2007, 2015)	10.0	12.1	9.8	10.8	12.4	10.6
Turkey (2011, 2013)	6.0	5.5	7.4	6.3	5.7	7.9
Vietnam (2007, 2015)	7.2	6.9	7.8	7.7	6.8	8.4
United States (1900, 1940)[b]	7.4	—	—	10.3	—	—

Sources: Labor force survey data; Goldin 2006.

Note: The mean is estimated on the basis of completed levels of education except for Sri Lanka because of data constraints. Sri Lanka includes partial-level competition. — = comparable data not available.

a. Bangladesh labor force survey data do not report completed years of education until 2013.

b. The US data are the mean years of schooling from Smith and Ward (1985) for female cohorts born 1866–85 (for 1900); 1886–1905 (for 1920, which is 8.5 years and not shown in table); and 1906–25 (for 1940)—each cohort generally representing women who were 15-to-34-year-olds in the years shown. The 1900–40 period represents roughly Phase I and Phase II of the jobs-to-careers transition described by Goldin (2006).

However, in Cambodia and Pakistan, although the years of education have increased among the female population, females still average less than five years of education, which is similar to or less than primary education. And in Bangladesh, most women have completed primary education but do not proceed to further studies.

Indicator Two: Marriage and Labor Force Participation

To assess marriage and labor force participation, this report uses the model further described in chapter 1 to analyze how households make labor supply decisions. In short, married couples usually want to combine income from working in the market with "household production" from working in the home. The worker who would earn less in the market often works more within the home. Thus, changes in expected earnings for either spouse can change the balance of work. That is why the difference between jobs and careers for women—reflecting the relative weight placed on women's work at home—helps explain how changes in expected wages affect female labor force participation (FLFP).

THE RISE OF MARRIED WOMEN IN THE US WORKFORCE

In other words, when a woman's work within the home is less valued, as when a woman has a career, an increase in the husband's wage is less likely to result in his wife giving up work outside the home. But if the family thinks of the wife's employment as a "job" and thus values her work within the home more highly in relative terms, an increase in the husband's wage could deter her from staying in the labor force.

Economists describe this difference with the terms "income effect" and "substitution effect." When household income rises, its members "buy" more household production by working less in the formal labor market. However, a wage increase also raises the opportunity cost of household production, so they buy less of it by working more. When a wage increase is associated with more hours worked in the labor market, economists say that the substitution effect dominates the income effect (Blau, Ferber, and Winkler 2010).

Traditional gender roles often result in women leaving a job and spending more time at home. Higher wages for women, however, may attract women to the labor force, such as in the decision to pursue a career. In this case, the substitution effect prevails, and women are more likely to return to work after marriage or even when husbands' wages increase.

One way to tell whether the income effect or the substitution effect dominates is to compare the average education level of working married women with that of the total population. Goldin (2006) argues that if the average married woman worker is less educated than the population average, the income effect dominates because the wages of less-educated workers are lower (lower market returns), and lower education levels are associated with jobs instead of careers. In the early 1900s, Goldin shows, US working women had lower education levels than the rest of the population. By the 1940s, however, the average married working woman had a higher education level than in the general population, suggesting that the substitution effect had come to dominate the income effect.

Rising labor force participation rates of married women and a rising share of female workers who are married are indications that workers' attitudes and perceptions about their jobs are changing. The mere length of time spent working in a job does not depend on an investment of time or money to prepare for the occupation. In the United States, for example, there was a relatively brief period in which women did not necessarily plan to remain in the labor force; therefore, although they were working, they did not invest in either training or education that would generate longer-term payoffs for women.

US statistics illustrate these changes. Only 8 percent of the employed were married in 1890. By 1930, this figure had risen to 26 percent and by 1950, to 47 percent. The labor force participation rate for married women aged 35–44 years increased from 10 percent in 1930 to 25 percent in 1950 and to 46 percent in 1970—a time span encompassing Phases II and III of the US jobs-to-careers transition (Goldin 2006). Further, US married women's labor supply continued to rise dramatically in the 1980s, with a smaller increase in the 1990s (Blau and Kahn 2007). The increase in the share of married female workers and an increase in the average age of female workers indicate a changing mindset. And as more women view their involvement in the labor force as long term, employers may be more likely to invest in female skill development and help reduce gender wage gaps.

JOBS-TO-CAREERS INDICATORS FOR MARRIED WOMEN IN CASE COUNTRIES

Which effect has been dominant in our sample countries: the income effect or the substitution effect? When the rising income that comes with more education is valued more in the labor market, the substitution effect dominates. But when it is valued less than household production, the income effect will dominate.

Education Level

Table 2.2 shows the ratio of the average years of education for married working females to that of the total married female population. A ratio greater than 1 indicates that the substitution effect dominates, which is evidence of a transition toward careers. On the other hand, a ratio below 1 indicates that the income effect dominates, which suggests

TABLE 2.2 Ratio of Married Working Women's Years of Education to All Married Women in Sample Middle-Income Countries, by Earliest and Latest Data Year

Country	Earliest data year	Latest data year	Min	Max
Bangladesh[a]	0.92	n.a.	n.a.	n.a.
	(2013)	n.a.	n.a.	n.a.
Cambodia	1.20	1.00	0.97	1.20
	(2007)	(2014)	(2011)	(2007)
Egypt, Arab Rep.	1.29	1.33	1.21	1.33
	(2009)	(2015)	(2010)	(2015)
Pakistan	0.57	0.53	0.49	0.65
	(2008)	(2015)	(2013)	(2011)
Sri Lanka	1.03	1.03	0.96	1.03
	(2007)	(2015)	(2013)	(2014)
Turkey	1.36	1.36	1.36	1.37
	(2011)	(2013)	(2011)	(2012)
Vietnam	1.03	1.02	1.02	1.03
	(2007)	(2015)	(2015)	(2010)

Source: Labor force survey data.

Note: The survey year for each statistic is in parentheses under the ratio. A ratio above (below) 1 indicates that the substitution effect (income effect) dominates. The higher (lower) the ratio, the likelier the prevalence of careers (jobs) for women. n.a. = not applicable.

a. Bangladesh labor force survey data do not report completed years of education until 2013.

the prevalence of jobs instead of careers. The results show several differences across the seven case countries:

- Two countries, Egypt and Turkey, have ratios significantly above 1. Working married women have higher education levels than married women overall, which is evidence that the labor market rewards investment in education—a positive sign of a transition toward careers.
- Three countries—Cambodia, Sri Lanka, and Vietnam—have ratios at or close to 1.
- Two countries, Bangladesh and Pakistan, have ratios lower than 1, suggesting the prevalence of women's jobs as opposed to careers.

When the average education of *working* married women is similar to or lower than that of the *total* married female population, it could mean that wages are not high enough to encourage women to pursue higher levels of education. Alternatively, it could mean that the labor market does not offer enough employment opportunities or the right incentives for more-educated women to join the workforce. The latter scenario seems most likely for Sri Lanka, given its higher average levels of education.

Labor Force Participation

Another measure is the labor force participation (LFP) rate of married women, given that when the income effect dominates, working women typically leave the labor force when they get married. The LFP rate of married workers is the share of both employed and unemployed people in the married working-age population (generally aged 15–65 years) who are seeking a job. Because marriage rates vary by age, it is important to control for age when evaluating LFP rates. In 1950 in the United States, the LFP rate of married women aged 35–44 years was 25 percent; this increased to 46 percent by 1970.

The share of the overall female workforce that is married increased or remained stable in all focus countries except Egypt (table 2.3). In addition, marriage seems to have a smaller effect over time in discouraging women from participating in the labor market. In fact, for working women aged 35–44 years, marriage rates in all countries are higher than they were in the United States in 1950 (47 percent).

Interestingly, marriage rates are lower among female apparel workers than in the overall working female population. However, apparel marriage rates have dramatically increased (by 7–18 percentage points) in a short period.

Mean Age at First Marriage

Because long-term careers require more human capital investment, careers are often associated with delayed marriage. One measure of age at first marriage is the singulate mean age at marriage (SMAM), which the United Nations Development Programme (UNDP) calculates using the marital status categories of men and women aged 15–54 years for each wave of the national survey data they collect. In the most recent year

TABLE 2.3 Marriage Rates of Working Women and FLFP Rates of Married Women in Sample Middle-Income Countries, by Earliest and Latest Data Years

		Marriage rate, working female population			Married FLFP rate	
Country	**Year**	**Overall**	**Apparel**	**36–45 years**	**Overall**	**36–45 years**
Bangladesh	2005	79	56	73	30	33
	2016	84	72	81	36	43
Cambodia	2007	50	28	66	47	48
	2014	58	37	74	96	96
Egypt, Arab Rep.	2009	72	24	84	25	28
	2015	67	31	84	24	25
Pakistan	2008	71	42	85	24	27
	2015	72	60	86	25	27
Sri Lanka	2008	69	51	85	39	48
	2015	72	59	86	38	47
Turkey	2011	67	45	79	28	36
	2013	67	53	78	30	40
Vietnam	2007	74	57	85	81	90
	2015	77	73	87	81	91

Source: Labor force survey data.

Note: "Overall" marriage rates are of all working females only. Female labor force participation (FLFP) rates are estimated using the female married population only, calculated as the share of both employed and unemployed married females of working age (15–65 years) who are seeking a job.

available from the UNDP for our seven case countries, the female SMAM is lowest in Bangladesh (18.8 years) and highest in Sri Lanka, Turkey, and Pakistan, at 23.4, 23.3, and 23.0 years, respectively (table 2.4). In the United States, the female median age of marriage was 21.2 in 1920, but the SMAM reached 27.5 by 2010.[1]

These ages show that, in Bangladesh, women are getting married just slightly above the age when women finish upper-secondary education, and in Cambodia, they are doing so before the age when one would typically complete tertiary education. The latter explains the results of table 2.1, which shows that in Bangladesh and Cambodia, most women do not continue studying beyond lower-secondary education. (Pakistan also has low female educational attainment, but its relatively higher female SMAM might indicate explanations other than marriage.) Therefore, if women switch to childcare activities after marriage, the relatively young marriage age suggests that women are withdrawing from the labor market with few years of experience. The impacts of such decisions can complicate women's reentry into the labor market later in life, halting the development of a career path.

In Egypt, Sri Lanka, Turkey, and Vietnam, where the female SMAM is 22 years or more (about the average age women complete a college degree), the shares of women

TABLE 2.4 Singulate Mean Age at Marriage for Females in Sample Middle-Income Countries, Early 2010s, and the United States, 1920

Country (year of data)	SMAM
Sri Lanka (2012)	23.4
Turkey (2013)	23.3
Pakistan (2013)	23.0
Vietnam (2014)	22.4
Egypt, Arab Rep. (2014)	22.0
Cambodia (2014)	21.6
Bangladesh (2014)	18.8
United States (1920)	21.2

Sources: "World Marriage Data 2019" data set, United Nations Department of Economic and Social Affairs (UN DESA), Population Division: https://population.un.org/MarriageData/Index.html; "Historical Marital Status Tables 1950 to 1990, and Current Population Survey," US Census Bureau: https://www.census.gov/data/tables/time-series/demo/families/marital.html.

Note: Singulate mean age at marriage (SMAM) is "the average length of single life expressed in years among those who marry before age 50. It is a synthetic indicator calculated from marital status categories of men and women aged 15–54 years at the census or survey date" (UN DESA 2013).

with at least upper-secondary education are 59, 43, 38, and 29 percent, respectively (from labor force survey data). Thus, women are deciding to delay marriage either (a) until they have enough education to pursue a career, or (b) until they have more labor market experience. Both explanations would better enable women to continue a career after an interruption due to childcare.

Indicator Three: Lifetime Labor Force Participation

As women come to envision employment as a "career"—in the sense of being a planned or intentional part of their identity—they anticipate working for a larger share of their lives. In the United States, women born from 1931 to 1940 were employed for more than 40 percent of their postschooling years up to around age 50. For those born from 1941 to 1950, the figure was 55 percent of their postschooling years (Goldin 2006). As for our analysis of the jobs-to-careers path for female apparel workers in LMICs, the key questions are these: What is the average age of women in the apparel workforce, and how does it compare with other industries among our sample countries?

The apparel industry attracts young workers, especially when exports begin to increase (Artuc et al. 2019; Goutam et al. 2017), and our results suggest that many of these workers stay in the industry. Indeed, the average age of female apparel workers increases over time (table 2.5). Similarly, the share of the youngest workers (aged 15–20 years) falls over time, while the share of older workers increases over time—which suggests that those who enter the workforce may end up staying rather than being continuously replaced by newer, younger workers. This is not the case in other industries, such as education, where the average age of females has declined.

Although apparel attracts women into the labor force, younger females seem less likely to go into apparel because the share of employment has not increased over time, yet the average age and marriage rates have increased. But if FLFP has remained stable, women must be going into other industries. When looking at the youngest age group of females (15–25 years), crop and animal production and apparel are the top employers in all our country cases, followed by either retail or education. Retail is one of the top three employers of this group in Cambodia, Sri Lanka, Turkey, and Vietnam.

Female apparel workers are younger than the overall female average across all industries and countries. Although the average age of female apparel workers increased over time (as shown in table 2.5), that age remains under 30 in Bangladesh, Cambodia, and Pakistan. When a country has maintained a younger average age of female workers in an industry over time, that suggests that its comparative advantage is based on labor costs, because younger females have less experience and are more likely to work for lower wages. It may also suggest that apparel is the only opportunity available for women with less than lower-secondary education. Thus, it is not surprising that the two countries most dependent on apparel exports and competing largely based on low wages—Bangladesh and Cambodia—also have the youngest workers. In Sri Lanka, Turkey, and Vietnam, the largest share of females in the apparel industry are 31–45 years old, whereas in all the other sample countries, the largest share is in the 21–30 age group.

TABLE 2.5 Average Age of Female Workers over Time in Selected Industries and Middle-Income Countries, 2000s–2010s

Change in average age (in years) between first and last data year

Country	Years	Overall	Non-agriculture	Crop and animal production	Apparel	Retail	Education
Bangladesh	2005–16	36 to 36	33 to 33	35 to 38	25 to 27	37 to 37	33 to 32
Cambodia	2007–14	37 to 36	34 to 32	40 to 40	24 to 26	41 to 39	39 to 35
Egypt, Arab Rep.	2009–15	38 to 35	38 to 38	39 to 31	29 to 30	35 to 38	39 to 40
Pakistan[a]	2008–15	34 to 34	31 to 32	35 to 35	28 to 29	40 to 40	32 to 32
Sri Lanka	2007–15	40 to 42	39 to 40	43 to 47	32 to 36	41 to 42	40 to 40
Turkey	2011–13	37 to 37	33 to 34	42 to 42	30 to 32	32 to 32	34 to 35
Vietnam	2007–15	38 to 40	37 to 38	40 to 44	30 to 32	40 to 42	37 to 36

Source: Labor force survey data.

Note: Overall and industry columns present the average ages during the earliest year and the latest year shown in a given country's "Years" column.

a. In Pakistan, the average age did not change between 2008 and 2015 in three industries: crop and animal production, retail, and education.

The story here may be that apparel jobs are at least good enough to keep women in the workforce but are less appealing to younger generations—and there are few, if any, alternative options for middle-aged women. Given the lack of other employment opportunities and often minimal reskilling programs in LMICs, females who start in the apparel industry are likely to stay in it while they remain in the workforce.

Indicator Four: Earnings Gaps between Men and Women

The male-female wage gap is one of the most pervasive and widespread labor market characteristics, given that on average, worldwide, men earn more than women. Wage gaps not only send a discouraging signal but also provide a financial disincentive for women to invest in labor market experience, training, and education. Exporting apparel increases the demand for female workers and, as a result, may affect the wage gap. Labor market experience, industry and occupation segregation, and government policies also play vital roles as determinants of pay gaps for equal work.

FACTORS BEHIND THE WAGE GAPS

In the United States, wage gaps were persistent even after the quiet revolution started (Goldin's Phase IV). In 1980, women's earnings were about 60 percent of men's wages (Goldin 2006) and by 2020 were close to 84 percent (Barroso and Brown 2020). The wage gap does not necessarily close when women start entering the labor market (Kabeer and Natali 2013); indeed, if women enter the labor market for some reason besides wages, the increase in the relative supply of women can even widen the gap. Furthermore, as women enter the labor market, they often start in lower-ranked occupations or are simply paid less than men for the same work, both of which can lower the average wage earned by women. In any given country, the factors driving gender wage gaps can be numerous, entrenched, and interconnected.

Experience and skills requirements. In the labor market, occupations within an industry differ in terms of activities, skills, education, and wages. Technical and managerial positions (which men usually hold) often earn higher salaries than operators or machinists, and they require more (and different) skills and education.

Gender norms. Moreover, gender norms exist in many industries and occupations; that is, men and women often choose to work in different industries and occupations. For example, men are more likely to take jobs in construction, industries that require using capital equipment or handling heavy loads, chemical production and use, engineering, and software development. Women tend to work in health services, education, domestic services, or assembly-line work associated with activities performed in the home (such as sewing and food preparation).

Employment segregation. In the United States, employment segregation by occupation accounted for 33 percent of the gender wage gap, employment segregation by industry for 18 percent, and experience for 14 percent, according to the Oaxaca-Blinder decomposition used by Das and Kotikula (2019). In fact, employment segregation is one of the primary contributors to gender wage gaps around the world. Women tend to be more concentrated in low-wage employment and in fewer sectors; men are more evenly distributed across sectors, occupations, and job types (Christian, Evers, and Barrientos 2013; Fontana 2009; ILO 2016). As a result, gender wage gaps can be significant.

Unequal pay for equal work. Furthermore, women may be paid less than men for the same work. This may be because of discrimination or because women's subordination is deeply entrenched. For example, men are more likely to switch jobs or ask for higher wages—either of which often leads to higher earnings over time, even in the same position (Pearlman 2019; Schultz 2019).

EMPIRICAL ANALYSIS OF WAGE GAPS

There are many different dimensions of both labor market characteristics (industry and occupation mix, output prices, and geographic differences) and individual worker characteristics (age, education, experience, industry, occupation, and others). Therefore, we apply a commonly used empirical approach—Mincerian equations—to explore the components that explain the wage gaps driving gender wage differentials and to see whether education or other policies might support the transition toward better-paid jobs and careers.

Previous literature has decomposed the gap between male and female workers and estimated the effect of the growth in female-intensive industries on increasing demand for female workers (Blau and Kahn 2017; Kis-Katos, Pieters, and Sparrow 2017; Sauré and Zoabi 2014). To analyze the evolution of the gender wage gap in each sample country, we use a Mincerian wage equation, where the dependent variable is "real monthly wages" and the explanatory variables are the different observable characteristics of both the labor market and the individual. We interpret the estimated coefficients as the contribution that each of the represented elements makes to total earnings. In our estimation, we include variables that identify female workers, the apparel industry (which includes textiles and leather), the interaction between females and the apparel industry variable, and variables representing discrete education levels by gender. We also include control covariates such as age, age squared, education, weekly hours worked, and industry sectors. Our estimation equation for worker i at time t is

$$\begin{aligned} lnWage_{it} &= \alpha + \beta_1 Female_{it} + \beta_2 Apparel_{it} + \beta_3 Female_{it} xApparel_{it} \\ &+ \beta_4 Education_{it} + \beta_5 Education_{it} xFemale_{it} + \beta_6 Age_{it} \\ &+ \beta_7 Age_{it}^2 + \beta_8 Hours_{it} + \sum_k \delta_k Industry_{kit} + e_{it}. \end{aligned} \quad (2.1)$$

Average Wage Gaps and Changes over Time

Figure 2.2 shows the results for all the sample countries at two points that cover the span of labor force survey data available. Across all industries, and controlling for education and weekly hours worked, females earn less than males in all countries and years. We do not find strong evidence of consistent decline in gender wage gaps for most countries in the period studied. The exceptions are Bangladesh, Cambodia, and Sri Lanka, where the gender wage differential decreased by 61.1, 18.6, and 20.1 percentage points, respectively. In these countries, wages increased for both genders, suggesting that wages grew faster for females than for males. These countries also have the highest dependence on apparel exports among our country cases. (For the full set of Mincerian regression results, see annex 2A, tables 2A.1–2A.7.)

In contrast, although wages increased for both females and males in Egypt, Pakistan, Turkey, and Vietnam, the wage gaps increased in those countries by 2 percentage points to almost 19 percentage points. Egypt experienced the biggest increase in the gender gap (about 19 percentage points), followed by Vietnam (10.6 points), where although wages increased for both genders, the number of weekly reported hours of work decreased. That decline in hours worked was bigger for women, meaning women were earning less but also working fewer hours than men when comparing 2007 with 2015. Pakistan, the country with the second largest gender gap increase (5.4 percentage points) and Turkey (with a 11.2 point increase) both reported increased weekly hours worked for males and females.

FIGURE 2.2 **Male-Female Wage Gap in Sample Middle-Income Countries, Earliest and Latest Data Years**

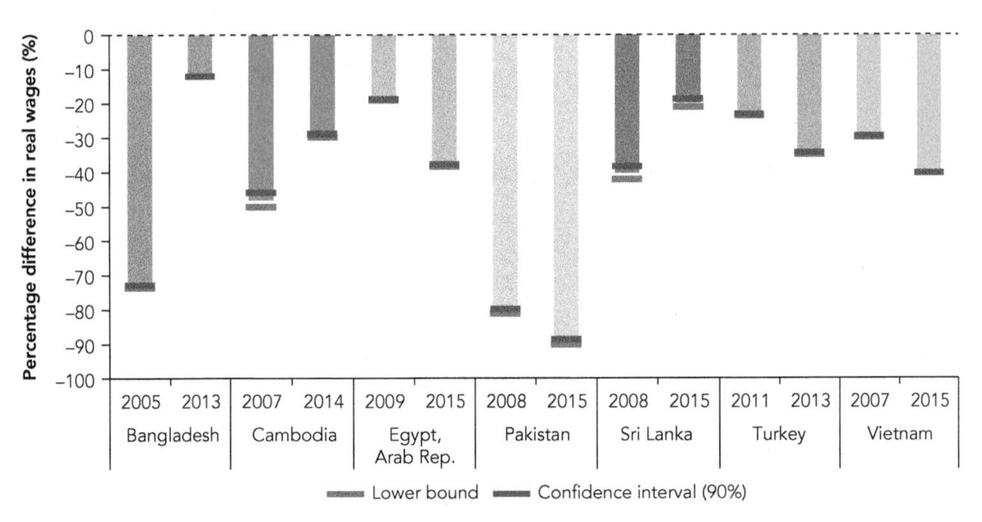

Source: Estimates of equation (2.1) using countries' labor force survey (LFS) data.

Note: Chart shows the percentage difference in real wages between males (at 0) and females, measured in the national currency. For 2005 and 2013 in Bangladesh, we use reported education levels as provided by the LFS data, as further discussed in annex 2A. For the full set of Mincerian regression results, see annex 2A, tables 2A.1–2A.7.

Wage Gaps by Education Level and Changes over Time

A further comparison of the wage gaps between men and women with the same education level shows similar differences across the sample countries but also highlights how educational attainment may offer significant wage returns for women (see figure 2.3). In Sri Lanka, the returns to completing primary education are lower for females than males in most years, and returns to lower-secondary education show a decreasing trend. However, having tertiary education or above is especially beneficial for Sri Lankan women, enabling them to earn more than 50 percent more than those who do not have tertiary education (see annex 2A, table 2A.5). It is possible that as Sri Lankan women have become more educated, the wage premium from primary education has decayed. As markets demanding workers with primary and secondary education encounter a labor supply whose average years of education exceed those levels, the wage benefits from a primary education decrease and those from higher education increase.

Not surprisingly, countries where women generally stop studying at primary school (such as Cambodia and Pakistan) have higher returns for women for higher levels of education. In Pakistan, for both primary and lower-secondary education, the wage differential for women is close to 70 and 90 percentage points, respectively. The low shares of women with at least some education—less than 30 percent of the female population, compared with 60 percent of the male population—might explain the huge differential.

These results suggest that returns to education might encourage women in most countries to invest or stay in school, at least until they have completed primary or lower-secondary education if they plan for a longer-horizon job. However, women's earnings relative to men's are falling in most countries, possibly because of women entering the labor market in lower-paid positions. Primary and lower-secondary education premiums seem to greatly benefit female workers more than males, but this is not sufficient to activate a career pathway.

Upper-secondary education premiums are even higher in all countries—for example, Pakistan is close to 90 percent and Vietnam is close to 50 percent—but the share of women with this level of education is still small in Bangladesh, Cambodia, and Pakistan. Further, higher returns for women with less education can encourage them to drop out of school and enter the workforce earlier. For occupations that require higher human capital, women need to continue beyond their lower-secondary studies before entering the labor market.

A career pathway that rewards labor market experience over education might still be feasible for women in countries where incentives are not sufficient for—and cultural norms preclude—continued studying. On the other hand, in Sri Lanka, women need to have more than a lower-secondary education to have better returns than males. The labor market greatly rewards Sri Lankan women who invest in education, and the gender wage gap is decreasing in that country.

FIGURE 2.3 **Difference between Males and Females in the Wage Returns from Education in Sample Middle-Income Countries, by Education Level, 2007–15**

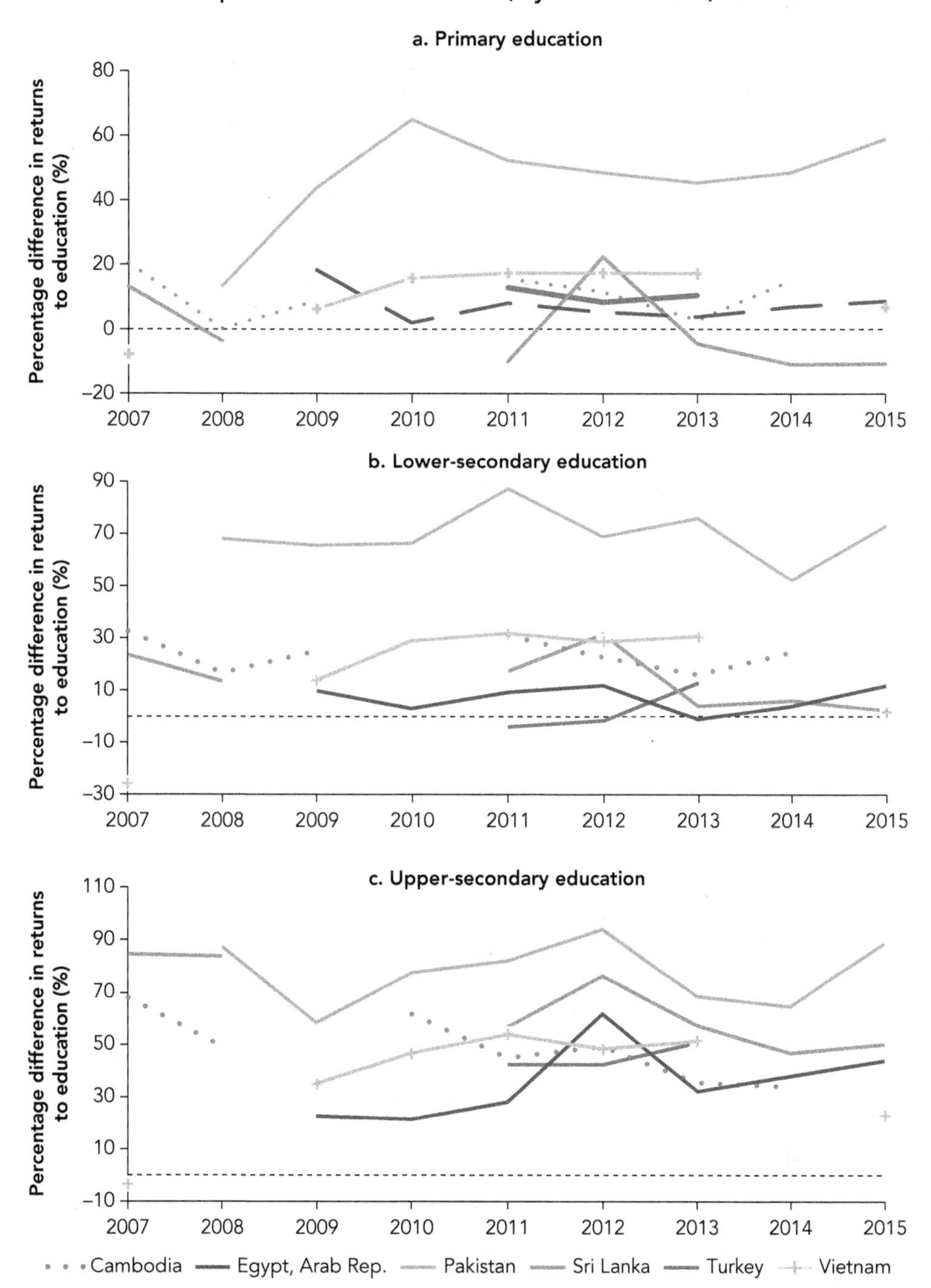

Source: Estimates of equation (2.1) using countries' labor force survey data.

Note: A comparison of panels b and c shows that women gain the most if they continue past lower-secondary education. Positive values indicate a higher wage premium for women than for men; negative values indicate lower returns for women than for men. The elaboration uses Mincerian equations and data from labor force surveys. For the full set of Mincerian regression results, see annex 2A, tables 2A.1–2A.7. Bangladesh is excluded because of data comparability issues, as further described in appendix A. Discontinuities in countries' data lines reflect labor force surveys rounds that we do not have access to.

Indicator Five: Distribution of Employment across Industries and Occupations

The fifth performance indicator is employment across industries and occupations. Different occupations require different education levels. Managers, professionals, technicians, and clerks have upper-secondary education or higher, while agricultural workers have less than primary education. Workers in mid-level sales or services and craft or plant operators have primary or lower-secondary education. And as figure 2.4 shows, the difference in education level between men and women is much larger across occupations than within occupations.

Thus, one critical factor in the wage differences between men and women is the segregation of men and women into different occupations. This suggests that women's ability to shift from "jobs" to "careers" with better wages depends on both (a) the availability of work (demand) that requires higher education, skills, and experience; and (b) the

FIGURE 2.4 **Average Years of Worker Education, by Occupation and Gender, in Sample Middle-Income Countries, Most Recent Year**

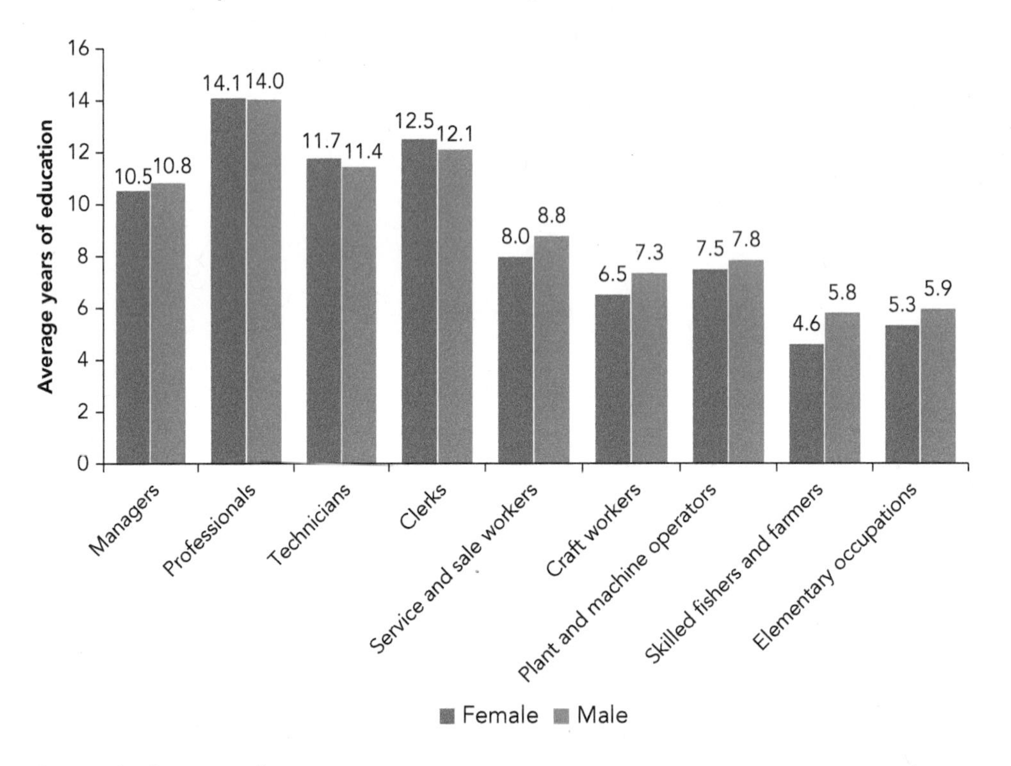

Source: Labor force survey data.
Note: The average number of years shown is the average from the seven countries (Bangladesh; Cambodia; Egypt, Arab Rep.; Pakistan, Sri Lanka, Turkey, and Vietnam) per occupation. The countries' latest years of data vary between 2013 and 2015.

degree to which women can access male-dominated, higher-wage occupations within industries.

In the United States, rising female education levels and higher demand for clerical workers were pivotal in the shifting of female employment from manufacturing to services (Goldin 2006). During the transition, two labor market indicators rapidly changed: a rise in the female intensity (ratio of female to male workers) of clerical workers and a drop in manufacturing's share of female (nonagricultural) employment.

In the late nineteenth century, US women rarely occupied office jobs such as clerks, bookkeepers, and copyists. But by 1930, more than half of bookkeepers were women (Goldin 2006). And the percentage of women working as clerical workers rose from 15 percent in 1890 to 48 percent in 1920 and up to 62 percent by 1950 (table 2.6). However, these were low-paid clerical occupations and did not include higher-paid ones such as accountants or auditors, which were held by men (Das and Kotikula 2019). Meanwhile, the share of female manufacturing workers decreased from 32 percent to 26 percent to 22 percent during the same periods, respectively.

How do our sample apparel producers compare? First, in terms of clerical occupations, our results show that none of these countries has reached a share of female employment close to that of US women during Phase II, when they started transitioning from manufacturing into clerical jobs. For example, Sri Lanka, Egypt, and Turkey have the biggest shares of female nonagricultural workers in clerical jobs, but they are not even half of the US Phase II level. Bangladesh and Cambodia are only at levels approaching the United States when it began Phase I (as women shifted from agricultural to factory work), while Pakistan's share of female clerical employment is close to zero.

As for the share of female nonagricultural employment in the manufacturing industry, Sri Lanka (at 24 percent) shows a share similar to the US Phase II—and in Sri Lanka and Turkey (11 percent), we might be observing the beginning of a transition from manufacturing to clerical occupations. However, the share of female manufacturing workers increased in Bangladesh, Cambodia, Pakistan, and Vietnam (not shown in table 2.6). In those countries, apparel still plays an important role in the country's exports and in generating jobs for women. Given the low share of women in clerical occupations, these countries may still be in the early stages of getting women into the labor force and generating a change in the mindset that precludes women from working. As for Egypt, neither clerical occupations nor the manufacturing sector are important sources of female employment; HSOs are.

Of course, clerical work is not the only career pathway for women. Between 1994 and 2016, employment shifts in Organisation for Economic Co-operation and Development (OECD) countries tended to demand more skill, and women benefited from this more than men. Evidence shows a reallocation from clerical occupations toward service and retail workers, technicians, and professionals—a trend that is more beneficial for women (Das and Kotikula 2019).

Notably, whether more women transition into the services sector is not necessarily determined by either the lack or existence of women of higher educational attainment.

TABLE 2.6 **Measures of Female Employment in Clerical and Manufacturing Occupations in Sample Middle-Income Countries, Relative to Phases of the US Jobs-to-Careers Transition**

	Female intensity[a] (%)		Share of female (nonagricultural) employment[b] (%)		Female intensity[a] (US phase equivalent)		Share of female (nonagricultural) employment[b] (US phase equivalent)	
Country	Clerical	Manufacturing	Clerical	Manufacturing	Clerical	Manufacturing	Clerical	Manufacturing
Bangladesh	16	25	2	41	PO	PO	PO	PO
Cambodia	41	41	6	35	PI	PO	PI	PO
Egypt, Arab Rep.	29	3	7	7	PI	PIV	PI	PIV
Pakistan	2	15	0	36	PO	PII	PO	PO
Sri Lanka	53	27	7	24	PII	PO	PI	PII
Turkey	42	12	12	11	PI	PII	PI	PIV
Vietnam	49	35	2	18	PII	PO	PO	PIII
US Phase 0 (1890)[c]	15	20	4	32	n.a.	n.a.	n.a.	n.a.
US Phase I (1900)[c]	24	19	6	30	n.a.	n.a.	n.a.	n.a.
US Phase II (1920)[c]	48	15	22	26	n.a.	n.a.	n.a.	n.a.
US Phase II (1930)[c]	52	13	23	19	n.a.	n.a.	n.a.	n.a.
US Phase III (1950)[c]	62	17	28	22	n.a.	n.a.	n.a.	n.a.

Sources: Goldin 1984; International Labour Organization ILOSTAT "Employment by Sex and Economic Activity" data set, 1969–2020.

Note: Clerical occupations (C) are represented by ISCO-08 code 4 (clerical support workers) and manufacturing occupations (M) by ISCO-08 codes 7 and 8 (craft and related trades workers as well as plant and machine operators and assemblers) (ILO 2012). All countries' data are from 2017 ILOSTAT, except Pakistan's, which are from 2018. We present rounded numbers to the closest integer. ISCO = International Standard Classification of Occupations; n.a. = not applicable.

a. Female intensity is the ratio of females to males in each occupation.

b. Share of female employment is the percentage of the total female working population who work in the specified type of occupation.

c. Goldin (2006) defines each US phase (P) roughly as follows: (I) late 1800s–1900: female agricultural workers move into factory work; (II) early 1900s: women shift increasingly from manufacturing to clerical jobs; (III) 1950–early 1970s: women increasingly work in mid-skill service occupations requiring higher education levels (teachers, nurses, and so on); (IV) late 1970s onward: women increasingly pursue long-term careers, regardless of spouses' incomes, that convey a greater sense of identity. Note that US data are not available after 1950 for female intensity and share of employment within clerical and manufacturing occupations.

Although Egypt, Sri Lanka, Turkey, and Vietnam have the human capital to activate education-related career pathways for women, this does not automatically translate into employment in higher-wage occupations. One reason is that several domestic-serving industries (such as education, human health services, and public administration) tend not to emerge until countries attain higher-income status.

Conclusion

Is there evidence that jobs created by export-oriented industries like apparel directly support women's pursuit of long-term, higher-paid careers—that is, a "quiet revolution"? Based on where our sample countries stand on the five indicators of a transition from jobs to careers, drawing on the US experience, the answer is no. However, apparel may well be helping indirectly.

STATUS OF THE OVERALL JOBS-TO-CAREERS TRANSITION

Figure 2.5 maps our sample countries based on economic development (using gross domestic product [GDP] per capita), FLFP, and their transition to career-oriented jobs

FIGURE 2.5 Relative Stage of Sample Countries in the Transition to Longer-Horizon Occupations for Women

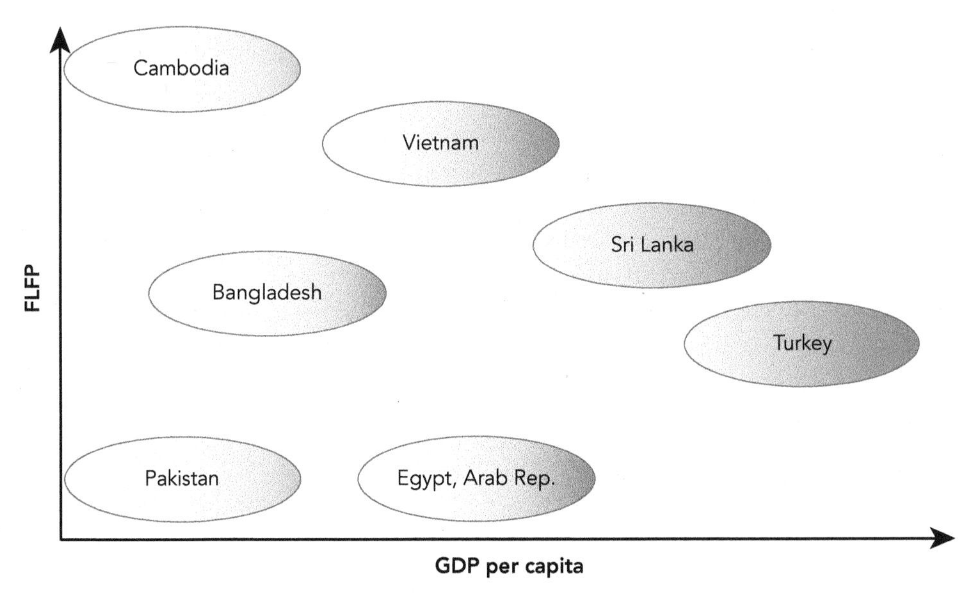

Sources: World Bank and International Labour Organization ILOSTAT data sets.

Note: Degree of shading is based on the share of working women in high-skill occupations, going from lighter to darker as the share increases. FLFP = female labor force participation; GDP = gross domestic product.

for women. Bangladesh, Cambodia, and Pakistan are farthest to the left because of low GDP per capita, the lowest average education levels among our sample countries, and the lowest shares of women in HSOs. Female workers in these are also the youngest, on average, among the country cases.

In Egypt and Pakistan, FLFP has historically been low, which may signal that other FLFP determinants—such as cultural norms—hinder women from participating in the labor market. Women employed in Pakistan are primarily in the agriculture sector, and in Egypt the largest share of working women are in HSOs (see chapter 1, box 1.3). Further, Egyptian women have a high unemployment rate, exceeding 21 percent for women with higher education.[2]

Working women in Sri Lanka, Turkey, and Vietnam are more highly educated on average than in the other countries, and they work in a wider variety of manufacturing and service industries (see chapter 3, table 3.3). The average age of female workers has also increased in these countries, as have female marriage rates and education overall. Thus, firms are slowly expanding and upgrading to include more women in career-related occupations.

Even though we recognize that the development path cannot be the same for any two countries—and, of course, the United States does not represent the *only* or even the *best* path—we encounter similarities in this chapter that can help explain the evolution of women's permanence in the labor market. For example, female apparel workers in all the sample countries are younger than the average across all industries. Given that relatively low labor costs are a requisite for competing in the global apparel industry, younger workers and first-time job seekers are common, because they are more likely to work for lower wages.

APPAREL SECTOR TRENDS

Nevertheless, the average age of female apparel workers is also increasing across countries. This suggests that the industry might be retaining women longer but becoming less appealing to younger generations. This trend implies at least two scenarios: (a) middle-aged women have few alternative options to apparel work, and (b) younger females choose to work in a different industry or continue in school.

The first scenario—longer retention of women into middle age—is feasible as long as labor demand limits the availability of career-related occupations. Several service industries (such as residential care and social work) do not emerge until countries reach a relatively high income per capita. Intersectoral upgrading and upward mobility within the apparel sector is also limited because the leading firms are usually foreign and maintain their better-paid positions in their home countries.

In the United States, the boom of clerical occupations signaled the start of women's transition from manufacturing to the services sector. Occupations associated with careers (such as management and professional services) require at least upper-secondary education. But the existence of women with that level of human capital does not guarantee significant job-to-career transitions. Four of our country cases—Egypt, Sri Lanka, Turkey, and Vietnam—have the human capital to activate the career pathway, yet there has been little increase in those countries' shares of women in clerical or managerial positions. Hence, females who start in the apparel industry are likely to stay in it while they remain in the workforce; that is, their "job" becomes a "career" in terms of length of work but not in the full sense used in this report. Staying in the workforce generally, and in the apparel industry in particular, is not necessarily associated with better wages, employment benefits, or working in occupations with more decision-making power.

The second scenario—the changing choices of younger women—is more positive in terms of development. Because female apparel workers are among the youngest across industries and the share of workers in the youngest age group has not increased in recent years, younger women may be postponing their entrance into the labor market and staying in school. The rise in education levels in all the sample countries seems to support this process. The exception is Pakistan, where apparel still brings young women into the labor market and where (as in Bangladesh and Cambodia) women are lagging in the educational attainment needed to activate career pathways.

THE JOBS-TO-CAREERS OUTLOOK FOR THE SAMPLE COUNTRIES

Bangladesh, Cambodia, and Pakistan

Apart from whether they become apparel workers, Bangladeshi and Cambodian women tend to stop studying after lower-secondary education and marry before the typical age of tertiary education graduation. In Pakistan, few women have formal education and marry around the age of 23, meaning that women there are not necessarily dropping out of school because of a decision to marry. Limited access to education or strong gender norms might be inhibiting Pakistani women's educational attainment.

If women drop out of work at a young age (for instance, because of childcare duties or other household activities after marriage), they lose years of labor market experience, which could complicate reentry with a better position years later. These characteristics help explain why Bangladesh, Cambodia, and Pakistan do not meet the conditions necessary for women's transition to longer-horizon employment—or as we call it, "careers"—based on higher human capital.

Egypt, Sri Lanka, Turkey, and Vietnam

The opposite happens in the other sample countries. Women marry, on average, at the age when they would be completing a college degree, suggesting that they are postponing marriage until they have either completed enough education to pursue a career or have gained more labor market experience. Both reasons are beneficial for women planning to stay longer in the labor market. In fact, that is what happens (except in Egypt, with its persistently low FLFP): the data suggest that, over time, more married women are becoming part of the workforce.

The stability of women in the labor market (regardless of marital status or children) is a necessary, but not sufficient, condition for the jobs-to-careers transition. In Sri Lanka, Turkey, and Vietnam, the rise in working married women along with their human capital suggests that conditions are present to transition toward a service-oriented female workforce. Egyptian women also share higher educational attainment, but the low overall FLFP might be a limiting factor for the transition to happen.

In Sri Lanka and Turkey, the broad distribution of employment across occupations signals that the transition is in its initial stages, but it has not yet started in Egypt or Vietnam, perhaps because of labor demand limitations. Because working women in these two countries are more highly educated, on average, than nonworking women, several overlapping dynamics could be at play: (a) the minimum wage women will accept is not available in the labor market; (b) spousal household income is preventing their labor participation; or (c) cultural norms are hindering female work.

What Role Can Apparel Jobs Play?

The bottom line is that apparel jobs offer opportunities for the least educated women but offer little incentive for the current generation to invest in the education needed to pursue HSOs. In most of the apparel exporting countries studied here, wage gaps between women and men have widened, probably because of occupational segregation, educational differences, or structural discrimination.

However, women's real wages have increased in all the sample countries. And large returns to education might encourage women to invest in their education—a necessary requirement for careers that require higher human capital. Yet only in Sri Lanka has the education wage premium diminished for initial levels of education, hence creating large incentives for women to continue in school past the lower-secondary level.

As more education propels long-term adjustment from jobs to careers, the big education wage premiums for women in all countries represent grounds for optimism. However, even as countries raise human capital and females stay longer in the labor market, labor demand has yet to increase to absorb these more-educated, more-experienced women into careers befitting their increasing skills.

Annex 2A: Mincerian Equation Results

There are many different dimensions of both labor market characteristics (industry and occupation mix, output prices, and geographic differences) and individual worker characteristics (age, education, experience, industry, occupation, and others). Therefore, we use Mincerian equations to explore the components that explain the wage gaps driving gender wage differentials and to see whether education or other policies might support the transition toward better-paid jobs and careers. Results are discussed in the main text.

TABLE A2.1 Bangladesh: Mincerian Equation Results with Education Categories

	2005	2010	2013	2016
Female	−0.731***	−0.062***	−0.12***	−0.24***
	(−38.07)	(−4.46)	(−7.69)	(−33.83)
Apparel	0.227***	0.097***	0.24***	0.29***
	(12.75)	(8.45)	(24.36)	(43.77)
Female * Apparel	0.143***	0.107***	0.12***	0.07***
	(4.43)	(4.83)	(9.87)	(6.81)
Age	0.039***	0.017***	0.02***	0.02***
	(24.29)	(15.68)	(22.06)	(31.53)
Age^2	−0.000***	−0.000***	−0.00***	−0.00***
	(−19.97)	(−12.01)	(−18.12)	(−26.29)
Primary	0.128***	−0.012	0.01	0.10***
	(3.85)	(−0.48)	(0.83)	(8.65)
Lower secondary/ Middle school	0.338***	−0.077***	0.10***	0.14***
	(10.43)	(−3.50)	(5.38)	(12.53)
Upper secondary/ High school	0.578***	−0.089*	0.06***	0.28***
	(11.15)	(−1.89)	(3.29)	(18.33)
Degree, M.S. or PhD	0.611***	−0.107***	0.01	0.19***
	(14.68)	(−2.71)	(0.40)	(13.72)
Primary * Female	0.143***	0.116***	0.06***	0.07***
	(11.58)	(14.58)	(7.36)	(14.15)
Lower secondary/Middle school * Female	0.275***	0.280***	0.03***	0.20***
	(21.51)	(35.40)	(2.98)	(38.68)
Upper secondary/High school * Female	0.662***	0.564***	0.17***	0.45***
	(28.89)	(34.30)	(18.05)	(59.77)
Degree, M.S. or PhD * Female	1.024***	0.861***	0.40***	0.86***
	(51.65)	(56.54)	(36.48)	(117.39)
Hours worked	0.011***	0.004***	0.00	0.00***
	(34.62)	(15.57)	(1.46)	(23.85)
Constant	5.138***	6.260***	6.87***	6.39***
	(147.28)	(244.76)	(333.61)	(447.24)
N	**22,943**	**41,892**	**21,629**	**72,226**

Source: World Bank.

a. Educational variable for reference: no education.

$^*p < .05$, $^{**}p < .01$, $^{***}p < .001$.

TABLE A2.2 Cambodia: Mincerian Equation Results with Education Categories

	2007	2008	2009	2011	2012	2013	2014
Female	−0.479***	−0.153	−0.202***	−0.345***	−0.278***	−0.163***	−0.293***
	(−3.80)	(−1.46)	(−5.10)	(−5.52)	(−4.65)	(−2.64)	(−10.10)
Apparel	0.565***	0.636***	0.430***	0.103*	0.270***	0.238***	0.270***
	(3.68)	(5.36)	(8.14)	(1.82)	(4.82)	(4.77)	(11.19)
Female * Apparel	0.154	0.145	0.183***	0.339***	0.132**	0.169***	0.164***
	(0.95)	(1.12)	(3.17)	(5.46)	(2.14)	(3.09)	(6.17)
Age	0.077***	0.045***	0.052***	0.039***	0.043***	0.034***	0.037***
	(8.17)	(5.36)	(14.98)	(9.11)	(10.24)	(8.52)	(17.98)
Age^2	−0.001***	−0.001***	−0.001***	−0.000***	−0.001***	−0.000***	−0.000***
	(−8.71)	(−5.24)	(−14.55)	(−8.93)	(−9.53)	(−7.90)	(−18.13)
Primary	0.361**	0.048	−0.022	0.041	0.074	0.022	0.137***
	(2.53)	(0.39)	(−0.48)	(0.58)	(1.10)	(0.33)	(4.16)
Lower secondary/ Middle school	0.249*	0.256**	0.020	0.077	0.042	0.032	0.142***
	(1.65)	(1.97)	(0.39)	(1.05)	(0.60)	(0.45)	(4.10)
Upper secondary/High school	0.683***	0.046	0.082	0.103	0.155*	−0.107	0.170***
	(3.92)	(0.30)	(1.38)	(1.25)	(1.92)	(−1.36)	(4.54)
Degree, M.S. or PhD	0.539**	0.082	0.084	0.177	0.066	0.120	0.224***
	(2.29)	(0.40)	(0.85)	(1.61)	(0.63)	(1.23)	(4.93)
Primary * Female	−0.156	−0.045	0.111***	0.116**	0.042	0.007	0.014
	(−1.55)	(−0.53)	(3.33)	(2.15)	(0.89)	(0.14)	(0.60)
Lower secondary/ Middle school * Female	0.078	−0.086	0.235***	0.233***	0.188***	0.130**	0.109***
	(0.73)	(−0.97)	(6.58)	(4.22)	(3.87)	(2.49)	(4.47)
Upper secondary/High school * Female	0.157	0.376***	0.441***	0.409***	0.286***	0.356***	0.228***
	(1.36)	(3.81)	(10.96)	(6.69)	(5.35)	(6.44)	(8.68)
Degree, M.S. or PhD * Female	0.795***	1.132***	1.069***	1.020***	0.959***	0.870***	0.735***
	(5.24)	(8.61)	(18.66)	(13.90)	(14.20)	(13.08)	(23.04)
Hours worked	0.015***	0.021***	0.016***	0.018***	0.019***	0.015***	0.013***
	(8.85)	(13.38)	(27.94)	(21.08)	(22.87)	(17.99)	(31.16)
Constant	9.748***	9.578***	9.881***	10.290***	10.233***	10.694***	10.935***
	(46.86)	(53.18)	(140.85)	(104.73)	(108.28)	(113.30)	(236.13)
N	**2,599**	**2,821**	**9,008**	**3,484**	**3,847**	**4,141**	**13,904**

Source: World Bank.

a. Educational variable for reference: no education.

$*p < .05$, $**p < .01$, $***p < .001$.

TABLE A2.3 Egypt, Arab Rep.: Mincerian Equation Results with Education Categories

	2009	2010	2011	2012	2013	2014	2015
Female	−0.191***	−0.256***	−0.232***	−0.431***	−0.322***	−0.338***	−0.380***
	(−9.95)	(−12.94)	(−11.01)	(−10.28)	(−15.77)	(−16.91)	(−19.49)
Apparel	−0.092***	−0.179***	−0.033*	−0.804***	−0.158***	−0.099***	−0.080***
	(−6.32)	(−11.33)	(−1.87)	(−23.25)	(−9.22)	(−5.97)	(−4.67)
Female * Apparel	−0.037	−0.122***	−0.059	0.146**	0.037	−0.050	−0.068**
	(−1.18)	(−3.78)	(−1.60)	(2.05)	(1.05)	(−1.53)	(−1.96)
Age	0.012***	0.024***	0.013***	0.035***	0.020***	0.018***	0.018***
	(11.11)	(20.47)	(10.35)	(13.97)	(15.84)	(14.15)	(14.27)
Age^2	0.000	−0.000***	−0.000**	−0.000***	−0.000***	−0.000**	−0.000***
	(0.15)	(−8.10)	(−2.46)	(−4.16)	(−2.70)	(−2.20)	(−3.26)
Primary	0.146***	−0.026	0.036	−0.013	−0.023	0.002	0.014
	(2.98)	(−0.54)	(0.74)	(−0.15)	(−0.49)	(0.05)	(0.32)
Lower secondary/ Middle school	0.072	−0.020	0.025	0.023	−0.084*	−0.026	0.028
	(1.44)	(−0.35)	(0.44)	(0.21)	(−1.65)	(−0.52)	(0.55)
Upper secondary/High school	0.130***	0.099***	0.164***	0.287***	0.188***	0.241***	0.286***
	(6.30)	(4.64)	(7.23)	(6.36)	(8.54)	(11.09)	(13.54)
Degree, M.S. or PhD	0.051**	0.021	0.140***	0.095**	0.146***	0.202***	0.269***
	(2.39)	(0.95)	(6.08)	(2.08)	(6.48)	(9.06)	(12.40)
Primary * Female	0.037***	0.046***	0.045***	0.066***	0.062***	0.068***	0.074***
	(3.91)	(4.67)	(4.37)	(3.30)	(6.14)	(6.75)	(7.37)
Lower secondary/ Middle school * Female	0.026**	0.051***	0.070***	0.098***	0.075***	0.069***	0.093***
	(2.47)	(4.60)	(5.99)	(4.18)	(6.67)	(5.88)	(7.62)
Upper secondary/High school * Female	0.096***	0.117***	0.116***	0.331***	0.137***	0.139***	0.155***
	(17.25)	(19.25)	(18.63)	(25.75)	(21.72)	(21.19)	(23.31)
Degree, M.S. or PhD * Female	0.335***	0.336***	0.341***	0.628***	0.345***	0.331***	0.372***
	(45.64)	(42.14)	(41.90)	(37.81)	(41.93)	(38.66)	(42.55)
Hours worked	0.002***	0.001***	-0.000	-0.001***	0.002***	0.002***	0.002***
	(10.73)	(5.19)	(-1.35)	(-2.92)	(8.93)	(9.16)	(9.57)
Constant	6.877***	6.738***	7.110***	6.472***	6.885***	6.952***	6.945***
	(312.61)	(281.04)	(282.24)	(124.89)	(268.01)	(263.41)	(263.95)
N	**57,370**	**60,995**	**65,287**	**62,814**	**57,387**	**57,026**	**57,908**

Source: World Bank.

a. Educational variable for reference: no education.

*$p < .05$, **$p < .01$, ***$p < .001$.

TABLE A2.4 Pakistan: Mincerian Equation Results with Education Categories

	2008	2009	2010	2011	2012	2013	2014	2015
Female	−0.804***	−0.755***	−0.838***	−0.917***	−0.849***	−0.911***	−0.794***	−0.893***
	(−19.01)	(−14.54)	(−19.41)	(−20.85)	(−18.41)	(−22.02)	(−20.26)	(−19.18)
Apparel	0.307***	0.407***	0.312***	0.350***	0.335***	0.367***	0.356***	0.275***
	(7.67)	(9.87)	(8.22)	(8.74)	(8.12)	(10.76)	(10.58)	(7.19)
Female * Apparel	−0.340***	−0.368***	−0.021	−0.262***	−0.323***	0.150	−0.069	−0.023
	(−4.38)	(−4.38)	(−0.24)	(−2.65)	(−3.57)	(1.50)	(−0.66)	(−0.20)
Age	0.074***	0.064***	0.070***	0.078***	0.074***	0.063***	0.071***	0.075***
	(23.04)	(18.88)	(20.42)	(21.49)	(21.69)	(20.09)	(23.97)	(22.19)
Age^2	−0.001***	−0.001***	−0.001***	−0.001***	−0.001***	−0.001***	−0.001***	−0.001***
	(−18.26)	(−14.11)	(−15.54)	(−15.95)	(−16.40)	(−14.06)	(−18.25)	(−16.94)
Primary	0.086	0.394***	0.583***	0.416***	0.409***	0.371***	0.404***	0.469***
	(0.72)	(3.90)	(5.27)	(3.65)	(3.66)	(4.26)	(4.55)	(5.10)
Lower secondary/ Middle school	0.433***	0.411***	0.487***	0.589***	0.407***	0.486***	0.286***	0.479***
	(6.87)	(5.95)	(7.36)	(9.19)	(6.12)	(7.71)	(4.67)	(6.93)
Upper secondary/ High school	0.385***	0.145*	0.279***	0.243***	0.356***	0.170**	0.128*	0.422***
	(5.56)	(1.84)	(3.91)	(3.27)	(4.66)	(2.45)	(1.88)	(5.54)
Degree, M.S. or PhD	0.391***	0.552***	0.392***	0.532***	0.463***	0.495***	0.310***	0.421***
	(6.97)	(8.52)	(6.75)	(9.09)	(7.74)	(9.37)	(6.11)	(7.37)
Primary * Female	0.049**	0.044*	0.066***	0.106***	0.076***	0.083***	0.082***	0.121***
	(1.96)	(1.73)	(2.66)	(3.97)	(2.76)	(3.50)	(3.62)	(4.65)
Lower secondary/ Middle school * Female	0.250***	0.245***	0.179***	0.285***	0.283***	0.274***	0.238***	0.251***
	(12.45)	(11.16)	(8.63)	(12.66)	(12.96)	(13.65)	(12.53)	(11.68)
Upper secondary/ High school * Female	0.490***	0.439***	0.498***	0.579***	0.584***	0.515***	0.518***	0.466***
	(17.71)	(15.02)	(17.59)	(19.66)	(19.91)	(19.04)	(20.95)	(17.08)
Degree, M.S. or PhD * Female	0.883***	0.807***	0.941***	0.959***	0.993***	0.942***	0.923***	0.930***
	(35.89)	(31.48)	(38.02)	(36.28)	(38.12)	(39.76)	(42.36)	(38.17)
Hours worked	0.003***	0.001	−0.000	0.001*	0.000	−0.001	0.000	0.001*
	(4.79)	(1.37)	(−0.77)	(1.91)	(0.42)	(−1.12)	(0.45)	(1.74)
Constant	6.792***	6.928***	6.991***	6.575***	6.851***	7.112***	7.004***	6.915***
	(89.43)	(87.89)	(93.13)	(79.99)	(85.69)	(101.96)	(102.39)	(89.83)
N	**7711**	**7810**	**7127**	**7307**	**7148**	**7993**	**7786**	**8105**

Source: World Bank.

a. Educational variable for reference: no education.

*$p < .05$, **$p < .01$, ***$p < .001$.

TABLE A2.5 Sri Lanka: Mincerian Equation Results with Education Categories

	2007	2008	2011	2012	2013	2014	2015
Female	−0.407***	−0.402***	−0.075	−0.303***	−0.269***	−0.236***	−0.199***
	(−3.72)	(−3.58)	(−0.65)	(−3.47)	(−2.98)	(−3.73)	(−2.69)
Apparel	0.493***	0.236***	0.271***	0.336***	0.335***	0.399***	0.351***
	(7.30)	(3.62)	(4.07)	(7.07)	(6.93)	(12.96)	(9.55)
Female * Apparel	−0.054	0.085	−0.071	−0.029	−0.040	−0.090**	0.037
	(−0.71)	(1.13)	(−0.91)	(−0.51)	(−0.71)	(−2.51)	(0.86)
Age	0.064***	0.061***	0.060***	0.060***	0.062***	0.057***	0.056***
	(12.83)	(12.53)	(12.53)	(16.71)	(18.19)	(24.39)	(22.22)
Age^2	−0.001***	−0.001***	−0.001***	−0.001***	−0.001***	−0.001***	−0.001***
	(−11.90)	(−11.66)	(−12.04)	(−15.92)	(−17.40)	(−23.33)	(−21.73)
Primary school * Female	0.078	−0.028	−0.334***	−0.003	−0.088	−0.129*	−0.237***
	(0.64)	(−0.22)	(−2.59)	(−0.03)	(−0.89)	(−1.84)	(−2.95)
Secondary school * Female	0.028	−0.059	−0.213*	−0.053	−0.193**	−0.135**	−0.256***
	(0.24)	(−0.50)	(−1.74)	(−0.58)	(−2.04)	(−2.05)	(−3.35)
High school, vocational or technical * Female	0.230**	0.258**	−0.166	0.103	0.056	0.009	−0.056
	(1.98)	(2.18)	(−1.36)	(1.13)	(0.60)	(0.14)	(−0.73)
Higher education * Female	0.165	0.255*	−0.060	0.018	−0.024	−0.011	−0.109
	(1.15)	(1.78)	(−0.42)	(0.18)	(−0.23)	(−0.15)	(−1.30)
Primary school	0.054	−0.008	0.233***	0.227***	0.043	0.020	0.130**
	(0.64)	(−0.09)	(2.60)	(3.35)	(0.62)	(0.40)	(2.34)
Secondary school	0.210**	0.197**	0.388***	0.370***	0.236***	0.197***	0.280***
	(2.55)	(2.38)	(4.50)	(5.66)	(3.54)	(4.18)	(5.18)
High school, vocational or technical	0.617***	0.578***	0.735***	0.661***	0.514***	0.461***	0.557***
	(7.28)	(6.81)	(8.31)	(9.89)	(7.54)	(9.60)	(10.15)
Higher education	1.156***	1.152***	1.162***	1.043***	0.889***	0.890***	1.046***
	(11.00)	(11.10)	(11.14)	(13.20)	(11.42)	(16.39)	(17.10)
Constant	7.123***	7.541***	7.520***	7.868***	8.121***	8.319***	8.364***
	(51.95)	(54.93)	(54.57)	(76.06)	(80.32)	(118.06)	(106.66)
N	**14,999**	**16,036**	**11,635**	**12,767**	**16,519**	**17,201**	**17,441**

Source: World Bank.

a. Educational variable for reference: no education.

$^*p < .05$, $^{**}p < .01$, $^{***}p < .001$.

TABLE A2.6 Turkey: Mincerian Equation Results with Education Categories

	2011	2012	2013
Female	−0.234***	−0.259***	−0.346***
	(−15.08)	(−17.16)	(−22.69)
Apparel	0.303***	0.276***	0.328***
	(28.36)	(25.42)	(29.18)
Female * Apparel	−0.005	0.004	−0.018
	(−0.44)	(0.38)	(−1.57)
Age	0.082***	0.082***	0.080***
	(90.92)	(94.07)	(91.23)
Age^2	−0.001***	−0.001***	−0.001***
	(−76.85)	(−80.36)	(−77.25)
Primary	0.013	−0.016*	−0.010
	(1.42)	(−1.75)	(−1.00)
Lower secondary/Middle school	0.116***	0.100***	0.115***
	(12.17)	(10.53)	(11.82)
Upper secondary/High school	0.288***	0.265***	0.267***
	(30.31)	(28.03)	(27.40)
Degree, M.S. or PhD	0.761***	0.746***	0.752***
	(77.15)	(76.41)	(74.82)
Primary * Female	−0.114***	−0.098***	−0.010
	(−6.77)	(−5.95)	(−0.64)
Lower secondary/Middle school * Female	0.073***	0.084***	0.142***
	(4.11)	(4.83)	(8.17)
Upper secondary/High school * Female	0.138***	0.160***	0.241***
	(8.19)	(9.74)	(14.53)
Degree, M.S. or PhD * Female	0.126***	0.159***	0.258***
	(7.56)	(9.91)	(15.89)
Hours worked	0.004***	0.004***	0.005***
	(32.63)	(31.60)	(39.03)
Constant	4.350***	4.413***	4.363***
	(215.13)	(218.63)	(212.99)
N	**92,141**	**94,891**	**97,079**

Source: World Bank.
a. Educational variable for reference: no education.
$^*p < .05$, $^{**}p < .01$, $^{***}p < .001$.

TABLE A2.7 Vietnam: Mincerian Equation Results with Education Categories

	2007	2009	2010	2011	2012	2013	2015
Female	−0.297***	−0.252***	−0.266***	−0.284***	−0.254***	−0.291***	−0.403***
	(−26.87)	(−26.97)	(−36.40)	(−44.17)	(−30.93)	(−36.08)	(−67.50)
Apparel	0.960***	0.503***	0.092***	0.145***	0.279***	0.322***	0.490***
	(49.65)	(13.74)	(12.22)	(20.60)	(31.50)	(37.46)	(54.61)
Female * Apparel	−0.025	−0.034	0.018**	0.032***	0.014	0.013	0.171***
	(−1.14)	(−0.82)	(2.30)	(4.16)	(1.51)	(1.40)	(17.03)
Age	0.106***	0.043***	0.044***	0.048***	0.052***	0.056***	0.058***
	(124.93)	(27.22)	(76.64)	(93.82)	(80.31)	(87.81)	(125.77)
Age^2	−0.001***	−0.001***	−0.001***	−0.001***	−0.001***	−0.001***	−0.001***
	(−112.62)	(−28.37)	(−69.04)	(−85.43)	(−75.35)	(−82.55)	(−126.14)
Primary	0.023*	−0.188***	0.051***	0.067***	0.055***	0.077***	−0.002
	(1.73)	(−4.06)	(5.62)	(8.33)	(5.35)	(7.73)	(−0.23)
Lower secondary/ Middle school	0.063***	−0.053	0.115***	0.144***	0.114***	0.148***	0.037***
	(4.82)	(−0.83)	(13.54)	(18.91)	(11.76)	(15.68)	(5.17)
Upper secondary/ High school	0.115***	0.164***	0.147***	0.196***	0.155***	0.209***	0.147***
	(7.83)	(4.47)	(17.24)	(25.81)	(15.95)	(21.88)	(18.77)
Degree, M.S. or PhD	0.160***	0.099***	0.116***	0.121***	0.077***	0.116***	0.200***
	(8.65)	(3.46)	(13.19)	(15.45)	(7.77)	(12.14)	(23.01)
Primary * Female	−0.102***	0.250***	0.107***	0.107***	0.119***	0.096***	0.071***
	(−10.46)	(10.87)	(18.76)	(20.93)	(18.38)	(14.86)	(14.04)
Lower secondary/ Middle school * Female	−0.320***	0.194***	0.177***	0.175***	0.173***	0.159***	−0.018***
	(−33.18)	(6.69)	(32.65)	(35.63)	(27.86)	(26.08)	(−3.77)
Upper secondary/ High school * Female	−0.145***	0.186***	0.320***	0.343***	0.328***	0.305***	0.081***
	(−13.51)	(6.94)	(56.33)	(66.51)	(50.11)	(46.87)	(14.87)
Degree, M.S. or PhD * Female	0.421***	0.659***	0.766***	0.818***	0.824***	0.774***	0.449***
	(30.33)	(30.96)	(122.86)	(145.20)	(116.40)	(111.79)	(68.17)
Hours worked	0.019***	0.016***	0.008***	0.015***	0.015***	0.015***	0.024***
	(107.45)	(54.94)	(71.12)	(148.44)	(103.31)	(110.32)	(236.81)
Constant	3.577***	5.583***	6.154***	5.703***	5.677***	5.605***	5.178***
	(181.75)	(161.49)	(500.01)	(509.76)	(392.54)	(392.17)	(465.57)
N	**307,286**	**30,388**	**174,732**	**230,826**	**143,802**	**145,003**	**374,916**

Source: World Bank.

a. Educational variable for reference: no education.

$*p < .05$, $**p < .01$, $***p < .001$.

Notes

1. US female median age of marriage (1920) is from "Historical Marriage Status Tables, 1950 to 1990, and Current Population Survey," US Census Bureau: https://www.census.gov/data/tables/time-series/demo/families/marital.html. US female SMAM (2010) is from the "World Marriage Data 2019" data set, United Nations Department of Economic and Social Affairs (UN DESA), Population Division: https://population.un.org/MarriageData/Index.html.
2. Unemployment data on Egyptian women with advanced education are from the International Labour Organization, ILOSTAT database. See https://data.worldbank.org/indicator/SL.UEM.ADVN.ZS?locations=EG.

References

Artuc, E., G. Lopez-Acevedo, R. Robertson, and D. Samaan. 2019. *Exports to Jobs: Boosting the Gains from Trade in South Asia*. South Asia Development Forum Series. Washington, DC: World Bank.

Atkin, D. 2016. "Endogenous Skill Acquisition and Export Manufacturing in Mexico." *American Economic Review* 106 (8): 2046–85.

Barroso, A., and A. Brown. 2020. "Gender Pay Gap in U.S. Held Steady in 2020." Report, May 25, Pew Research Center, Washington, DC. https://www.pewresearch.org/?p=257386.

Becker, G. 1975. *Human Capital: A Theoretical and Empirical Analysis, with Special Reference to Education.* 2nd ed. Cambridge, MA: National Bureau of Economic Research.

Blau, F., M. Ferber, and A. Winkler. 2010. *The Economics of Women, Men, and Work.* 6th ed. Upper Saddle River, NJ: Prentice-Hall/Pearson.

Blau, F., and L. Kahn. 2007. "Changes in the Labor Supply Behavior of Married Women: 1980–2000." *Journal of Labor Economics* 25 (3): 393–438.

Blau, F., and L. Kahn. 2017. "The Gender Wage Gap: Extent, Trends, and Explanations." *Journal of Economic Literature* 55 (3): 789–865.

Christian, M., B. Evers, and S. Barrientos. 2013. "Women in Value Chains: Making a Difference." Revised Summit Briefing No. 6.3, Capturing the Gains, Manchester, UK. https://assets.publishing.service.gov.uk/media/57a08a22ed915d3cfd0005e6/ctg_briefing_note_6.3.pdf.

Das, S., and A. Kotikula. 2019. "Gender-Based Employment Segregation: Understanding Causes and Policy Interventions." Jobs Working Paper, Issue No. 26, World Bank, Washington, DC.

Fontana, M. 2009. "The Gender Effects of Trade Liberalization in Developing Countries: A Review of the Literature." In *Gender Aspects of the Trade and Poverty Nexus: A Macro-Micro Approach,* edited by M. Bussolo and R. De Hoyos, 25–50. Washington, DC: World Bank; New York: Palgrave Macmillan.

Goldin, C. 1984. "The Historical Evolution of Female Earnings Functions and Occupations." *Explorations in Economic History* 21 (1): 1–27.

Goldin, C. 2006. "The Quiet Revolution That Transformed Women's Employment, Education, and Family." *American Economic Review* 96 (2): 1–21.

Goldin, C., and L. Katz. 2008a. "Mass Secondary Schooling and the State: The Role of State Compulsion in the High School Movement." In *Understanding Long-Run Economic Growth: Geography, Institutions, and the Knowledge Economy*, edited by D. L. Costa and N. R. Lamoreaux, 275–310. National Bureau of Economic Research Conference Report. Chicago: University of Chicago Press.

Goldin, C., and L. Katz. 2008b. "Why the United States Led in Education: Lessons from Secondary School Expansion, 1910 to 1940." In *Human Capital and Institutions: A Long-Run View*, edited by D. Eltis, F. Lewis, and K. Sokoloff, 143–78. Cambridge: Cambridge University Press.

Goutam, P., I. A. Gutierrez, K. B. Kumar, and S. Nataraj. 2017. "Does Informal Employment Respond to Growth Opportunities? Trade-Based Evidence from Bangladesh." Working Paper WR-1198, RAND Corporation, Santa Monica, CA.

ILO (International Labour Organization). 2012. *International Standard Classification of Occupations, ISCO-08, Volume I: Structure, Group Definitions and Correspondence Tables.* Geneva: ILO.

ILO (International Labour Organization). 2016. *Report IV: Decent Work in Global Supply Chains.* Report ILC.104/IV for the International Labour Conference, 105th Session, 2016. Geneva: International Labour Organization.

Kabeer, N., and L. Natali. 2013. "*Gender Equality and Economic Growth: Is There a Win-Win?*" Working Paper No. 417, Institute of Development Studies, Brighton, UK.

Kis-Katos, K., J. Pieters, and R. Sparrow. 2017. "Globalization and Social Change: Gender-Specific Effects of Trade Liberalization in Indonesia," Discussion Paper No. 10552, Institute of Labor Economics (IZA), Bonn.

Pearlman, J. 2019. "Occupational Mobility for Whom?: Education, Cohorts, the Life Course and Occupational Gender Composition, 1970–2010." *Research in Social Stratification and Mobility* 59: 81–93. doi:10.1016/j.rssm.2018.11.009.

Sauré, P., and H. Zoabi. 2014. "International Trade, the Gender Wage Gap and Female Labor Force Participation." *Journal of Development Economics* 111: 17–33.

Schultz, M. A. 2019. "The Wage Mobility of Low-Wage Workers in a Changing Economy, 1968 to 2014." *RSF: The Russell Sage Foundation Journal of the Social Sciences* 5 (4): 159–89.

Smith, J., and M. Ward. 1985. "Time-Series Growth in the Female Labor Force." *Journal of Labor Economics* 3 (1): S59–S90.

UN DESA (United Nations Department of Economic and Social Affairs). 2013. "World Fertility Report: 2012." Report, UN DESA Population Division, New York.

CHAPTER 3

What Are the Barriers to Career Development?

Key Messages

- This report identifies three main barriers for middle-income countries to address to expand female career opportunities.
- First, low service sector demand due to insufficient national income (low gross domestic product [GDP] per capita) makes it difficult for women to transition from jobs to careers. Occupations associated with careers mostly occur in professional service industries that barely exist in lower-middle-income countries.
- Second, "careers" (unlike "jobs") often require upper-secondary or tertiary education, yet many lower-middle-income countries lack a sufficient share of the population with the education to qualify for high-skill occupations. In addition, graduates must have the required skills for the labor market.
- Third, social, cultural, and legal barriers are at play that limit female participation in the workforce. In several country cases, women are underrepresented even in traditionally female-dominated industries.

Introduction

So far, this report has made the case that although apparel cannot directly enable women to shift from jobs to careers, it can indirectly lay the foundation for the transition. However, as chapter 2 has shown, our seven apparel exporting countries of focus—Bangladesh, Cambodia, the Arab Republic of Egypt, Pakistan, Sri Lanka, Turkey, and Vietnam—have not made this transition. This finding suggests the persistence of barriers that hinder the transition from jobs to careers.

This chapter further defines "jobs" versus "careers" using industrial and occupational data. It complements the approach in chapter 2, which looked at the jobs-to-careers transition in terms of five indicators of women's workforce involvement (Goldin 2006): investment in human capital, marriage and labor force participation, lifetime labor force participation, earnings gaps between men and women, and distribution of employment across occupations and industries.

Careers are important because they imply a change in mindset toward planned long-horizon employment, investment in human capital, and lifetime labor-market continuity. Careers can even form part of a person's identity, having significant implications for life decisions about when to get married or have children (Goldin 2006). Careers are also attractive for the compensation received as a return on either the investment in education or the required experience or skill to have such occupations. It is perhaps not surprising, therefore, that some occupations are more likely to be associated with careers than others.

For many reasons, women have traditionally been more prominent than men in certain occupations—a phenomenon of employment segregation, as further discussed below. To that end, this chapter focuses on identifying which occupations are most often associated with careers and explores the current labor market trends in our sample countries. The first part of this chapter identifies industries that collectively account for most of the female labor market globally and by country income level. It then presents a breakdown of industries by occupation, including the skill and education levels typically required.

The analysis continues by examining three barriers that low- and middle-income countries face in seeking to expand female career opportunities:

- *Low service sector demand.* Lower-middle-income countries have insufficient income and low demand for professional service industries (such as social work and residential care facilities) that have traditionally provided careers for women in higher-income countries.
- *Low education levels.* Many lower-middle-income countries have an insufficient share of the population with the education to qualify for mid- or high-skill occupations.
- *Societal and cultural norms.* Social, cultural, and legal barriers are at play that limit female participation in the workforce; in several country cases, women are

underrepresented even in industries that are traditionally female-dominated in terms of total share of employees.

Importantly, we show that many of the female-dominated occupations are often associated with certain industries as well and that barriers to career development can be linked to the development of these occupations and industries. Careers related to high-skill occupations (HSOs) are not equally divided across all industries, and the apparel industry has few career-oriented opportunities. And because of low wages in apparel manufacturing, mediocre labor market returns to gross domestic product (GDP), and therefore minimal increases in GDP per capita, the industry's own characteristics can be a barrier (as further discussed in chapter 4).

Global Patterns of Female Labor Intensity

Around the world, the distribution of males and females across industries and occupations is far from even. Men and women have traditionally gravitated toward certain industries and occupations for a range of potential reasons. Employment segregation by gender refers to the distinction between "female jobs" and "male jobs" because gender-based segmentation of labor markets results in the underrepresentation of one gender (Bergmann 1974). Industry and occupational segregation by gender means that men have historically dominated the industrial sector in every region of the world, whereas women have recently dominated the services sector in every region except South Asia, Sub-Saharan Africa, and the Middle East and North Africa (Woetzel et al. 2015).

This employment segregation is one of the primary contributors to the gender wage gap globally (Das and Kotikula 2019). In fact, jobs traditionally held by women are characterized by low earnings, low training, and few opportunities for upward mobility (Das and Kotikula 2019; Li et al. 1998; Schultz 2019).

How are the differences in the distribution of women and men across occupational categories estimated? This is typically done by using methods similar to those in income inequality measurements, such as the segregation curve derived from the Gini index (Silber 2012).[1] Segregation indexes usually incorporate simple or complex forms of the proportion of males and females in the occupations analyzed, as done in Blau, Brummund, and Yung-Hsu (2012) and Gradín (2020). Most indexes measuring occupational segregation over time also account for the possible effects of occupational structure changes—a byproduct of shifts in the economy's occupational mix due to the decline or rise of a specific sector or industry, as initially proposed by Fuchs (1975).

Because we are looking at a snapshot in time and at occupations individually, we use two simple approaches to measure industry and occupation segregation: The first is to consider the share of all working women employed in each industry. The second uses the ratio of females to males within each industry to consider the female intensity of different industries and occupations. Among manufacturing industries at the global level, tobacco product manufacturing and apparel manufacturing are the most female intensive, with ratios of 4.3 and 1.3, respectively.[2] In fact, only those two manufacturing industries employ more women than men.

Which sectors and industries employ the most females globally? According to International Labour Organization labor force and household survey data,[3] the concentration of female employment in 2017 varied systematically across countries in relation to GDP per capita (figure 3.1). Agriculture is the biggest sectoral employer of females in low-income countries (53 percent), tying with services (42 percent each) in lower-middle-income countries.

But as country income rises, a notable shift occurs. The share of women employed in agriculture drops to 11 percent in upper-middle-income countries and is only 2 percent in high-income ones.[4] Conversely, the female concentration in services rises steadily by income level, from 32 percent in low-income countries to 42 percent in lower-middle-income, 74 percent in upper-middle-income, and 87 percent in high-income countries.

Manufacturing accounts for the lowest share of female employment across income levels except in high-income countries. In that sector, apparel is the most important employer of females, followed by food products, accounting for 3 percent

FIGURE 3.1 **Sectoral Shares of Total Female Employment, by Country Income Level, 2017**

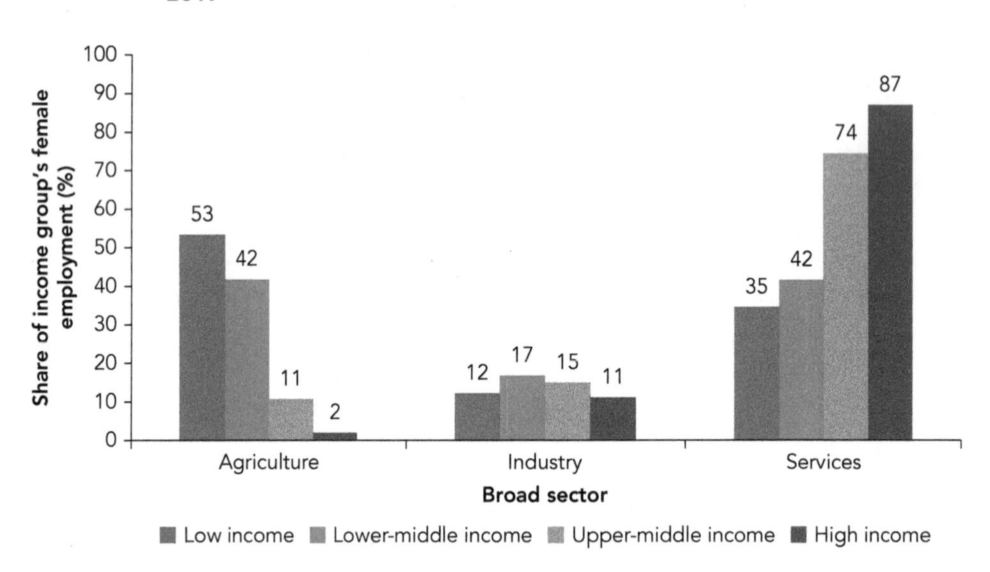

Source: International Labour Organization ILOSTAT data, "Employment by sex and economic activity (thousands), Annual" (1947–2020).

Note: The data cover 118 countries globally across regions. Broad sectors are defined under the International Standard Industrial Classification (ISIC) system, which groups economic activities into agriculture (including forestry, fishing, and mining); manufacturing (here, "industry"); and services. Country income categories are according to World Bank classifications.

and 2 percent of all female employment in 2017, respectively.[5] Middle- and high-income countries maintain similar shares of total employment in manufacturing with slightly under 25 percent of the workforce. The female share in manufacturing, however, drops from 17 percent in lower-middle-income countries to 11 percent in high-income countries.[6]

The drop in female manufacturing employment from middle- to high-income countries is driven by the apparel industry. In high-income countries, textiles, apparel, and leather account for only 1 percent of female employment, compared with 7 percent in lower-middle-income countries (table 3.1). This shows that employment in apparel manufacturing is not sustainable; female apparel workers will eventually need to find employment in other industries as country income rises.

The pattern that this shift forms, as shown in figure 3.1, is similar to the U-shape found when female labor force participation (FLFP) and national income are compared, consistent with the "feminization U hypothesis" discussed in chapter 1. In low- and lower-middle-income countries, FLFP rates are high because of the large concentration of women working in labor-intensive agriculture and domestic service industries. In upper-middle and high-income countries, FLFP increases again as service sectors expand and generate higher-wage opportunities for women.

TABLE 3.1 **Shares of Total Female Employment, by Country Income Group, Selected Industries, 2017**

Percent

Industry (ISIC4[a] code)	Low income	Lower-middle income	Upper-middle income	High income	All income levels
Crop production (01)	45	44	13	1	23
Textiles, apparel, leather (13–15)	4	7	5	1	5
Apparel (14)	3	5	3	1	3
Other manufacturing (10–12, 16–33)	6	7	8	7	7
High-skill services (84–86)	8	11	19	31	19
Mid-skill services (47, 56)	23	16	25	16	18
Low-skill services (96–97)	5	6	12	4	6
Residential care, social work (87–88)	0	0	1	8	3
Financial services (64–69)	1	1	3	8	4
All other services not listed above	6	6	12	23	13
Countries (no.)	6	21	21	34	82

Source: International Labour Organization ILOSTAT data, "Employment by sex and economic activity (thousands), Annual" (1992–2020).

Note: The data cover 82 countries globally across regions. Country income categories are according to World Bank classifications. Shares across the income groups may not total 100 percent because of rounding.

a. ISIC4 = *International Standard Industrial Classification of All Economic Activities (ISIC), Rev. 4* (UN DESA 2008).

The Three Female Employment Groups

Now that we know which industries and occupations tend to employ more women than others, we can try to organize them in a way that highlights patterns in industries, occupations, education levels, average wages, and shares of workers with formal work arrangements (table 3.2). An in-depth analysis of female employment across the seven sample countries suggests that employment tends to fall into three groups (further described below) that together illustrate the transition from jobs to careers. For this classification, we focus on the technical requirements rather than the labor market permanence and job experience components of careers.

Group 1: Agriculture and informal domestic service industries. Employment in this group can often be considered "jobs," and these industries and occupations are primarily in low- and lower-middle-income countries. Workers tend to have no formal education or primary education. The group includes agricultural, elementary, or sales and service occupations—corresponding to International Standard Classification of Occupations (ISCO) codes 6, 9, and 5, respectively. Work is almost entirely informal (over 95 percent), and wages are generally below minimum wage and the lowest among all industries (see appendix A, tables A.3 and A.4). Geographically, agricultural employment is in rural areas that do not overlap with employment opportunities in the other groups. Most female employment in Bangladesh and Pakistan falls into Group 1.

Group 2: Light manufacturing and retail and food/beverage services. Employment in this group can be considered in transition between "jobs" and "careers." Light manufacturing includes apparel, textiles, leather, and food manufacturing, which tend to be the most labor-intensive *and* female-intensive manufacturing industries globally, with employment demand driven by exports and the domestic market. The primary occupations are craft workers or plant operators (ISCO codes 7 and 8), and workers generally have primary or lower-secondary education. Wages are higher than in Group 1 and near the minimum wage. Informal employment is mid-range (generally 60–70 percent). On average, men in light manufacturing industries tend to work about 10 hours more per week than women. Group 1 and 2 industries are more evident in Cambodia and Vietnam. Sri Lanka and Turkey are transitioning between Group 2 and Group 3.

Retail and food/beverage services are mid-skill industries where there is demand from the national market. Employment growth, however, is also driven by foreign tourism. Christian, Evers, and Barrientos (2013) find that 70 percent of workers in tourism are female, which suggests that foreign demand is a driver of female employment. Employment often overlaps geographically with light manufacturing (in urban and industrial areas). The main occupations are sales and service workers (ISCO code 5). Workers generally have primary or lower-secondary education and earn similar wages to production workers. Informal employment accounts for about 90 percent of workers, and women tend to work more hours per week than in light manufacturing, averaging around 48 hours per week.

TABLE 3.2 Characteristics of Female Employment Groups in Sample Middle-Income Countries

Industry	ISIC4/ISIC3.1[a]	Main occupations	Educational attainment	Share of informal employment	Weekly hours (male, female)	Average monthly wages
Crop and animal production	01/01	Agricultural, elementary	None, primary	High (98%)	41, 31	Low
Activities of households	97/95	Elementary	None, primary	High (>95%)	51, 40	Low
Other personal services	96/93	Sales/service	Lower secondary	High (>95%)	42, 39	Low–mid
Food manufacturing	10/15	Craft	Primary, lower secondary	Mid (70%)	52, 43	Mid
Textile manufacturing	13/17	Craft/plant	Lower secondary	Mid (60%)	53, 39	Mid
Apparel manufacturing	14/18	Craft/plant	Lower secondary	Mid (60%)	54, 43	Mid
Leather manufacturing	15/19	Craft/plant	Lower secondary	Mid (60%)	53, 50	Mid
Retail trade services	47/52	Sales/service	Lower secondary	High (90%)	54, 48	Mid
Food and beverage services	56/55	Sales/service	Primary	High (90%)	56, 48	Mid
Public administration[b]	84/75	Service, professionals, technicians, clerks, managers	Tertiary, upper secondary	Low (<10%)	50, 45 43, 42	High
Education	85/80	Professionals	Tertiary	Low (<20%)	39, 37	High
Human health services	86/85	Professionals, technicians	Tertiary, upper secondary	Low (<30%)	45, 43	High
Computer or electronics manufacturing	26/—[c]	Plant	Upper secondary	Low (30%)	49, 53	High
Financial services	64/65	Professionals, managers, clerks	Tertiary primary	Low (10%)	45, 45	High

Source: Labor force survey data, latest year available (between 2013 and 2015).

Note: Informality groups: Low: <30 percent; Mid: 50–75 percent; and High: >80 percent, based on country data. Groups are color coded: Group 1 is orange, Group 2 is blue, and Group 3 is green. Formality implies that workers have access to social benefits through their jobs and should be guaranteed minimum wage. The sample includes seven middle-income countries: Bangladesh, Cambodia, the Arab Republic of Egypt, Pakistan, Sri Lanka, Turkey, and Vietnam.

a. The ISIC4 or ISIC3.1 codes refer, respectively, to Rev. 4 and Rev. 3.1 of the *International Standard Industrial Classification of All Economic Activities (ISIC)*.

b. The two sets of average weekly hours for public administration reflect International Standard Classification of Occupations (ISCO) code 5 (top row) and ISCO code 3 (bottom row).

c. Industry is not included in ISIC 3.1.

Group 3: Skilled professional service industries. Employment in this group can be considered "careers." These industries—education, human health services, and public administration—are chiefly driven by domestic demand. Economists might describe these industries as "income elastic" in the sense that they expand as national income increases. Workers have upper-secondary or tertiary education, and the occupations include managers, professionals, technicians, clerks, and service workers (ISCO codes 1–5). More than 70 percent of this employment is formal, and average weekly hours are close to 40. This group would also include workers in more advanced manufacturing industries such as computers and electronics, although Vietnam is the only country participating in this industry. Residential care and financial services are also in this group but become more important in upper-middle and high-income countries.

The Three Barriers to Career Progression

That none of our sample countries has made the jobs-to-careers transition (see chapter 2) suggests that they face barriers to the expansion of women's opportunities. For that reason, our study focuses on both identifying and evaluating barriers not just to employment but also to careers.

As noted earlier, three barriers emerge: (a) low demand for professional service industries (due to low GDP); (b) low education levels; and (c) low female participation in industries that employ the most women globally. These barriers are not mutually exclusive and often represent barriers for both men and women. We analyze them with a focus on maximizing participation in Group 2 and enabling a move into Group 3, given that our sample countries are middle-income ones.

BARRIER ONE: LOW DEMAND FOR SERVICES DUE TO LOW GDP

The first barrier—low demand for activities originating in the services sector—is one that low- and lower-middle-income countries inevitably must overcome as part of their economic development. GDP per capita is simply not high enough to create enough demand for the service jobs that offer careers for both women and men.

Occupational Characteristics by Country Income Level

In keeping with a shift in employment from agriculture to the industrial and service sectors as countries get richer, the share of total employment in agriculture falls and the share in services rises, although the rise for females in services is even more pronounced. In addition, the total demand for low-skill occupations in agricultural and elementary occupations (ISCO codes 6 and 9) falls from 44 percent in lower-middle-income countries to 25 percent in upper-middle-income countries, and the demand for HSOs (ISCO codes 1–3) rises from 13 percent to 25 percent, although the rise for females is again more pronounced (rising from 15 percent to 32 percent) (figure 3.2).

FIGURE 3.2 Decomposition of Occupations in Women's and Total Employment Worldwide, by Broad Category and Country Income Level, 2017

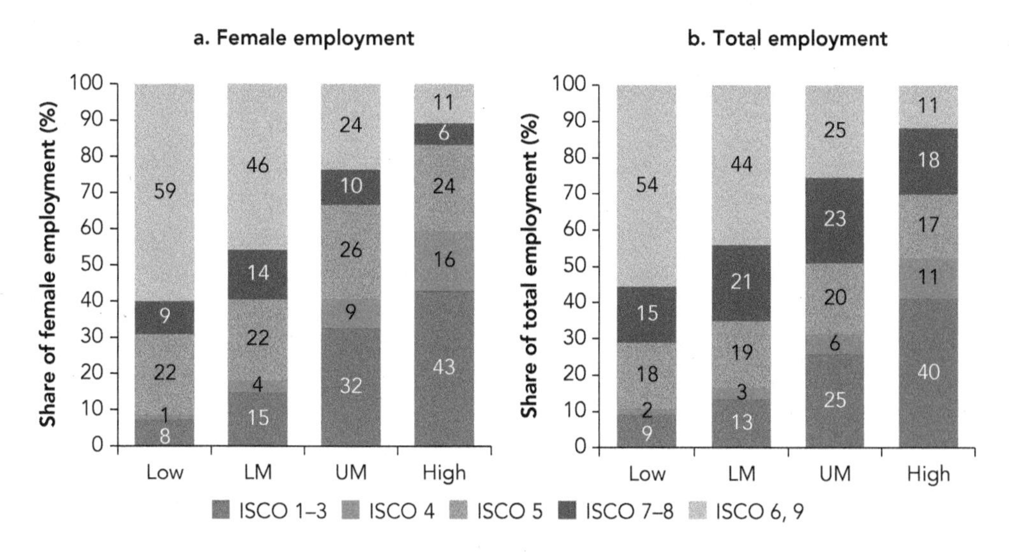

Source: ILOSTAT data, International Labour Organization.

Note: Data cover 102 countries using the International Standard Classification of Occupations ISCO-08 (ILO 2012)—including more countries than in the International Standard Industrial Classification of All Economic Activities (ISIC) 2-digit analysis used for table 3.2. (All countries' data are from 2017 ILOSTAT, except Pakistan's, which are from 2018. The sample excludes India because its use of the earlier ISCO-88 Index raised comparability issues.) By broad category, ISCO groups 1–3 include managers, professionals, and technicians and associate professionals; ISCO 4, clerical support workers; ISCO 5, services and sales workers; ISCO 7 and 8, craft and related trades workers as well as plant and machine operators and assemblers; and ISCO 6 and 9, skilled agricultural, forestry, and fishery workers as well as elementary occupations. Country income categories are according to World Bank classifications. LM = lower-middle income; UM = upper-middle income.

At the same time, production occupations increase in importance for middle-income countries before decreasing again for high-income countries. Mid-skill service industries (such as retail and food/beverage services) are important for countries across income levels, but they are most important in upper-middle-income countries. Occupational analysis supports this, given that sales/service occupations maintain a similar share across income levels overall as well as for females. Between lower-middle-income and high-income countries, the share of clerical workers (ISCO group 4) increases overall from 3 percent to 11 percent and for females from 4 percent to 16 percent, with the main increase occurring in upper-middle- to high-income countries. In upper-middle-income countries, HSOs (ISCO groups 1–3) in 2017 accounted for 25 percent of overall employment, compared with only 13 percent in lower-middle-income countries, yet it was 15 percentage points lower than high-income countries.

Certain industries that have been traditionally important for females (such as social work and residential care activities) are only prominent in high-income countries, accounting for 8 percent of female employment in 2017.[7] As table 3.1 shows, these industries are virtually nonexistent in low- and middle-income countries, accounting for less than 1 percent of female employment. Similarly, financial services account for 8 percent of female employment in high-income countries, compared with 2 percent in Sri Lanka and 1 percent in Cambodia, Turkey, and Vietnam. Other high-skill industries (like education, human health services, and public administration) are important across income levels, but they are most important to female employment in the richest countries.

Consumer spending mimics shifts in employment from agriculture to services (Merotto and Casanovas 2020), with consumption of services and nonessential goods rising as income does. Lower-income countries have less demand for services, given that most of the income earned is needed to purchase food and essential products. And without the domestic demand for service industries and the HSOs needed to support them, there will be low employment in these industries and occupations.

One way to visualize the shift in the labor market during the jobs-to-careers transition is by looking at how employment characteristics (occupations, education, and demand) change as country income rises (figure 3.3). It shows that in lower-middle-income countries, agricultural and elementary occupations, which require primary education levels or less, still account for the largest share of workers. Drivers of growth in employment demand are often from foreign exports of goods (and, for some countries, from services), with remaining employment serving domestic demand for goods and services. But in high-income countries, the driver is demand for services for the domestic market and for services that add value to products produced in foreign markets and consumed globally—and these occupations require upper-secondary and tertiary education.

Demand for Skills by Country Income Level

Another way to assess women's role in the labor force is to ask the following: In low-skill, mid-skill, and high-skill occupations, what share of employment is female, depending on country income levels? Our results show that in low- and lower-middle-income countries, females account for less than half of employment across all occupation groups at all skill levels (figure 3.4). But as countries rise from lower-middle to upper-middle-income status, females account for higher shares of HSOs, clerks, and sales and service workers and for lower shares of production workers.

These results suggest that returns from employment in the occupations available in lower-middle-income countries (Group 2, including light manufacturing and food/beverage services) are likely insufficient to draw women into the workforce, especially given the extra education (primary or beyond) needed and the number of hours worked relative to wages received. Alternatively, there may not be enough jobs available, or the jobs are being taken by men because of cultural norms.

Across all lower-middle-income countries, females account for 40 percent of HSOs. In our sample countries, Cambodia, Sri Lanka, and Vietnam are above the average; Bangladesh, Egypt, and Pakistan are below the average.[8] Turkey is well below the average

FIGURE 3.3 Employment Characteristics across Country Income Levels

	Low income	Lower-middle income	Upper-middle income	High income
Demand	Domestic goods and services	Foreign exports (goods, some services)	Foreign exports (services, some goods)	Domestic services
	Foreign exports (select goods)	Domestic goods and services	Domestic services	Foreign exports services
Upper-secondary, tertiary	Managers, Professionals, Technicians	Managers, Professionals, Technicians	Managers, Professionals, Technicians; Clerical	Managers, Professionals, Technicians; Clerical
Primary, lower-secondary	Sales/Service; Production	Sales/Service; Production	Sales/Service; Production	Sales/Service; Production
None, primary	Agriculture and elementary	Agriculture and elementary	Agriculture and elementary	Agriculture and elementary

Source: Adapted from Frederick 2021, with permission from the Duke University Global Value Chains Center, Durham, NC. Further permission required for reuse.

Note: The top row ("Demand") shows the sources of employment demand growth—divided into goods and services as well as by the location of the ultimate consumer (domestic or foreign). The bubble size is proportional to the share of employment in the occupational groups they display. The background shading across rows represents the average education levels of workers: dark gray for tertiary or upper-secondary education; gray for primary or lower-secondary education; and light gray for none or primary education. Country income categories are according to World Bank classifications.

for upper-middle-income countries (34 percent compared with 52 percent). And the female share of HSOs is highest in Vietnam—our only case country where females represent more than half of HSOs.[9]

BARRIER TWO: LOW EDUCATION LEVELS

The second barrier—low education levels—also arises as a country moves up the development curve, and it applies to both women and men. It matters greatly in the jobs-to-careers transition because of its integral link with the requirements for each occupation, regardless of industry. Where do our sample countries stand in terms of

FIGURE 3.4 **Female Share of Employment, by Occupation Group and Country Income Level, 2017**

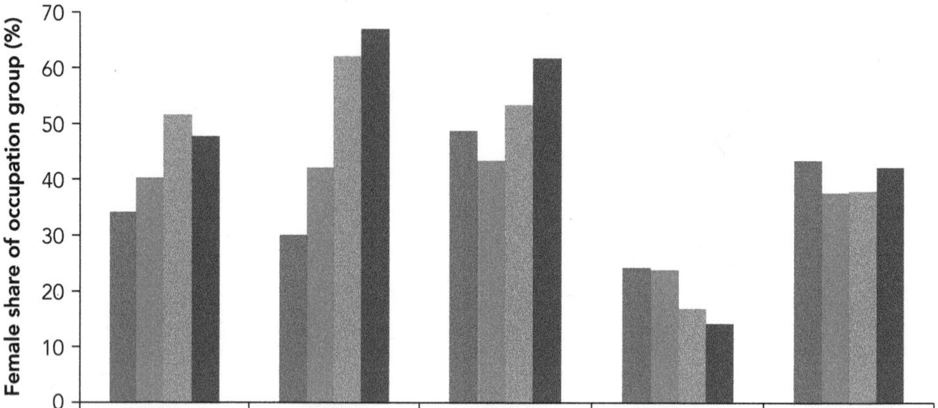

Female share of occupation group (%)

	ISCO 1–3	ISCO 4	ISCO 5	ISCO 7–8	ISCO 6, 9
Low	34	30	49	24	43
LM	40	42	43	24	38
UM	52	62	53	17	38
High	48	67	62	14	42

Low LM UM High

Source: International Labour Organization ILOSTAT data, "Employment by sex and occupation (thousands), Annual" (1969–2020).

Note: Data cover 102 countries using the International Standard Classification of Occupations ISCO-08 (ILO 2012), including more countries than in the International Standard Industrial Classification of All Economic Activities (ISIC) 2-digit analysis used for table 3.2. (All countries' data are from 2017 ILOSTAT, except Pakistan's, which are from 2018. The sample excludes India because its use of the earlier ISCO-88 Index raised comparability issues.) By broad category, ISCO groups 1–3 include managers, professionals, and technicians and associate professionals; ISCO 4, clerical support workers; ISCO 5, services and sales workers; ISCO 7 and 8, craft and related trades workers as well as plant and machine operators and assemblers; and ISCO 6 and 9, skilled agricultural, forestry, and fishery workers as well as elementary occupations. Country income categories are according to World Bank classifications. LM = lower-middle income; UM = upper-middle income.

upper-secondary education, which is key for moving up from jobs to careers? All but Egypt, Sri Lanka, and Turkey fall below the level needed for HSOs (figure 3.5).

In Cambodia and Pakistan, the proportion of females with enough education to partake in careers is below the average of all lower-middle-income countries.[10] In these countries plus Bangladesh, larger shares of employed males than employed females have at least an upper-secondary education, and the share of men in careers is slightly higher.[11] Thus, these countries may need to expand upper-secondary education overall, especially for females. Another pressing obstacle is the shares of women without any formal education in Cambodia and Pakistan, at 42 percent and 74 percent, respectively.[12]

Turkey and Vietnam have similar proportions of male and female workers who have completed upper-secondary education, and in Vietnam, females account for a slightly higher share of careers. The share of the workforce in Vietnam and Turkey with

FIGURE 3.5 **Share of Workers with at Least Upper-Secondary Education, by Gender, in Sample Middle-Income Countries**

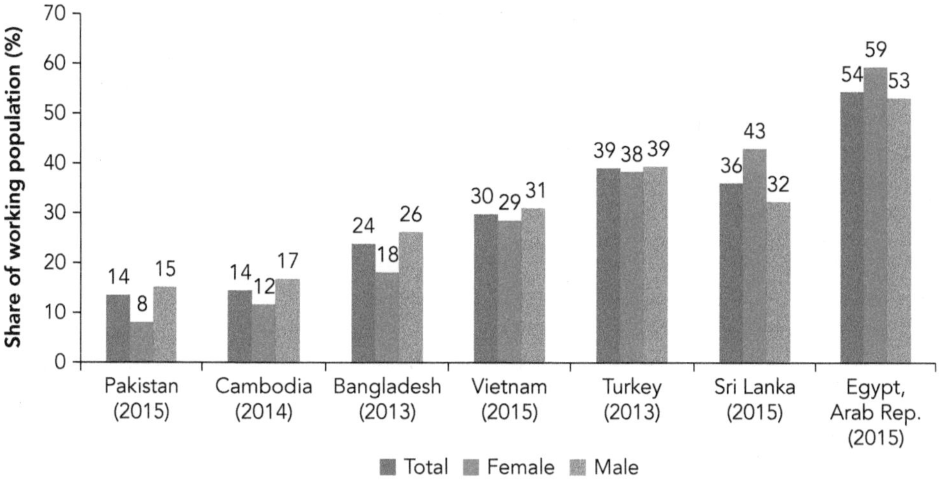

Source: Labor force survey data.
Note: Years in parentheses designate the year of country data.

upper-secondary education or higher exceeds the share of the workforce in HSOs in lower-middle-income countries (13 percent) and upper-middle-income countries (25 percent), respectively (as shown in figure 3.2).

Is Higher Education Always Enough?

Among our sample countries, Egypt and Sri Lanka have the highest shares of the female workforce with upper-secondary education or more, who would hence meet or exceed the level typically required for HSOs in high-income countries, and more employed women than men in those countries have completed upper-secondary education. Women's education levels appear sufficient to fulfill career occupations, suggesting that the problem—that these countries show little sign of a jobs-to-careers transition—may stem from either the lack of demand for career occupations or the lack of targeted educational programs to match the needs of specific industries and occupations.

The higher-education system in Egypt may also be misaligned with the country's market for high-skill labor. Although most working women there have attained at least upper-secondary education, higher education had long focused on conferring credentials for coveted local public sector jobs rather than on teaching tradable skills in demand by the private sector (World Bank 2020a). By the time this focus on education for public sector employment ended (in the late 1990s), women lacked the skills needed for private sector employment and have since had a difficult time finding jobs (Kabeer 2013).

Education and Occupational Mobility

Low human capital can complicate the insertion and permanence of women in the labor market. Having access to education not only helps them to acquire skills but is often related to lower fertility rates and higher mobility across occupations and industries. Given the asymmetric childcare responsibilities between women and men in households, childbirth can hinder women from entering the labor market or reentering it later. Less-educated women are less likely to return at all and are slower to resume work after childbirth (Dex, Ward, and Joshi 2005).

Low- and mid-skilled workers with lower-secondary education or less can benefit from work experience to increase their probabilities of upward mobility. However, women in these occupations often leave work after childbirth and, upon their return, have higher chances of being demoted or taking a part-time job. In other words, when experience in a particular occupation is interrupted, upward mobility becomes less feasible (Schultz 2019). In such cases, education may help as a safeguard.

Women with low formal educational qualifications who enter the labor market often complete an apprenticeship that ties them to their initial occupation—and, most likely, the industry as well—because it is a job-specific investment. In contrast, those with upper-secondary education tend to have higher mobility because their skills are not necessarily specific to one occupation and they have broader knowledge that could be used in other occupations. In fact, women with secondary education tend to be in less sex-differentiated labor markets because it is easier to leave their initial occupation even if it had been in a female-dominated sector (Li et al. 1998). Thus, the low shares of women with such education levels in Bangladesh, Cambodia, and Pakistan could also explain their lower mobility toward better-paid occupations outside the apparel industry.

Alternatively, women in the other sample countries, despite being more educated, might still be choosing jobs under different constraints such as mobility limitations due to lack of secure transportation. Moreover, a lack of business networks might contribute to their exclusion from available career opportunities (UNIDO 2018). Women tend to have smaller professional networks than men, which limits the information women have regarding the needs, expectations, and requirements of employers and investors. Networks are not only important for job referrals and acquisition but also affect women's expectations, aspirations, and acquisition of skills.

One study in Pakistan found that men have more active employment searches than women. To understand why, the researchers looked at how people search for employment and found that personal networks were the predominant search method (Xu et al. 2021). Relatedly, another study in Pakistan found that women also primarily (75 percent of respondents) obtain information about school or training institutes through their personal connections (JICA 2017). However, those networks tend to be small; 62 percent of the women sampled had no working female friends. Furthermore, referrals from networks were the most common hiring method of firms (Xu et al. 2021), and the most common reason cited by apparel companies for their limited hiring of females was the lack of female applicants (JICA 2017).

BARRIER THREE: SOCIETAL AND CULTURAL NORMS

The third barrier relates to societal and cultural norms that lead to unfavorable workplace practices, regulations, laws, and behaviors toward women—or that in other ways inhibit or dissuade women from working. One way to test for the existence of this type of barrier is to check for low FLFP in general as well as in the industries that employ the most women globally.

Mapping Where Social, Cultural, or Legal Barriers Exist

To do this, we take the industries that we have already identified as collectively accounting for most of the female labor market globally and estimate employment ratios for them (table 3.3). We use simple ratios between the number of women and men in each occupation to show occupational segregation in our sample countries. Ratios closer to 1.0 have a more equal distribution of males and females in an occupation, while lower ratios signal a larger proportion of men. Naturally, we do not expect to observe ratios close to 1.0 across all industries, but low ratios in industries that traditionally employ more women may suggest there are underlying social, cultural, or legal barriers to FLFP.

Our results show that HSOs in high-skill service industries (education and human health services) tend to favor female employment. In Egypt, Sri Lanka, Turkey, and Vietnam, women account for more HSOs in these two industries than men. But in Bangladesh, Cambodia, and Pakistan, women account for less than half of the HSOs in the education industry. As for human health services, they account for less than half of the HSOs in Bangladesh and Pakistan. These are also the countries with the lowest average education levels and the ones where fewer working women than men have upper-secondary education or higher.

For middle-income countries transitioning from jobs to careers, the occupational tendencies within Group 2 are particularly relevant. The Group 2 workforce is composed of either production workers or sales and service workers plus career occupations. In these occupations, females are mostly underrepresented in our case countries. Females also account for a greater share of lower-skill occupations relative to their representation in HSOs within the mid-skill manufacturing and service industries (table 3.3).

This analysis shows the following:

- In Bangladesh, Egypt, Pakistan, and Turkey, men account for more than half of the workforce in all Group 2 industries and occupations, except among apparel production workers in Bangladesh and Pakistan.[13]
- In the retail and food/beverage service industries, female-to-male ratios among sales and service workers are particularly low in Pakistan (0.0 and 0.0), Bangladesh (0.1 and 0.1), Egypt (0.3 and 0.0), and Turkey (0.4 and 0.2). But in Cambodia and Vietnam, female-to-male worker ratios are greater than 2.0.

TABLE 3.3 Ratio of Female-to-Male Employment in Select Industries and Occupations, Sample Middle-Income Countries, Mid-2010s

Industry	ISIC4/ISIC3.1[a]	Turkey 2013		Egypt, Arab Rep. 2015		Pakistan 2015		Bangladesh 2016		Sri Lanka 2015		Cambodia 2014		Vietnam 2015	
		1–3	7–8/5	1–3	7–8/5	1–3	7–8/5	1–3	7–8/5	1–3	7–8/5	1–3	7–8/5	1–3	7–8/5
Food[b]	10/15	0.2	0.2	0.0	0.1	0.0	0.0	0.1	0.3	0.3	1.0	n.a.	1.0	1.0	1.2
Textiles[b]	13/17	0.4	0.9	0.0	0.1	0.0	0.7	0.1	0.8	0.8	2.9	n.a.	6.7	1.3	1.5
Apparel	14/18	0.2	0.9	0.1	0.6	0.0	1.0	0.1	1.1	1.0	3.8	2.0	3.3	1.9	4.6
Leather	15/19	0.0	0.1	0.0	0.0	0.0	0.3	0.2	0.2	0.2	2.3	0.0	2.9	2.5	3.1
Retail services	47/52	0.5	0.4	0.1	0.3	0.0	0.0	0.2	0.1	0.4	0.7	0.9	2.5	1.1	2.2
Food and beverage services	56/55	0.1	0.2	0.0	0.0	0.0	0.0	0.1	0.1	0.3	0.4	1.2	2.0	1.1	2.2
Education[b]	85/80	1.1	n.a.	1.1	n.a.	0.7	n.a.	0.7	n.a.	2.9	n.a.	0.7	n.a.	2.8	n.a.
Human health services[b]	86/85	1.7	n.a.	1.8	n.a.	0.4	n.a.	0.7	n.a.	2.0	n.a.	1.1	n.a.	1.6	n.a.
All industries[b]	**All**	**0.4**	**n.a.**	**0.3**	**n.a.**	**0.2**	**n.a.**	**0.3**	**n.a.**	**0.7**	**n.a.**	**0.5**	**n.a.**	**1.0**	**n.a.**

Source: Labor force survey data.

Notes: Columns headed with "1–3" represent International Standard Classification of Occupations (ISCO) codes 1, 2, and 3 (managers, professionals, and technicians). Columns headed with "7–8/5" represent ISCO codes 7 and 8 (craft workers and plant operators) and in the retail and food/beverage rows, ISCO code 5. Ratios are between the number of women and men in each occupation. Ratios of 1.0 or higher (shaded in green) designate equal or larger proportions of women. Ratios of less than 1.0 (shaded in orange) designate a larger proportion of men. Low ratios in industries that traditionally employ more women may suggest there are underlying social, cultural, or legal barriers to female labor force participation.

a. ISIC4/ISIC3.1 numbers designate economic activities classified in the *International Standard Industrial Classification of All Economic Activities (ISIC)* Rev. 4 and Rev. 3.1, respectively.

b. n.a. = not applicable, meaning that no occupations under the designated ISCO code (column heading) are relevant to the industry in this row.

Looking at the occupational breakdown within manufacturing industries, apparel is the only one where female-to-male ratios in HSOs are greater than 1.0, even though this is evident in only three countries—Cambodia, Sri Lanka, and Vietnam—and the number of HSOs is limited (as further discussed in chapter 4). Females still account for a small share of the HSOs in apparel in Bangladesh, Egypt, Pakistan, and Turkey. Females also account for a lower share of production workers in these countries. However, apparel is one of the few industries where production workers have female-to-male ratios greater than 1.0 in Bangladesh and Pakistan, and although this ratio is below 1.0 in Egypt and Turkey, apparel has the highest ratio among the manufacturing industries.

In other words, women in middle-income countries primarily work in a select number of industries in mid-skill occupations, including sales/service and production workers. However, most of our sample countries show that women are underrepresented even in traditionally female-dominated industries. This suggests that even if income and education levels increase, pervasive cultural barriers to women in the workplace still must be addressed in some countries. On the positive side, the female-intensive apparel industry has proven to be one of the few industries where women have gained some traction. There is still room for these countries to expand female participation in apparel across occupations, and the strategies and best practices used in apparel can provide valuable lessons for other industries as these countries continue to develop.

Indicators of Legal and Economic Barriers

So what might be hindering women's participation in these key industries and occupations? Regressive laws—such as those that restrict women from working in certain jobs or from being the head of a household—can perpetuate discriminatory norms (Klugman et al. 2014). In fact, countries with low FLFP across industries and occupations (namely, Bangladesh, Egypt, Pakistan, and Turkey) also tend to be those where sexism (Bertrand 2020) and occupational segregation are more prevalent.

The World Bank's Women, Business and the Law Index is composed of eight indicators: Mobility, Workplace, Pay, Marriage, Parenthood, Entrepreneurship, Assets, and Pension (World Bank 2020b). These indicators align with different areas of the law and the economic decisions women make at various stages of their lives. The index provides a framework to build evidence concerning the links between legal gender equality and women's economic inclusion.[14] Regionally, the Middle East and North Africa and South Asia have the lowest index scores—49.6 and 62.3, respectively.

As for our country cases, Egypt has the lowest score (45.0) and Turkey the highest (82.5) (table 3.4). Although a low score in any indicator indicates room for improvement, the low scores related to workplace and pay are particularly relevant to this report. Regarding the workplace indicator, in Bangladesh and Sri Lanka the law does *not* prohibit gender-based employment discrimination, and in Egypt a woman cannot get a job in the same way as a man. The pay indicator covers four areas:

TABLE 3.4 **Women, Business, and the Law Index Scores, by Indicator, in Sample Middle-Income Countries and the United States**

Country	Mobility	Workplace	Pay	Marriage	Parenthood	Entrepreneurship	Assets	Pension	Overall
Egypt, Arab Rep.	50	75	0	0	20	75	40	100	45.0
Bangladesh	100	50	25	60	20	75	40	25	49.4
Pakistan	75	100	25	60	20	75	40	50	55.6
Sri Lanka[a]	100	75	25	100	20	75	80	50	65.6
Cambodia	100	100	75	80	20	100	100	25	75.0
Vietnam	100	100	75	100	80	100	100	0	81.9
Turkey	100	100	75	80	80	75	100	50	82.5
United States	100	100	75	100	80	100	100	75	91.3

Source: World Bank 2020b; historical data from the Women, Business and the Law database: https://wbl.worldbank.org/en/wbl-data.

Note: Countries are listed in order of lowest to highest overall score. Scores for Bangladesh, Cambodia, Egypt, Sri Lanka, and Turkey have remained the same on the annual index from 2017 to 2021. Scores for Pakistan (entrepreneurship and overall) and Vietnam (pay and overall) improved between 2020 and 2021; however, 2021 values are not shown in the table. The 2020 index indicators are based on data from June 2, 2017, to September 1, 2019.

a. Sri Lanka's scores on the Parenthood indicator differ between the published report (40) and raw data (20). The raw data list 20 in all years and include responses for questions, so that value is used for the Parenthood score and for calculating the overall score.

- *Whether the law mandates equal remuneration for work of equal value.* Among our country cases, laws stipulating equal pay exist only in Turkey and Vietnam.
- *Whether women can work the same night hours as men.* Pakistan and Sri Lanka have laws that inhibit women from working similar night hours as men.[15]
- *Whether women can work jobs deemed as dangerous.* Bangladesh and Egypt have laws that limit female participation in certain areas.
- *Whether women can work in the same industries as men.* All country cases except Cambodia have laws limiting female employment in at least one industry in the index.

Most of our case countries—Bangladesh, Egypt, Pakistan, Sri Lanka, and Vietnam—have laws related to working in factories that limit women's ability to work.[16] In Bangladesh, women receive the same treatment as adolescents before the law when it comes to working in manufacturing.[17] In this sense, women are not allowed to clean, adjust, or lubricate any part of machinery while it is in motion. Women in Pakistan and Sri Lanka have similar restrictions and cannot work in occupations that involve cleaning machines in motion (World Bank 2020b). Although restrictions in most countries involve only the manufacturing or mining industries, Vietnam has legal limitations that cover 38 different jobs in different sectors, including jobs aboard seagoing ships. Additionally, there are 39 other jobs that pregnant and nursing women cannot hold.[18]

These are just examples to illustrate a more important underlying concern—that these countries choose to *legally* restrict women from making their own employment decisions. If there are health and safety reasons that suggest a woman should avoid certain occupational tasks, these concerns can be communicated to employers and workers without restricting female participation. In most cases, however, these limitations have no supporting documentation or rationale for limiting female participation and appear to be driven by social and cultural norms.

The bottom line is that, among our country cases, there is a general correlation between countries that have (a) gender-based legal barriers and cultural beliefs against women working outside the home, and (b) low FLFP overall as well as in the industries that employ the most women globally.

Conclusion

Given that lower-middle-income countries often struggle with helping women make the transition from jobs to careers, it is natural to ask what barriers they might be encountering. This chapter identifies and analyzes three barriers that policy makers will need to address in our sample countries (Bangladesh, Cambodia,

Egypt, Pakistan, Sri Lanka, Turkey, and Vietnam). Several findings emerged from this analysis:

- Although HSOs account for 13 percent of employment in lower-middle-income countries, they make up 25 percent of women's employment in upper-middle-income countries and 40 percent in high-income ones. Similarly, several professional service industries that have been traditionally important for females are prominent only in high-income countries. We find that returns from employment in the occupations available in lower-middle-income countries are perhaps insufficient to draw women into the workforce, especially given the extra education needed and the number of hours worked relative to the wages received.
- Education levels in three sample countries (Bangladesh, Cambodia, and Pakistan) are insufficient to meet the needs of career occupations, particularly for women. But in the other countries (Egypt, Sri Lanka, Turkey, and Vietnam), education levels for women are not only sufficient but also equal to or higher than those for men. Thus, the problem is likely to stem from low demand in select industries and misalignment between education and workforce development.
- In most of our case countries, certain laws either (a) limit women's ability to undertake certain occupations, to earn, or to move between occupations equally to men; or (b) are lacking in protections against discrimination in the workplace. Moreover, gender norms further limit women's involvement in the labor force or diminish the workplace environment, deterring them from staying in the workforce. This is particularly evident in Bangladesh, Egypt, Pakistan, and Turkey, which have lower FLFP rates, higher levels of sexism, and—except in Turkey—lower gender equality based on the World Bank's Women, Business and the Law indicators. They also have low female-to-male ratios in industries that traditionally employ more women.

If countries primarily engage in industries that mostly provide "jobs" (such as in apparel manufacturing), the opportunities for career advancement are quite limited. Furthermore, when these jobs provide low wages, there are minimal returns to national income that would increase demand for the professional service industries that women often transition into in higher-income countries. The following chapter explores this further.

Notes

1. The Gini coefficient is the most commonly used measure of the inequality of the distribution of income (or consumption) in an economy. A Gini value of 0.0 indicates perfect equality, and a value of 1.0 indicates perfect inequality.

2. International Labour Organization (ILO), "Employment by sex and economic activity, ISIC level 2" (1992–2020) data, https://www.ilo.org/shinyapps/bulkexplorer40/?lang=en&segment=indicator&id=EMP_TEMP_SEX_EC2_NB_A.
3. For details on the data sources, see appendix A.
4. ILO, "Employment by sex and economic activity (thousands), Annual" (1947–2020) data, https://www.ilo.org/shinyapps/bulkexplorer20/?lang=en&segment=indicator&id=EMP_TEMP_SEX_ECO_NB_A.
5. ILO, "Employment by sex and economic activity, ISIC level 2" (1992–2020).
6. ILO, "Employment by sex and economic activity (thousands), Annual" (1947–2020).
7. ILO, "Employment by sex and economic activity, ISIC level 2" (1992–2020).
8. Female share of HSOs by country (highest to lowest): Vietnam (52 percent), Cambodia (43 percent), Sri Lanka (42 percent), Turkey (34 percent), Egypt (26 percent), Bangladesh (26 percent), and Pakistan (20 percent).
9. ILO, "Employment by sex and occupation (thousands), Annual" (1969–2020) data, https://www.ilo.org/shinyapps/bulkexplorer40/?lang=en&segment=indicator&id=EMP_TEMP_SEX_EC2_NB_A.
10. ILO, "Employment by sex and occupation (thousands), Annual" (1969–2020).
11. ILO, "Employment by sex and occupation (thousands), Annual" (1969–2020).
12. ILO, "Employment by sex and occupation (thousands), Annual" (1969–2020).
13. In Pakistan, apparel and tobacco manufacturing are the only industries where men do not outnumber women, but there are no industries where the proportion of women is higher than men among HSOs or sales and service workers.
14. *Women, Business and the Law* index data are available for 190 economies. The indicators for the 2020 index are based on data from June 2, 2017, to September 1, 2019. Scores by indicator are based on the number of questions (four or five). For example, a score of 50 means the indicator includes four questions, and the country's results were yes for two questions and no for two questions.
15. In Sri Lanka, see the Shops and Office Employees Act, Sec. 10; Employment of Women, Young Persons, and Children Act No. 47 of 1956, Secs. 2–3. In Pakistan, see the Sindh Shops and Commercial Establishment Act, Sec. 7(4).
16. In Egypt, see the Decree of Minister of Manpower and Immigration No. 183 of 2003, Arts. 1 and 2(A); Decree of Minister of Manpower and Immigration No. 155 of 2003, Art. 1. In Bangladesh, see the Labor Act, Secs. 39, 40, and 87. In Pakistan, see the Sindh Factories Act, Secs. 31(2) and 36. In Sri Lanka, see the Factories Ordinance No. 45 of 1942, Secs. 25, 67, and 67A (2). In Vietnam, see Circular No. 26/2013/TT-BLDTBXH, Lists Part A-I-32. In Turkey, there are no laws specific to factories, but there are laws in other industries covered in the Women, Business and the Law Index.
17. See the Bangladesh Labour Act, 2006, Arts. 87, 39, and 40: https://www.ilo.org/dyn/travail/docs/352/A%20Handbook%20on%20the%20Bangladesh%20Labour%20Act%202006.pdf.
18. See "Circular Promulgating the List of Jobs in Which the Employment of Female Workers Is Prohibited," Circular No. 26/2013/TT-BLDTBXH, Art. 23: https://www.ilo.org/dyn/natlex/docs/MONOGRAPH/97047/128483/F-256917122/VNM97047%20Eng.pdf.

References

Bergmann, B. 1974. "Occupational Segregation, Wages and Profits When Employers Discriminate by Race or Sex." *Eastern Economic Journal* 1 (2): 103–10.

Bertrand, M. 2020. "Gender in the Twenty-First Century." *AEA Papers and Proceedings* 110: 1–24.

Blau, F., P. Brummund, and A. Yung-Hsu. 2012. "Trends in Occupational Segregation by Gender 1970–2009: Adjusting for the Impact of Changes in the Occupational Coding System." Working Paper 17993, National Bureau of Economic Research, Cambridge, MA.

Christian, M., B. Evers, and S. Barrientos. 2013. "Women in Value Chains: Making a Difference." Revised Summit Briefing No. 6.3, Capturing the Gains, Manchester, UK. https://www.gov.uk/research-for-development-outputs/women-in-value-chains-making-a-difference.

Das, S., and A. Kotikula. 2019. "Gender-Based Employment Segregation: Understanding Causes and Policy Interventions." Jobs Working Paper, Issue No. 26, World Bank, Washington, DC.

Dex, S., K. Ward, and H. Joshi. 2005. "Changes in Women's Occupations and Occupational Mobility over 25 Years." Paper for Women and Employment Survey, Centre for Longitudinal Studies, Institute of Education, University of London.

Frederick, S. 2021. "GVC Employment Characteristics." Report, Duke University Global Value Chains Center, Durham, NC.

Fuchs, V. 1975. "A Note on Sex Segregation in Professional Occupations." *Explorations in Economic Research* 2 (1): 105–11.

Goldin, C. 2006. "The Quiet Revolution That Transformed Women's Employment, Education, and Family." *American Economic Review* 96 (2): 1–21.

Gradín, C. 2020. "Segregation of Women into Low-Paying Occupations in the United States." *Applied Economics* 52 (17): 1905–20. doi:10.1080/00036846.2019.1682113.

ILO (International Labour Organization). 2012. *International Standard Classification of Occupations, ISCO-08, Volume I: Structure, Group Definitions and Correspondence Tables.* Geneva: ILO.

JICA (Japan International Cooperation Agency). 2017. "Social and Gender Survey Report." Report of 2016–17 survey by the JICA Project for Skills Development and Market Diversification (PSDMD) of Garment Industry in Pakistan, Lahore.

Kabeer, N. 2013. *Paid Work, Women's Empowerment and Inclusive Growth: Transforming the Structures of Constraint.* New York: UN Entity for Gender Equality and the Empowerment of Women (UN Women).

Klugman, J., L. Hanmer, S. Twigg, T. Hasan, J. McCleary-Sills, and J. Santamaria. 2014. *Voice and Agency: Empowering Women and Girls for Shared Prosperity.* Washington, DC: World Bank.

Li, J. H., M. Buchmann, M. König, and S. Sacchi. 1998. "Patterns of Mobility for Women in Female-Dominated Occupations: An Event-History Analysis of Two Birth Cohorts of Swiss Women." *European Sociological Review* 14 (1): 49–67.

Merotto, D., and E. Casanovas. 2020. "Which Comes First—the Chicken, the Egg, or the Demand for Poultry Products? Engels Law and the Design of Jobs Strategies in Low-Income Countries (LICs)." Jobs and Structural Change Blog Series #8, February 17. World Bank, Washington, DC. www.jobsanddevelopment.org/which-comes-first-the-chicken-the-egg-or-the-demand-for-poultry-products-engels-law-and-the-design-of-jobs-strategies-in-low-income-countries-lics/.

Schultz, M. A. 2019. "The Wage Mobility of Low-Wage Workers in a Changing Economy, 1968 to 2014." *RSF: The Russell Sage Foundation Journal of the Social Sciences* 5 (4): 159–89.

Silber, J. 2012. "Measuring Segregation: Basic Concepts and Extensions to Other Domains." In *Research on Economic Inequality* Vol. 20, edited by J. A. Bishop and R. Salas, 1–35. Bingley, UK: Emerald Publishing. doi:10.1108/S1049-2585(2012)0000020004.

UN DESA (United Nations Department of Economic and Social Affairs). 2008. *International Standard Industrial Classification of All Economic Activities (ISIC), Rev. 4.* New York: United Nations.

UNIDO (United Nations Industrial Development Organization). 2018. "Mainstreaming Gender in Cluster Development." Report of the Department of Trade, Investment and Innovation, UNIDO, Vienna.

Woetzel, J., A. Madgavkar, K. Ellingrud, E. Labaye, S. Devillard, E. Kutcher, J. Manyika, R. Dobbs, and M. Krishnan. 2015. "The Power of Parity: How Advancing Women's Equality Can Add $12 Trillion to Global Growth." Report, McKinsey Global Institute, San Francisco.

World Bank. 2020a. *Convergence: Five Critical Steps toward Integrating Lagging and Leading Areas in the Middle East and North Africa*. Washington, DC: World Bank.

World Bank. 2020b. *Women, Business and the Law 2020.* 6th ed. Washington, DC: World Bank.

Xu, S., V. Jain, H. Khan, and K. Vyborny. 2021. "Barriers Faced by Women in Labour Market Participation: Evidence from Pakistan." International Growth Centre blog, March 23. https://www.theigc.org/blog/barriers-faced-by-women-in-labour-market-participation-evidence-from-pakistan/.

CHAPTER 4

How Does an Apparel Export Strategy Fit into the Jobs-to-Careers Transition?

Key Messages

- Apparel exporting creates many jobs—tending to be more formal and higher paying than other opportunities available to women with less than secondary education—but few careers.
- Even though apparel exporting provides jobs and tends to employ the most women among manufacturing industries, it is still only a small portion of the labor market and alone has minimal impact on female labor force participation unless apparel is a country's only export.
- Apparel exporting represents a temporary country strategy because of cost competitiveness and power dynamics between buyers (apparel brand owners) and developing-country manufacturers.
- Low- and middle-income countries (LMICs) rarely move from apparel manufacturing to apparel services, and no such country has moved into global branding or retailing.
- But LMICs can use apparel exporting to boost human capital, which would enable movement to other industries and higher wages to promote domestic services.

Introduction

The era of global value chains (GVCs) took off in the 2000s, part of a process that began in the 1980s as global manufacturing industries expanded significantly and multinationals in high-income countries moved production to low- and middle-income countries (LMICs). This shift in production generated formal sector jobs particularly for females in LMICs, which engaged in lower-skill, lower-value-adding activities while high-income countries engaged in higher-skill, career-oriented activities and occupations. However, participation in labor-intensive GVCs—such as apparel manufacturing—has its limits in supporting women's transitions from jobs to careers. One reason is that manufacturing creates few career-related occupations. Another is that wages are generally low (close to minimum wage) and wage increases are minimal.

This report contends that, in recent decades, apparel exporters in middle-income countries have made progress in the jobs-to-careers transition for women. It bases that conclusion on the progress that our seven case countries—Bangladesh, Cambodia, the Arab Republic of Egypt, Pakistan, Sri Lanka, Turkey, and Vietnam—have made on five performance indicators (such as investment in human capital and patterns of marriage and labor force participation), as chapter 2 examined in detail. Apparel has been important to exports in these countries, all of which have been key apparel exporters globally. And all of them (except Egypt) have been among the top 10 global apparel exporters at some point over the past three decades. But, as chapter 3 established, they also face three barriers to expansion of female career opportunities: (a) low national demand for higher-skill service industries; (b) low education levels; and (c) social and cultural norms that hinder female participation in industries that are important to women's employment globally.

This chapter explores how a strategy for apparel export growth fits into the jobs-to-careers transition. It begins by describing the characteristics of the apparel industry and GVCs. It then analyzes how our case countries participate in the apparel industry (checking on labor market indicators) and provides an overview of the workforce and opportunities for upward occupational mobility. It concludes with options for LMICs to improve their participation in apparel GVCs.

A key finding is that an apparel export–led industrialization path benefits workers in the short term. But unless countries expand other industries and invest in education and skill development, their apparel exports are not sufficient to induce the transition from jobs to careers.

A Profile of the Apparel Industry

Apparel is one of the world's most globalized manufacturing industries and often starts a country down the export-oriented industrialization path—in part by bringing rural women into the formal economy (English 2013). Further, low barriers to entry, including low start-up costs and minimal capital investment, help create entry-level jobs for young, unskilled women (Cammett 2006; Keane and Willem te Velde 2008; Nattrass and Seekings 2018).

The apparel industry is the world's top manufacturing employer of females, and it is female intensive for technical, economic, and practical reasons that are often rooted in social norms. Before mass production, women traditionally made garments at home as part of their household activities. Women were more likely than men to learn how to sew, which established a historical social norm that women operate sewing machines. Moreover, gender norms associate capital-intensive work as masculine and light manufacturing work as feminine (Tejani and Milberg 2016)—in some cases, associating females with technical advantages in using sewing machines, on the assumption that women have greater manual dexterity and nimbler fingers than men (Elson and Pearson 1981).

With the advent of global production, a combination of economics and availability reinforced these social norms. Globalization has often been associated with "feminization" of labor—described as the rise in the female share of employment, integration of women into the labor force, or increased participation of women in the global labor force (Palpacuer 2008)—particularly since the mid-1970s. Feminization took place almost entirely in labor-intensive industries including textiles, garments, and electronics (Tejani and Milberg 2016).

Moreover, producers observed several characteristics that made hiring women particularly attractive. Women are often willing to work for lower wages than men, are less likely to unionize, are generally easier to hire under informal contracts, and are more productive than men (Duboc 2013; Elson and Pearson 1981; Ghosh 2002; Rahman and Islam 2013; Safa 1994; Tejani and Milberg 2016). They may be more willing to take low-paying jobs to support educational opportunities for children (Tokatli, Kızılgün, and Cho 2011). They tend to be more patient than men and willing to work longer hours performing routine assembly operations, resulting in higher productivity. And they tend to have a better work ethic, are more reliable, and have lower absenteeism than men (Christian, Evers, and Barrientos 2013; Ghosh 2002; Safa 1994).

Prior studies of the textile and apparel industries emphasize their value in creating short-term employment opportunities and supporting inclusive development (Keane and Willem te Velde 2008; Nattrass and Seekings 2018; Whitfield, Staritz, and Morris 2020). Few countries, however, have achieved sustained economic growth, skill transfer, upgrading, and market diversification by participating in the textile and apparel sector (Van der Ven 2015). Since the advent of global sourcing in the 1980s, no country has rivaled the global dominance of apparel brands and lead firms from Europe, Japan, and the United States (Frederick 2016).

Furthermore, as an economy's technology improves, female employment shares fall (English 2013). For example, the Republic of Korea; Taiwan, China; and Malaysia experienced declines in female employment in both textiles and apparel from 1981 to 2008. This decline in female shares of employment in apparel—and in manufacturing in general—was associated with substantial technological upgrading and shifts toward less labor-intensive manufacturing industries (Kucera and Tejani 2014).[1]

Global Value Chain Participation and Development

How can LMICs—in particular, apparel exporters—position themselves to reap the greatest benefits of integrating into a GVC? A good starting point is a better understanding of specific industries' structure (including the workers, firms, and countries involved along the entire chain) and the drivers of industrial organization, governance, and upgrading. These relationships are highly dynamic, and the ways in which firms and countries enter and improve their positions in GVCs differs depending on their current position, objectives, and governance. Here, governance refers to relationships between buyers, sellers, service providers, and regulatory institutions (box 4.1).

BENEFITS AND LIMITS OF BUYER-SUPPLIER RELATIONSHIPS ALONG THE CHAIN

Apparel GVCs are "buyer-driven" (Gereffi 1994), with higher profit margins in the higher-value-added activities (design, sales, marketing, and finance) that have high

BOX 4.1 The Role of Governance in Global Value Chains

Global value chain (GVC) governance describes the authority and power relationships that determine where and how resources are allocated along the GVC (Gereffi 1994; Gereffi, Humphrey, and Sturgeon 2005).

Governance from Firms

GVC "lead firms" add the most consumer value to the final product or service. They create the value of products and services to the consumer through marketing, branding, retailing, and design, and they determine who will produce the product, and where, to maximize their returns.

These firms are offshoring production to low- and middle-income countries, which are chosen based on a sliding scale that considers cost competitiveness along with other factors that vary in importance by firm and industry, including quality, capacity, capabilities, compliance, geography, and social factors (such as ease of doing business, cultural affinity, and relationship longevity) (Frederick 2016).

Governance from Institutions

Rules and regulations, from local to international, govern how firms and countries compete. The regulating institutions can be public or private, industry-specific or economywide.

The interplay of public and private governance influences where activities take place. For example, import tariffs and trade agreements play significant roles in shaping the geography of global apparel production. But for electronics, automobiles, or medical devices, the more significant governing factors are product and process standard compliance, capabilities, and quality (Frederick and Bamber 2018).

barriers to entry, whereas the lower-value-added activities (manufacturing and assembly) have low barriers to entry and are highly competitive. The two main cost components are labor and import tariffs. From the suppliers' perspective, taking on more sophisticated, more knowledge-intensive activities is referred to as functional upgrading (Humphrey and Schmitz 2002). The limited propensity of functional upgrading to the higher-value-added, service-related segments of GVCs is related to the literature on the "middle-income trap"—a phenomenon whereby countries gain a higher income status from increased exports but later get stuck at that level after losing a competitive edge (Engel and Taglioni 2017).

Over the past decade, GVCs have provided opportunities for LMICs with limited domestic demand for goods and services to produce products for high-income countries under the direction of global buyers—which, in turn, has boosted employment and income, especially for women. GVCs have also benefited high-income countries by enabling buyers to manufacture goods in countries with lower costs, which in the case of apparel is a function of low wages (along with import tariffs). As a result, these buyers have become more profitable, and consumers in high-income countries have benefited from lower apparel prices.

For LMICs, however, participation in the same GVC has a ceiling. As illustrated in figure 4.1, high-income countries control the most lucrative activities along the chain

FIGURE 4.1 **Relationships of GVC Activities and Country Roles to Occupational Skill and Country Income Levels**

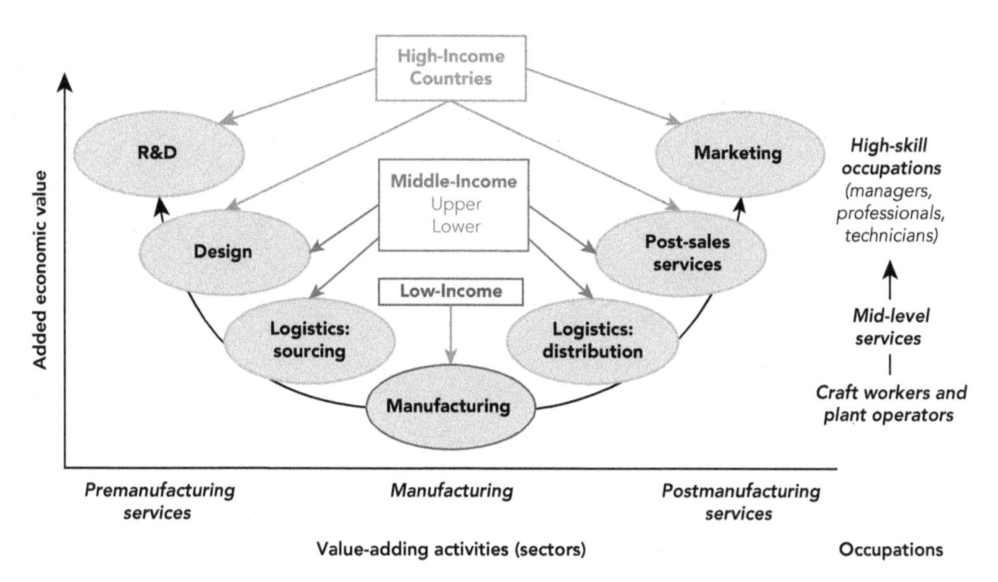

Source: Updated from Fernandez-Stark, Frederick, and Gereffi 2011; Frederick 2010. © World Bank.
Note: Yellow circles represent service sector industry and high-skill or sales or service occupations. Red outlines designate manufacturing and craft or production workers. (In some countries, elementary occupations are also used as helpers). GVC = global value chain; R&D = research and development.

(such as research and development and marketing), which are in the services sector. These lead firms set the price of the final product and create "value" in the eyes of the consumer through branding (box 4.2). But LMICs get locked into low-value-added activities—that is, manufacturing—because there is little room to move into the high-skill activities and because countries must keep labor costs low to remain globally competitive. Thus, although GVC integration can lead to large-scale job creation, it can also lead to sustained low wages and inequalities for low-skilled and female workers (Farole 2016).

Over time, however, some lead firms have started outsourcing some of the service industry activities to their most capable suppliers (Frederick 2015). This begins with preproduction and postproduction services such as shipping the final product to the buyer at an agreed-upon selling price (also referred to as freight on board) and input sourcing. Other suppliers may also provide technical design services (such as converting creative ideas into patterns) or assist with new product development (becoming original design manufacturers). In some cases, buyers may also consult with their most strategic first-tier suppliers on creative design, but buyers always maintain the final decision-making power. These activities provide more career-like opportunities, but few workers are needed in a factory in these positions.

What apparel manufacturing offers to workers are (a) formal jobs; (b) female employment; (c) knowledge of production systems, assembly-line manufacturing, and lean manufacturing concepts; and (d) supervisor and middle-management experience (if these positions are not filled by expats) (Frederick and Bamber 2018). But on the flip side, it offers only limited opportunities for functional upgrading and associated careers

BOX 4.2 The Four Stages of an Apparel Global Value Chain

The apparel GVC represents a series of industries that span the agriculture, manufacturing, and services sectors (Frederick 2019b). Its four stages, intertwined with the textile industry, are as follows (Frederick 2015; Frederick and Staritz 2012):

- *Other input suppliers.* These supply raw material, including natural fibers such as cotton and wool; man-made fibers such as polyester, nylon, and acrylic; and other inputs such as trim, machinery, and chemicals or dyes.
- *Textile component suppliers.* These supply yarn, fabric, and finishing.
- *First-tier suppliers.* These are final product manufacturers and intermediaries. Apparel manufacturers or vendors are responsible for cutting and sewing fabric into a final garment. These activities have historically been quite labor intensive, with low start-up and fixed costs and simple technology.
- *Lead firms.* These are the buyers, global apparel brands, and retailers. They do not own manufacturing facilities but outsource production of their products to a global network of suppliers. They are responsible for the service activities that add the most value to apparel products, including consumer research, new product development, creative design, branding, and retailing.

that require tertiary education or related computer and interpersonal (soft) business skills. And workers do not gain experience using advanced machinery or knowledge of how to operate in industries in which standards and regulations are important (Frederick and Bamber 2018).

CHARACTERISTICS OF APPAREL MANUFACTURERS

Most apparel exporting countries have two groups of manufacturing firms, which differ in their firm and workforce characteristics: (a) large, foreign-owned exporters, which have a global orientation; and (b) small and medium-size firms, which are based in and selling to regional or domestic markets (table 4.1). These differences can be seen in

TABLE 4.1 Characteristics of Apparel Manufacturers in Exporting Countries, by Scale of Operation

Characteristic	Global orientation	Domestic or regional orientation
Firm structure	• Multiunit companies	• Single locations
Ownership	• Foreign owned	• Domestically owned or predominately domestically managed companies
Size, production orientation	• Large factories (500–5,000 employees), large volume of production	• Mid-size (10–499 employees)
Year established and history	• Many established to take advantage of trade agreements or preferential labor costs	• Varied historical backgrounds—from family companies before exporting to recently established
Buyers and markets	• Export oriented • Buyers: EU and US brands	• Local and regional markets • Subcontractors to globally oriented firms
Geographic locations	• Development zones	• Development zones • Countrywide
Share of activity in country	• Generally account for small share (by number) of total firms • Likely account for >90%, if not more, of country's total apparel exports • Often 1–3 firms account for a sizable share of total apparel exports	• Account for small share of country's direct exports • Share of country's total apparel industry's firms and employment depends on whether data can be separated from microenterprises
What is most important to these companies?	• Predictability and stability • Cost • Time to market or lead time • Importance to their buyers	• Knowledge-intensive skills and support • Marketing, retailing, branding • Business ownership • Design (creative and technical)

Source: Frederick 2021.
Note: Apparel microenterprises (such as tailors and small retailers) are excluded from the table descriptions because they are not a target group for exporting. EU = European Union; US = United States.

our country cases: for example, female apparel workers in export-oriented parts of the country are more educated and earn higher wages than in other areas, with only a few exceptions.[2]

In addition, apparel microenterprises (such as tailors, dry cleaners, and small retailers) operate in the local market and are typically service oriented. But they are not a target group for exporting or for scaling up operations even though they are part of the apparel industry ecosystem.

The Multifiber Arrangement, Export Dependence, and Women

Another way to view the dynamics of GVCs is through a historical lens. The 1974 Multifiber Arrangement (MFA) and its predecessors (1962–2004)[3]—which aimed to protect domestic industries in high-income countries—also provided an opportunity for many LMICs to enter global exporting through apparel. In fact, apparel was many countries' first export industry, accounting for a significant share of exports. The MFA also expanded employment opportunities for women in the historically male-dominated manufacturing sector.

IMPACT OF MFA PHASEOUT

During the MFA phaseout (2005–08), however, the importance of apparel to a country's export basket declined in many countries—going from a peak of about 9 percent of all countries' exports (industry global mean share) in 2002 to 4.5 percent in 2015 before leveling off (figure 4.2). The apparel industry is unique in exhibiting a clear rise and fall in countries' dependence on the industry for exports, and this pattern aligns with the creation and phaseout of the MFA. The global apparel trade increased from 2000 to 2008, declined during the 2008–09 Global Financial Crisis, recovered by 2010, and has since leveled off. The end of the MFA and the economic crisis led to a consolidation of apparel exporting countries (Frederick and Staritz 2012).

This issue of apparel export dependence is worth further investigation because it offers a window into possible current outcomes for the female labor force. To estimate dependence, we began by determining the threshold of apparel's importance to a country's export portfolio between 1975 and 2015. We first calculated the apparel industry's global mean share of exports by determining apparel's share of each country's total exports in each year and averaging all countries' apparel share of exports between 1975 and 2015. Apparel's global mean share was 5.8 percent. We also calculated the apparel industry's share of total world exports over the same time, which was 2.9 percent.

FIGURE 4.2 **Apparel's Share of Global Exports, 1975–2015**

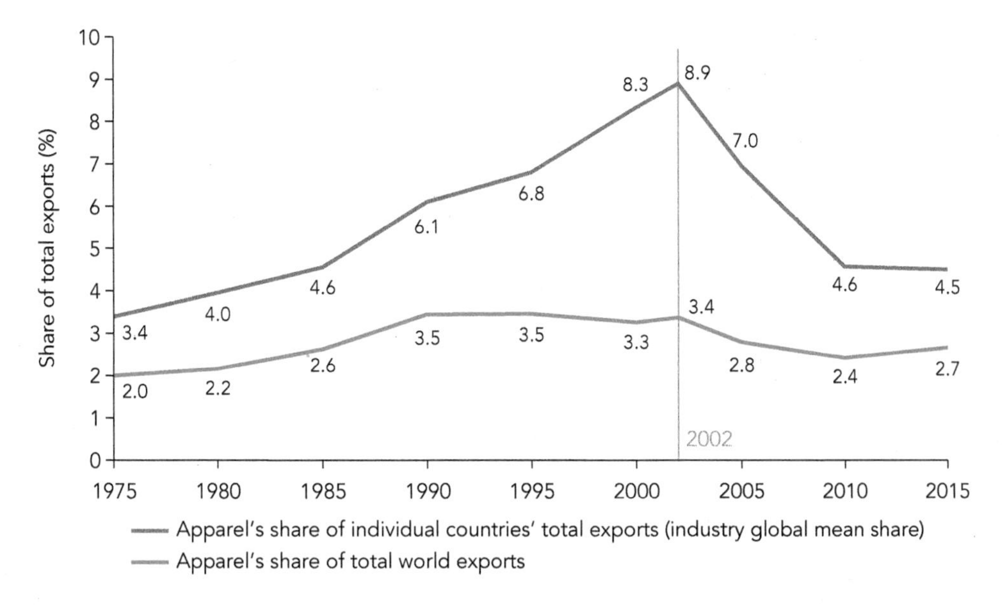

Source: United Nations Comtrade database, representing Standard Industrial Trade Classification 1-digit (SITC1), code 84 (articles of apparel and clothing accessories).
Note: Exports are represented by world imports of apparel (as designated under SITC1, code 84). All 182 countries in the UN Comtrade database are included. The "industry global mean share" is apparel's share of each country's total exports in each year, averaged for all countries.

DEVELOPMENT OF APPAREL EXPORTS, BY COUNTRY AND DECADE

Next, we divided countries worldwide based on the peak year for apparel's share of each country's exports, by decade: 1970s, 1980s, 1990s, 2000s, and 2010s (table 4.2). By this classification, the countries fell into five groups:

- Apparel was the primary entry point for exporting and represented, at its peak, more than 30 percent of the country's exports.
- Apparel exports occurred alongside other exports, with apparel's export share peaking at 15–30 percent of exports.
- Apparel exports occurred, but they peaked at a range of 6–14 percent of the country's exports.
- Apparel never became a significant part of the country's export portfolio (even if the country was a top global exporter), accounting for less than 2.9 percent of the country's exports and peaking at less than 6 percent.
- Apparel exports were never important (and the country was never a top global exporter), with apparel exports accounting for less than 2.9 percent of the country's average exports.

TABLE 4.2 Classification of Apparel Exporting Economies, by Decade and Share of Peak Apparel Exports

Decade of peak apparel export share	Apparel export shares averaging above 5.8%, 1975–2015		Apparel export shares averaging 2.9–5.8%, 1975–2015	Top global apparel exporters but below world average (2.9%)
	Peak share >30%	Peak share 15–30%	Peak share 6–14%	Peak share <6%
Late 1960s–1970s[a]	Timor-Leste (89%); **Hong Kong SAR, China (41%)**	**Korea, Rep. (25%); Taiwan, China (18%);** Uruguay (16%)	Israel (7%)	**Austria** (4%), **Belgium** (3%), **Japan** (3%), **France** (3%), **United Kingdom** (2%), **Netherlands** (1%)
1980s[b]	St. Kitts and Nevis (35%)	Cyprus (27%), Belize (18%)	Thailand (10%), **Italy (9%),** Panama (9%)	n.a.
1990s[c]	Tunisia (47%), Jamaica (33%), **Turkey (33%)**	Greece (26%), Portugal (24%), Costa Rica (23%), Croatia (20%), Philippines (18%), Lithuania (18%), China (16%), India (16%)	Lebanon (14%), Poland (13%), Estonia (13%), Hungary (12%), Serbia (11%), **Indonesia (8%),** Colombia (6%), Czech Republic (6%), Slovak Republic (6%)	**Mexico** (6%), **Germany** (2%), **United States** (1%)
2000s[d]	Lesotho (98%), **Cambodia (84%)**, Macao SAR, China (82%), Maldives (75%), Honduras (63%), Mauritius (61%), El Salvador (58%), Madagascar (52%), Dominican Republic (51%), Nicaragua (43%), Fiji (43%), Lao PDR (42%), Nepal (37%), Jordan (36%), Albania (34%), Morocco (33%), North Macedonia (32%), Guatemala (31%)	Romania (28%), Eswatini (25%), Bulgaria (21%), Vietnam (19%), Moldova (16%)	Egypt, Arab Rep. (13%), Kenya (11%), Peru (9%)	n.a.
2010s[d,e]	**Bangladesh (88%),** Haiti (88%), Sri Lanka (55%), Myanmar (40%), Pakistan (39%)	n.a.	Armenia (14%), Syrian Arab Republic (7%)	n.a.

(Table continues next page)

TABLE 4.2 **Classification of Apparel Exporting Economies, by Decade and Share of Peak Apparel Exports** *(continued)*

Decade of peak apparel export share	Apparel export shares averaging above 5.8%, 1975–2015		Apparel export shares averaging 2.9–5.8%, 1975–2015	Top global apparel exporters but below world average (2.9%)
	Peak share >30%	Peak share 15–30%	Peak share 6–14%	Peak share <6%
Non-apparel exporters (below world average and never top global exporters)	***Africa:*** Algeria; Angola; Benin; Burkina Faso; Burundi; Cameroon; Chad; Congo, Dem. Rep.; Côte d'Ivoire; Equatorial Guinea; Ethiopia; Gabon; Gambia, The; Ghana; Guinea; Liberia; Libya; Malawi; Mali; Mozambique; Namibia; Niger; Nigeria; Rwanda; Senegal; Sierra Leone; Somalia; South Africa; Suriname; Tanzania; Togo; Uganda; Zambia; Zimbabwe ***Americas:*** Argentina; Aruba; Bahamas, The; Brazil; Canada; Cayman Islands; Chile; Cuba; Ecuador; Martinique (territorial collectivity of France); Paraguay; Trinidad and Tobago; Venezuela, RB ***Asia:*** Afghanistan, Azerbaijan, Georgia, Kazakhstan, Malaysia, Papua New Guinea, Russian Federation, Singapore, Uzbekistan ***Europe:*** Belarus, Denmark, Finland, Iceland, Ireland, Latvia, Luxembourg, Norway, Slovenia, Spain, Sweden, Switzerland, Ukraine ***Middle East:*** Bahrain; Iran, Islamic Rep.; Iraq; Kuwait; Oman; Qatar; Saudi Arabia; United Arab Emirates; Yemen, Rep. ***Oceania:*** Australia, New Zealand			

Sources: Frederick 2021; United Nations Comtrade database, representing Standard Industrial Trade Classification (SITC) 1-digit code 84 (articles of apparel and clothing accessories).

Note: Apparel exporting economies are listed in order of highest to lowest percentage of export share within a table cell. **Bolded text** indicates an economy that was a top 10 global apparel exporting economy at some point. Top 10 exporters are based on individual economies (EU countries are not grouped). Orange shading designates economies whose apparel exports peaked before 1970; green shading, those that peaked between 1990 and the present; and red shading, non-apparel exporters. EU = European Union; n.a. = not applicable (no country in this category).

a. Among the economies whose apparel exports peaked between 1960 and 1980, the peak years are as follows (earliest to latest): Japan (1965); Austria (1966); Belgium (1966); Israel (1971); Korea, Rep. (1971); the Netherlands (1971); Taiwan, China (1971); France (1972); Hong Kong SAR, China (1975); United Kingdom (1978); Uruguay (1978); Timor-Leste (1979).

b. Among the economies whose apparel exports peaked between 1980 and 1990, the peak years are as follows (earliest to latest): Panama (1982); St. Kitts and Nevis (1984); Belize (1985); Cyprus (1987); Italy (1987); Thailand (1987).

c. Among the economies whose apparel exports peaked between 1990 and 1999, the peak years are as follows (earliest to latest): the Philippines (1990); Lebanon (1991); Portugal (1991); Germany (1992); India (1992); Indonesia (1992, 1998); China (1993); Colombia (1993); Costa Rica (1993); the Czech Republic (1993); Greece (1993); Hungary (1993); Poland (1993); the Slovak Republic (1993); Tunisia (1993); Turkey (1993); Croatia (1994); Estonia (1994 [first data year 1992]); Jamaica (1995); Egypt, Arab Rep. (1998); Morocco (1998); Serbia and Montenegro (1998 [now Serbia]); United States (1998); Lithuania (1999 [first data year 1992]); Mexico (1999); Dominican Republic (1999).

d. Among the economies whose apparel exports peaked in 2000 or after, the peak years are as follows (earliest to-latest): Fiji (2000); Maldives (2000); Mauritius (2000); Myanmar (2000); Nepal (2000); Sri Lanka (2000); Albania (2001); Bulgaria (2001); Honduras (2001); North Macedonia (2001); Romania (2001); El Salvador (2002); Nicaragua (2002); Cambodia (2003); Eswatini (2003); Lao PDR (2003); Lesotho (2003); Peru (2003); Vietnam (2003); Kenya (2004); Macao SAR, China (2005); Jordan (2006); Moldova (2006); Madagascar (2007); Haiti (2016); Syrian Arab Republic (2016); Pakistan (2017); Armenia (2018); Bangladesh (2018).

e. In the 2010s, apparel export shares were still on the rise, flat, or oscillating. Economies that are "flat" or oscillating reached peak export share and have generally continued to maintain that share or have fluctuated with multiple peaks.

In the late 1960s, top apparel exporters included the European Union countries; Hong Kong SAR, China; Japan; and the United States—but except in Hong Kong SAR, China, apparel never accounted for a significant share of any economy's exports. In the 1970s, Korea and Taiwan, China, reached peak apparel export shares and were among the top global exporters through the 1980s and early 1990s. Top apparel exporters from the 1960s and 1970s are now the lead firm economies and key first-tier suppliers in the apparel GVC.

The countries where apparel exports peaked in the 1990s and the 2000s—and some that are still on the rise—began exporting apparel during the MFA years (1974–2005) and are of particular interest. For the economies in the first column of table 4.2 (split into two sub-columns), apparel accounted for at least 5.8 percent of exports over the 40-year time frame (1975–2015). For the economies in the second column, apparel accounted for 2.9–5.8 percent of exports during that period.

What stands out in our results is apparel's high share of exports at its peak in each economy. Most economies that peaked in the 1990s and earlier had peak apparel export shares below 30 percent. Those peaking in the 2000s were far more dependent on apparel exports, with apparel in several economies representing over 50 percent of exports at some point. South Asian apparel exporters are unique in that all are generally dependent on apparel exports, and apparel's share of total exports is either still increasing (as in Bangladesh and Pakistan) or remains flat (as in Sri Lanka). But in Cambodia and Vietnam, the apparel share of exports has peaked and is declining.

Can Apparel Exports Increase Jobs and Female Labor Force Participation?

A 2020 report, *Women and Trade: The Role of Trade in Promoting Gender Equality*, identifies several ways that trade can improve female labor market outcomes (World Bank and WTO 2020). Given that the apparel industry is both female intensive and labor intensive, one might assume there is a correlation between apparel exports and rising demand for female labor. A simple time-series comparison of female labor force participation (FLFP) rates and apparel export shares confirms this for select countries, such as Bangladesh and Pakistan, from the 1990s through 2017.

STATISTICAL ANALYSIS

Plotting FLFP and apparel share of exports suggests a positive correlation between apparel exports and FLFP (figure 4.3). To test this hypothesis, we did a robust statistical analysis.[4] Results show that the t-stat reaches its maximum when the breakpoint dummy is at a 93 percent share of exports. However, the apparel-share-of-exports coefficient becomes positive and is relevant (1 percent statistical significance) when countries reach 82 percent of exports, and the positive effect continues until a 98 percent share of exports (figure 4.4). In other words, apparel exporting has a positive and

FIGURE 4.3 **Correlation between FLFP Rates and Apparel Export Shares**

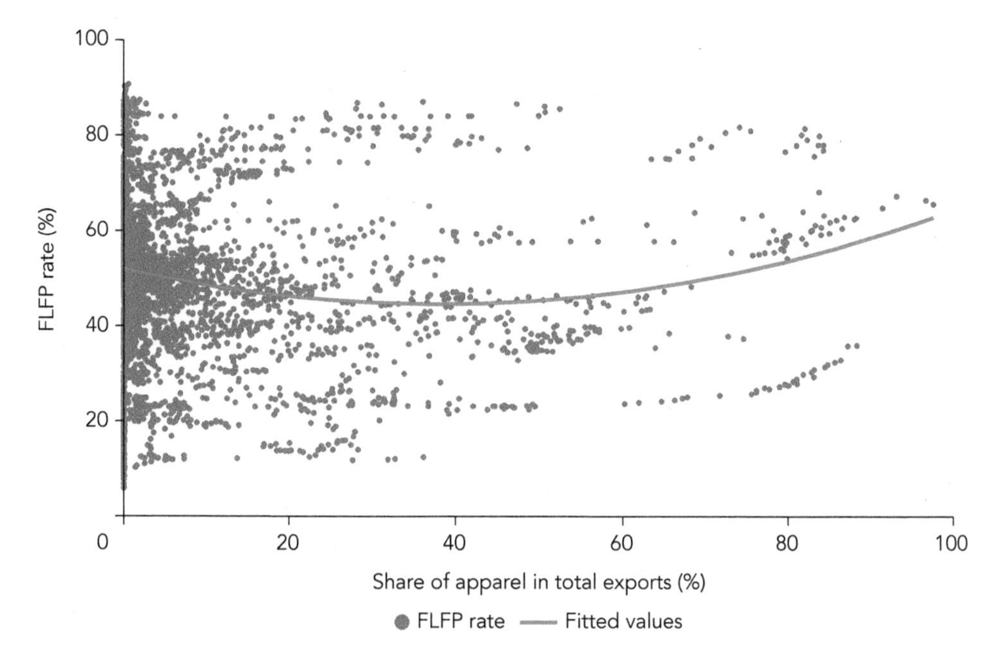

Sources: United Nations Comtrade database and International Labour Organization estimations of female labor force participation (FLFP) rates.
Note: The sample includes all 182 countries in the UN Comtrade database. The time-series comparison of FLFP rates and apparel export shares uses data from the 1990s through 2017.

statistically significant effect on FLFP only in countries whose exports are heavily concentrated in apparel. Only five countries have had an apparel share above 81 percent for at least two years: Bangladesh, Cambodia, Haiti, Lesotho, and Timor-Leste.

Such a high apparel share of exports is problematic because the country depends on a single industry's performance, making it vulnerable to external negative demand shocks. Further, when analyzing country cases, we find no consistent pattern of FLFP in apparel exporting countries below the 82 percent threshold and when comparing apparel exporting to nonexporting countries: most countries had similar FLFP rates in the beginning of the MFA phaseout and 10 years after (1995 and 2015).

FLFP RATES AND TRENDS, BY ECONOMY

Table 4.3 provides FLFP rates for select apparel exporting economies, with some nonapparel exporters included for reference. Economies in the green-shaded columns are positive examples where the economies either increased their FLFP rates to exceed the 2015 world average or maintained FLFP rates at or above the world average. Economies in the yellow-shaded columns have room for improvement, since their FLFP rates increased or stayed the same but nonetheless either (a) remained below or close to the

FIGURE 4.4 **Regression Analysis of Apparel Export Shares and FLFP Rates**

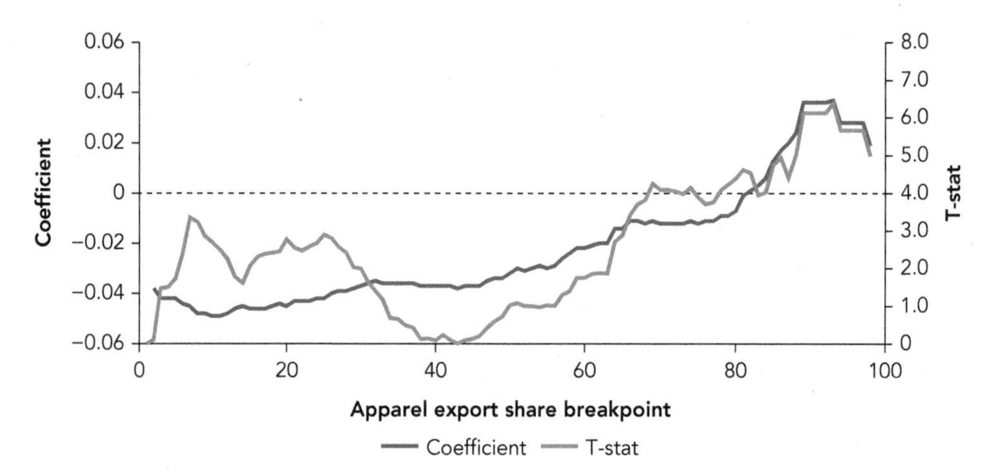

Sources: Regressions using United Nations Comtrade database and International Labour Organization estimations of female labor force participation (FLFP) rates.
Note: To show the effect of apparel exports on FLFP, 100 regressions were performed, using data from the 1990s through 2017, from all 182 countries in the UN Comtrade database, including fixed effects and robust standard errors. The FLFP rate was regressed against log GDP, a dummy variable that identifies countries with GDP above the mean, apparel exports share, and a dummy variable that interacts the apparel share of exports with a number between 1 and 100. This latter variable serves as a breakpoint to establish the cutoff of higher statistical significance for the correlation.

world average, or (b) decreased but still exceeded the world average in 2015. Economies in the red-shaded columns have negative trends whereby FLFP rates declined and are below the world average. For reference, the world average FLFP fell from 51 percent in 1995 to 48 percent in 2015.

The apparel exporting economies with the most positive FLFP outcomes are in

- *East and Southeast Asia:* Cambodia; China; Macao SAR, China; Indonesia; the Lao People's Democratic Republic; Myanmar; the Philippines; Thailand; and Vietnam;
- *Latin America and the Caribbean:* Belize, Costa Rica, the Dominican Republic, El Salvador, Guatemala, Haiti, Honduras, Jamaica, Nicaragua, and Panama; and
- *Sub-Saharan Africa:* Lesotho and Madagascar.

Yet FLFP has also greatly increased in recent decades in some non-apparel exporting countries such as Chile, Qatar, and Saudi Arabia.

The apparel exporters that show average or improving FLFP rates but still have rates well below the world average are Bangladesh, Pakistan, and Sri Lanka. Maldives and Nepal exhibit big increases in FLFP, but neither country is a significant apparel exporter, and their apparel export share values peaked in 2000. In Albania, India, and Romania, on the other hand, the FLFP rate declined well below the world average, even though those countries are MFA apparel exporters. Turkey and countries in the Middle East and North Africa (such as Egypt, Jordan, Lebanon, Morocco, and Tunisia) are also underperformers—with similar FLFP rates below the world averages in both 1995 and 2015.

TABLE 4.3 **FLFP Rates and Trends for Apparel Exporting and Nonexporting Economies, 1995–2015**

	FLFP rates increase		FLFP rates stay flat or oscillate			FLFP rates decrease	
Country group	**< World average**	**≥ World average**	**≥ World average**	**Near world average (48–51%)**	**< World average**	**≥ World average**	**< World average**
Apparel exporters under the MFA (1990–2000s)	**Bangladesh (26–32%),** Eswatini (43–47%), Greece (37–45%), Hungary (41–47%), Italy (34–40%), Maldives (28–45%), Mauritius (39–46%), **Pakistan (13–24%)**	Belize (36–48%); Costa Rica (36–48%); Dominican Republic (38–50%); Haiti (58–61%); Macao SAR, China (48–67%); Nicaragua (34–49%); Portugal (49–54%)	**Cambodia (77–74%),** Nepal (82–82%), Lao PDR (80–77%), Madagascar (84–84%), **Vietnam (72–73%)**	Bulgaria (51–49%), El Salvador (43–45%), Fiji (40–40%), Guatemala (40–39%), Honduras (46–48%), Indonesia (49–51%), Philippines (48–49%)	**Egypt, Arab Rep. (21–22%);** Jordan (12–14%); Lebanon (21–23%); Morocco (23–23%); **Sri Lanka (36–36%);** Tunisia (23–25%); **Turkey (31%–31%)**	China (73–63%), Jamaica (65–57%), Lesotho (68–60%), Myanmar (61–52%), Thailand (66–61%)	Albania (54–46%), India (31–22%), Romania (62–45%)
Non-apparel exporters (reference countries)	Afghanistan (15–19%), Iraq (8–14%), Saudi Arabia (15–22%)	Brazil (47–53%), Chile (36–50%), Colombia (53–58%), Ecuador (49–52%), Panama (43–51%), Paraguay (53–56%), Qatar (46–59%)	Bahamas, The (68–68%)	Argentina (48–48%); Russian Federation (54–55%); Venezuela, RB (47–49%)	Algeria (12–15%), Senegal (33–35%)	n.a.	n.a.

Source: International Labour Organization (ILO), "Labour force participation rate by sex and age" (1990–2030) data.
Note: ILO modeled estimates are of female labor force participation (FLFP) rates, 15 years of age and older, in 1995 and 2015. **Bolded text** indicates the seven case countries. Green-shaded columns show economies that either maintained FLFP rates at or above the world average or increased their FLFP rates to exceed the 2015 world average. Yellow-shaded columns show economies that either (a) maintained or increased their FLFP rates but remained below or near the world average, or (b) decreased FLFP rates but still exceeded the world average in 2015. Red-shaded columns show economies whose FLFP rates declined and are below the world average. The world average FLFP rate fell from 51 percent in 1995 to 48 percent in 2015. MFA = Multifiber Arrangement; n.a. = not applicable (no country in this category).

Among our selected case countries, only Cambodia and Vietnam have FLFP rates above the world average. In Egypt, Sri Lanka, and Turkey, low FLFP persisted across time and below the world average. Only in Bangladesh and Pakistan did FLFP increase while also remaining well below the world average.

Clearly, increasing the FLFP rate is a multidimensional challenge. Although an apparel industry creates jobs for women, the FLFP rate does not depend on the industry unless the country's export basket heavily relies on apparel.

Further, export-oriented apparel factories cluster in a few geographic areas across our sample middle-income countries: In Bangladesh, 70 percent of apparel workers are in Dhaka; in Cambodia, 43 percent are in Phnom Penh and Kandal; in Egypt, 41 percent are in Cairo, Giza, and Alexandria combined; in Pakistan, 58 percent are in Punjab State; in Sri Lanka, 44 percent are in Western Province; in Turkey, 58 percent are in Istanbul; and in Vietnam, 64 percent are in the Ho Chi Minh City and Hanoi regions.

The apparel industry is more geographically concentrated than the overall workforce in these countries, and apparel employment also concentrates in different geographic areas than agricultural employment, which is the largest employer of women across countries (map 4.1). Hence, if countries have low worker mobility (because of low human capital or high transportation costs, for example), it is difficult for the apparel-driven benefits to spill over outside highly apparel-concentrated regions.

MAP 4.1 Employment Concentration in the Agriculture and Apparel Sectors of Bangladesh, Cambodia, and Vietnam, 2013

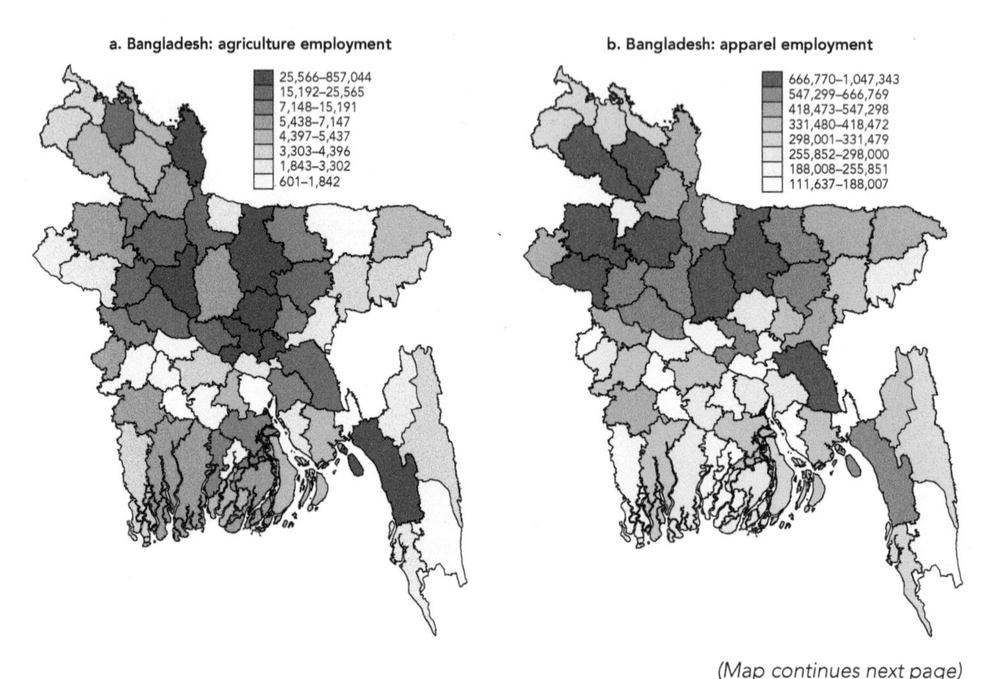

(Map continues next page)

MAP 4.1 **Employment Concentration in the Agriculture and Apparel Sectors of Bangladesh, Cambodia, and Vietnam, 2013** *(continued)*

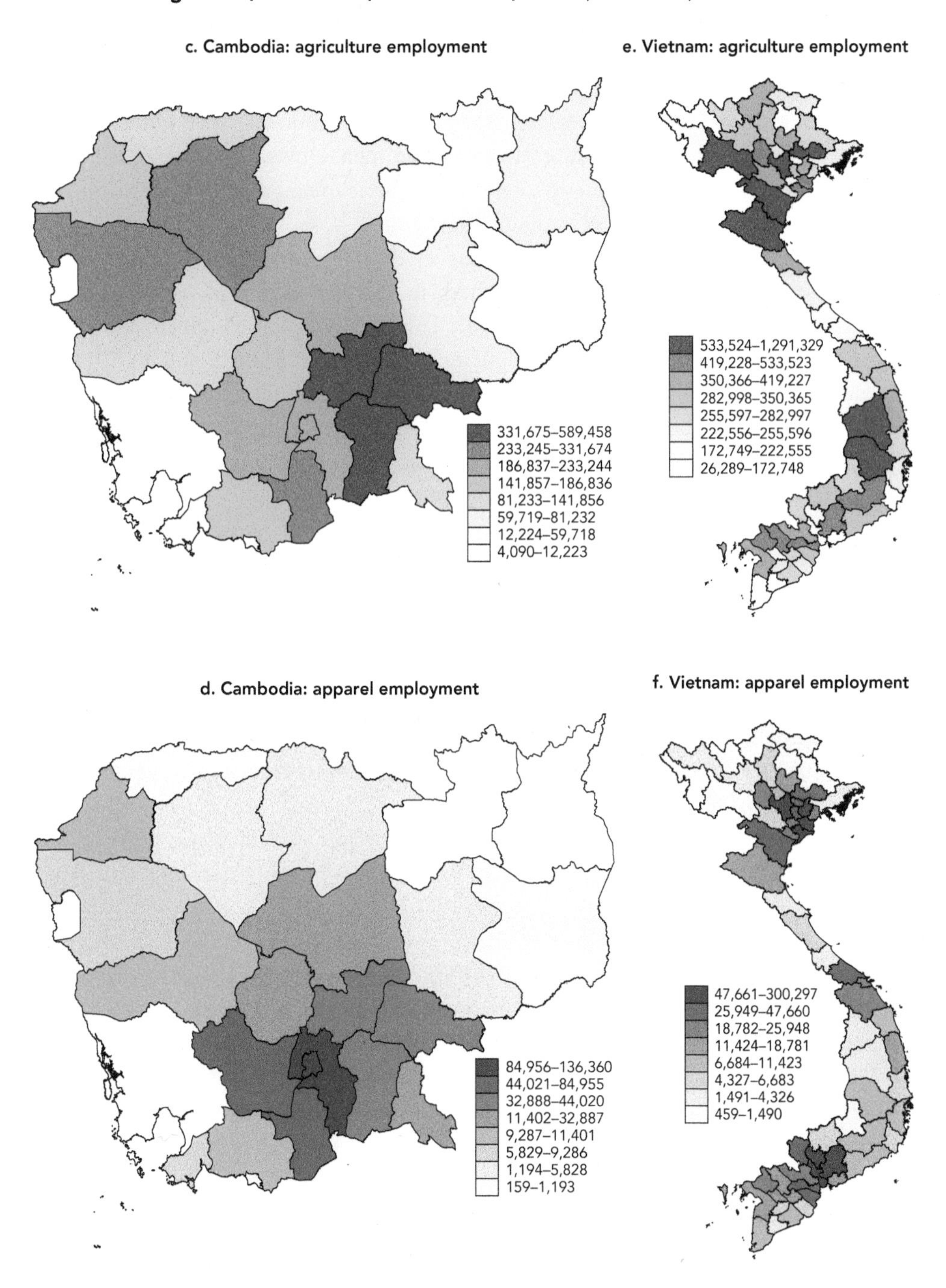

Source: Labor force survey data. © World Bank.

OVERALL FINDINGS

In other words, although apparel exporting creates jobs for women, the jobs generated are not usually enough to increase national FLFP rates unless the sector is unusually large, because manufacturing overall accounts for the smallest global labor force share compared with agriculture and services. Apparel is a labor-intensive manufacturing industry that globally employs more women than men. However, although the global apparel industry employed approximately 16.4 million females in 2017, crop and animal production alone employed 124.8 million females.[5]

A subnational analysis of labor force survey data supports these findings. Across country cases, the FLFP rates are highest in the agriculture-focused regions of Bangladesh, Cambodia, Egypt, Pakistan, Sri Lanka, Turkey, and Vietnam. As such, a positive, significant correlation between industry-specific exports and FLFP would occur only if a country heavily depends on one female-intensive industry, such as in Bangladesh and Cambodia. Thus, apparel must exceed a very high 81 percent of a country's total exports to translate into a larger share of women participating in the national labor market.

The Apparel Workforce: Opportunities for Upward Mobility?

Characteristics of the global apparel industry present challenges that are beyond the control of the apparel exporting countries. One challenge is that career progression in terms of technical requirements for apparel production workers is very limited; workers can move from being operators to filling a limited number of supervisor or quality-control positions with minimal wage increases. Another challenge is that about 85 percent of apparel factory workers globally earn the national minimum wage regardless of experience.

Few advancement opportunities. There are two types of workers in the apparel industry: (a) production workers, and (b) knowledge-intensive, service occupations (table 4.4). Over 75 percent of workers are involved in production. Minor advancements on the factory floor provide relatively small wage returns. For example, an operator who can use multiple types of sewing machines is more valuable because she can fill in when others are absent in certain production lines. But these advancements are limited by the firm's business model; many apparel factories produce only basic garments that require limited operations and provide little skill development.

At the low end, production workers and elementary occupations account for most of the apparel occupations across countries, ranging from 84 percent in Egypt to 98 percent in Cambodia. At the high end, those in career occupations—managers, professionals, and technicians—are more educated and better paid than craft and plant operators, but they account for less than 13 percent of the apparel workforce. Few skilled positions

TABLE 4.4 Employee and Wage Profile of the Apparel Value Chain, Global Estimates, 2017–19

Stage	Position	Share of workforce (%)	Education	Tasks or skills	Wages
Production	Sewing machine operators (55%)	75	Primary education; on-the-job training	Sewing machine operation	Low
	Other assembly-related (15%)		Primary or technical	Cutters, packers, spreaders, helpers	Low-Medium
	Supervisors and inspectors (5%)		Secondary education; technical	Communication skills	Medium
Services[a]	Sourcing and logistics (backward links)	15	Tertiary; university degree in business	Purchasing, organizational, computer, communication	Medium
	Sales, merchandising (forward links)		Tertiary; university degree in business	Customer service, order taking, finding buyers	Medium-High
	Design		Tertiary; university or apparel-specific degree	Creativity, computer-aided design (CAD)	Medium-High
	Administrative	10	Upper secondary or tertiary; university degree in business	Sales, finance, customer service	Medium
	Top management (general manager, factory manager, department managers, quality manager)		Tertiary; university degree in business, industrial engineering	Business, interpersonal, communication	High

Wage Levels	Low	Low-Medium	Medium	Medium-High	High
	Hourly; Minimum wage or piece rate	Hourly	Hourly or salary; approximately twice wages of an operator	Salary	Highest-paid employees; salary

Source: Frederick 2017, 2019a.

a. Services account for approximately 10–30 percent of the workforce depending on the firm's business model. The sector accounts for a larger share of the workforce in companies that sell their own brands, because workers are needed for brand development, market research, retailing, and creative design.

are needed in a typical factory, and those workers require higher education in different subject areas. These positions are filled by university graduates with degrees in business or engineering or by upper-secondary graduates who also have either practical experience or postsecondary training.

Across countries, the apparel industry's requirements range from primary to lower-secondary education, with less than 8 percent of workers having a university degree. For production workers and elementary occupations, even a few years of secondary education may have an adverse impact on employment prospects because of actual and perceived factors in some countries. Rahman and Islam (2013) provide insight from employers in Bangladesh, who imply that the ideal worker is younger than 35 and has only primary education, because more-educated workers have higher salary expectations and a greater awareness of labor rights. Furthermore, workers with education beyond lower-secondary may find apparel manufacturing unappealing because of the low wages and the routine nature of the work.

Persistently low wages. As for wages—the most primary cost component—our country cases provide results similar to prior studies on textile and apparel wages. Wages are better than for the alternatives in agriculture and have increased over time (Keane and Willem te Velde 2008; Nattrass and Seekings 2018). Yet they are often lower than in other manufacturing industries (Keane and Willem te Velde 2008), and a higher share of manufacturing employment in textiles and apparel is associated with lower average manufacturing wages (Gimet, Guilhon, and Roux 2015).

In all countries except Egypt, average monthly apparel wages are below the country's average for the manufacturing sector. (For more information, see appendix A, tables A.5 and A.6.) In Pakistan, Turkey, and Vietnam, average monthly apparel wages are also below the minimum wage. The benefits of female participation in GVCs come from the greater number of jobs available rather than from an opportunity to work in higher-paying jobs (Hollweg 2019).

Disparities in functional upgrading and social norms. Yet another factor that affects female labor market outcomes and occupational upgrading in the export-oriented apparel industry is firm ownership and strategy. Cambodia, Sri Lanka, and Vietnam—countries with low social barriers to female employment—started in apparel production largely because of foreign investment or joint ventures. On the positive end, Sri Lanka and Vietnam have engaged in more upgrading, which has required investing more in human capital and retaining skilled workers. This is evidenced by the increasing average age of workers, larger shares of married female workers, and an increasing share of workers with secondary education.

In contrast, in the Cambodian apparel industry—propelled almost entirely by Asian foreign investors—apparel factory owners based in other countries control the decision to minimize upgrading and keep wages low as part of their overall internationalization strategy. Apparel career occupations are in the parent company countries or are held by expats in Cambodia.

In Bangladesh, Egypt, and Turkey, domestic firms are responsible for the decision to keep wages and education low to remain cost-competitive and to maintain a more male-dominated labor force. The countries with the lowest female shares of apparel employment and the lowest FLFP rates all have predominantly domestic firms, and social norms and laws in these countries also limit gender workplace equality. Domestic-owned firms are more likely to embody the cultural and social norms and values of the country.

Relatedly, foreign-owned firms often invest in countries with similar sociocultural backgrounds. When they do engage in business with countries with different social norms, they are subject to national laws but not beholden to local norms. As such, doing business with countries with fewer barriers to gender equality may help overcome barriers from social norms.

Conclusion

An apparel export-led industrialization path benefits workers in the short term, but without expanding other industries and further investing in education or skill development, apparel exports are not sufficient to induce the transition from jobs to careers for women. Apparel exporting is typically a key portion of a country's export basket for only a limited number of years before the country can no longer remain globally cost-competitive.

Countries reap the most benefits by engaging with an eye toward workforce investment and using apparel manufacturing as a springboard to other sectors. Countries that stay in apparel without upgrading can continue to remain competitive at the low end, but this does not advance a country along the jobs-to-careers trajectory. It is important for countries to be aware of these alternative paths and to develop a longer-term strategy to achieve professional development; otherwise, if they lose competitive advantage, they may become stuck in the "middle-income trap."

For country policy makers, the most important points are to use the opportunities the apparel industry offers while remaining aware of the industry's limits to advancement and the transitory nature of its GVC participation. Countries can use apparel to raise their human capital—hence better enabling movement to other industries—and to increase wages to promote domestic services. They can choose to keep wages low to remain a competitive global supplier, or they can invest, promote, and enable educational expansion and industrial diversification. Finally, these strategies do not have to be mutually exclusive, because different strategies can be promoted in different geographical regions.

Notes

1. Kucera and Tejani (2014) analyze changes in female shares of manufacturing employment over nearly three decades (1981–2008) across 36 countries. They break manufacturing into three industry groups based on labor intensity.
2. In Cambodia, females' wages are not the highest in the country's exporting center Phnom Penh; and in Turkey, females are not the most educated in its exporting hub of Istanbul.
3. The quota system started with the Long-Term Arrangement Regarding International Trade in Cotton Textiles and Substitutes (LTA) under the auspices of the General Agreement on Tariffs and Trade (GATT) in 1962. The LTA was extended to materials other than cotton in 1974 and became known as the MFA.
4. We ran 100 regressions of the FLFP rate against log GDP, a dummy variable that identifies countries with gross domestic product (GDP) above the mean, apparel exports share, and a dummy variable that interacts the apparel share of exports with a number between 1 and 100. The latter variable serves as a breakpoint to establish the cutoff of higher statistical significance for the correlation. The regressions used data from 182 countries, including fixed effects and robust standard errors.
5. International Labour Organization (ILO), "Employment by sex and economic activity, ISIC Level 2 (1992–2020)" data, https://www.ilo.org/shinyapps/bulkexplorer40/?lang=en&segment=indicator&id=EMP_TEMP_SEX_EC2_NB_A.

References

Cammett, M. 2006. "Development and the Changing Dynamics of Global Production: Global Value Chains and Local Clusters in Apparel Manufacturing." *Competition & Change* 10 (1): 23–48.

Christian, M., B. Evers, and S. Barrientos. 2013. "Women in Value Chains: Making a Difference." Revised Summit Briefing No. 6.3, Capturing the Gains, Manchester, UK. https://www.gov.uk/research-for-development-outputs/women-in-value-chains-making-a-difference.

Duboc, M. 2013. "Where Are the Men? Here Are the Men and the Women! Surveillance, Gender, and Strikes in Egyptian Textile Factories." *Journal of Middle East Women's Studies* 9 (3): 28–53.

Elson, D., and R. Pearson. 1981. "'Nimble Fingers Make Cheap Workers': An Analysis of Women's Employment in Third World Export Manufacturing." *Feminist Review* 7 (1): 87–107.

Engel, J., and D. Taglioni. 2017. "The Middle-Income Trap and Upgrading along Global Value Chains." In *Global Value Chain Development Report 2017: Measuring and Analyzing the Impact of GVCs on Economic Development*, 119–39. Washington, DC: World Bank.

English, B. 2013. "Global Women's Work: Historical Perspectives on the Textile and Garment Industries." *Journal of International Affairs* 67 (1): 67–82.

Farole, T. 2016. "Do Global Value Chains Create Jobs? Impacts of GVCs Depend on Lead Firms, Specialization, Skills, and Institutions." *IZA World of Labor* (291): 1–11.

Fernandez-Stark, K., S. Frederick, and G. Gereffi. 2011. "The Apparel Global Value Chain: Economic Upgrading and Workforce Development." Report, Duke Center on Globalization, Governance & Competitiveness (Duke CGGC), Durham, NC.

Frederick, S. 2010. "Development and Application of a Value Chain Research Approach to Understand and Evaluate Internal and External Factors and Relationships Affecting Economic Competitiveness in the Textile Value Chain." Dissertation, North Carolina State University, Raleigh, NC.

Frederick, S. 2015. "Case One: Pro-Poor Development and Power Asymmetries in the Apparel GVC." In *Pro-Poor Development and Power Asymmetries in Global Value Chains,* edited by A. Abdulsamad, S. Frederick, A. Guinn, and G. Gereffi, 7–22 and 75–79. Report prepared for Oxfam America by the Duke Center on Globalization, Governance & Competitiveness, Durham, NC.

Frederick, S. 2016. "Benchmarking South Asia in the Global Apparel Industry." In *Stitches to Riches? Apparel Employment, Trade, and Economic Development in South Asia,* edited by G. Lopez-Acevedo and R. Robertson, 39–76. Washington, DC: World Bank.

Frederick, S. 2017. "Apparel Skills Mapping and Functional Upgrading in Vietnam: Jobs Diagnostic." Unpublished manuscript, World Bank, Washington, DC.

Frederick, S. 2019a. "Apparel Skills Mapping and Functional Upgrading in Cambodia: Jobs Diagnostic." Unpublished manuscript, World Bank, Washington, DC.

Frederick, S. 2019b. "Global Value Chain Mapping." In *Handbook on Global Value Chains,* edited by S. Ponte, G. Gereffi, and G. Raj-Reichert, 29–53. Northampton, MA: Edward Elgar Publishing.

Frederick, S. 2021. "GVC Employment Characteristics." Unpublished report, Duke University Global Value Chains Center, Durham, NC.

Frederick, S., and P. Bamber. 2018. "Central America in Manufacturing Global Value Chains (GVCs)." Research report prepared for the Inter-American Development Bank by the Duke Global Value Chains Center, Durham, NC.

Frederick, S., and C. Staritz. 2012. "Developments in the Global Apparel Industry after the MFA Phaseout." In *Sewing Success? Employment, Wages, and Poverty Following the End of the Multi-Fibre Arrangement,* edited by G. Lopez-Acevedo and R. Robertson, 41–86. Washington, DC: World Bank.

Gereffi, G. 1994. "The Organization of Buyer-Driven Global Commodity Chains: How U.S. Retailers Shape Overseas Production Networks." In *Commodity Chains and Global Capitalism,* edited by G. Gereffi and M. Korzeniewicz, 95–122. Westport, CT: Praeger.

Gereffi, G., J. Humphrey, and T. Sturgeon. 2005. "The Governance of Global Value Chains." *Review of International Political Economy* 12 (1): 78–104.

Ghosh, J. 2002. "Globalization, Export-Oriented Employment for Women and Social Policy: A Case Study of India." *Social Scientist* 30 (11/12): 17–60.

Gimet, C., B. Guilhon, and N. Roux. 2015. "Social Upgrading in Globalized Production: The Case of the Textile and Clothing Industry." *International Labour Review* 154 (3): 303–27.

Hollweg, C. 2019. "Global Value Chains and Employment in Developing Economies." In *Global Value Chain Development Report 2019: Technological Innovation, Supply Chain Trade, and Workers in a Globalized World,* 63–81. Geneva: World Trade Organization.

Humphrey, J., and H. Schmitz. 2002. "How Does Insertion in Global Value Chains Affect Upgrading in Industrial Clusters?" *Regional Studies* 36 (9): 1017–27.

Keane, J., and D. Willem te Velde. 2008. "The Role of Textile and Clothing Industries in Growth and Development Strategies." Research report, Overseas Development Institute (ODI), London.

Kucera, D., and S. Tejani. 2014. "Feminization, Defeminization, and Structural Change in Manufacturing." *World Development* 64: 569–82.

Nattrass, N., and J. Seekings. 2018. "Trajectories of Development and the Global Clothing Industry." *Competition & Change* 22 (3): 274–92.

Palpacuer, F. 2008. "Bringing the Social Context Back In: Governance and Wealth Distribution in Global Commodity Chains." *Economy and Society* 37 (3): 393–419.

Rahman, R., and R. Islam. 2013. "Female Labour Force Participation in Bangladesh: Trends, Drivers and Barriers." Asia-Pacific Working Paper Series, International Labour Organization, Geneva.

Safa, H. 1994. "Export Manufacturing, State Policy, and Women Workers in the Dominican Republic." In *Global Production: The Apparel Industry in the Pacific Rim*, edited by E. Bonacich, L. Cheng, N. Chinchilla, N. Hamilton, and P. Ong, 247–67. Philadelphia: Temple University Press.

Tejani, S., and W. Milberg. 2016. "Global Defeminization? Industrial Upgrading and Manufacturing Employment in Developing Countries." *Feminist Economics* 22 (2): 24–54.

Tokatli, N., Ö. Kızılgün, and J. E. Cho. 2011. "The Clothing Industry in Istanbul in the Era of Globalisation and Fast Fashion." *Urban Studies* 48 (6): 1201–15.

Van der Ven, C. 2015. "Where Trade and Industrial Policy Converge: How Developing Countries Can Utilize Trade Preferences to Generate Sustainable, Local Growth in the Garment Sector." *The International Lawyer* 49 (1): 49–92.

Whitfield, L., C. Staritz, and M. Morris. 2020. "Global Value Chains, Industrial Policy and Economic Upgrading in Ethiopia's Apparel Sector." *Development and Change* 51 (4): 1018–43.

World Bank and WTO (World Trade Organization). 2020. *Women and Trade: The Role of Trade in Promoting Gender Equality*. Washington, DC: World Bank.

CHAPTER 5

How to Speed Up the Jobs-to-Careers Transition

Key Messages

- The export-oriented apparel industry can provide an indirect launching pad for women to transition from jobs to careers if countries adopt complementary policies to boost human capital.
- This report makes four policy recommendations to increase the probability that women will enter the labor market and to create an environment that supports female career development.
- Recommended industry policies: (a) increase participation of female production workers in export-oriented apparel manufacturing and related industries, and (b) increase the number of female supervisors and upgrade jobs within apparel to manufacturing-related services.
- Recommended cross-cutting policies to empower women: (a) increase access to education, especially at the upper-secondary level; and (b) break glass ceilings.

Introduction

A large and growing body of research shows that globalization—and the export-oriented apparel industry in particular—generally creates formal employment opportunities. This industry is one of the main manufacturing employers of women. It provides an important step into formal manufacturing work for those with primary to lower-secondary education, even if it is not the only way for low-skilled females to enter the formal workforce. And because the apparel industry is both female intensive and labor intensive, studies show that higher apparel exports go hand in hand with higher female labor force participation (FLFP).

But most, if not all, of this research focuses either explicitly or implicitly on "jobs" and only rarely hints at the importance of "careers." In contrast, our report seeks to shift the paradigm of how we think of women's participation in the labor force by demonstrating the importance of the distinction between jobs and careers. Notably, we associate the jobs-to-careers transition with a change of mindset within the household about how work is viewed. In other words, people who shift from jobs to careers adopt a long-run view of their labor market experience—one that is associated with more education, tenure, promotions, and identity.

APPAREL EXPORTS: LAUNCHING PAD OR BOUNDARY?

In the global value chain (GVC) literature, the concept of functional upgrading is closely related to the transition from jobs to careers—but the pathway is not automatic. Unlike in the United States a century ago, today's highest-value activities are carried out by global lead firms in higher-income countries. And even if some of those positions were hosted in the producing countries, the shift from production workers to high-skill occupations (HSOs) would require higher education and different skills than workers in our studied countries possess.

Moreover, certain high-skill service industries that are an important source of female employment in high-income countries do not exist in low- and middle-income countries (LMICs). Foreign demand for manufacturing or service industries can help drive this change. And an export-oriented path can contribute to rising education and income levels to create an economy that demands domestic (national) services. But our evidence suggests some countries have leveraged this opportunity better than others. The latter are those who have kept wages low to remain globally competitive by continuing to hire younger, less-educated workers—a strategy that will continue to create jobs but does little to further develop workers' skills or boost national income.

From a policy perspective, our central questions are these: How can females move from jobs to careers, and can apparel be a launching pad for greater female inclusion? This report finds answers by checking the progress of the jobs-to-careers transition in seven middle-income, apparel exporting countries: Bangladesh, Cambodia, the Arab Republic of Egypt, Pakistan, Sri Lanka, Turkey, and Vietnam (as discussed in chapter 2).

We find that although some are making significant progress, others continue to struggle, raising the possibility of barriers in the path.

We identify three main barriers (further discussed in chapter 3):

- Low demand for career-related occupations in the service sector due to insufficient national income (low gross domestic product [GDP] per capita)
- Low education levels
- Societal and cultural norms that inhibit or dissuade women from working.

Besides, apparel manufacturing has its own drawbacks. One is limited opportunities for career advancement, because it needs few HSOs. Another is that nearly all apparel workers are on the production line, executing tasks that require little training or education (see chapter 4).

Even so, a historical analysis of apparel exporting countries validates the temporary importance of apparel manufacturing to countries' export portfolios. An intuitive yet important takeaway from this report is that economic diversification beyond apparel will eventually be necessary to increase female and male engagement in careers. Women who start in the apparel industry are increasingly staying in it as long as they remain in the workforce; that is, their "jobs" become "careers" in terms of length of work but not necessarily in the sense of better wages, benefits, or long-term planning. Growth driven by export-oriented manufacturing industries and foreign demand is still necessary to increase per capita income and demand for higher-paid, high-skill careers across all countries. As such, apparel exporting countries should maximize the opportunities they have available through the apparel industry from jobs to careers and transfer the lessons learned as they continue to develop.

In the United States—where what Goldin (2006) calls the "quiet revolution" took over 100 years to complete—nineteenth-century manufacturing offered the opportunity for young, unmarried females with lower-secondary education to move to mill houses to work in apparel factories (Goldin 1984). Their experience, and the income provided by employment in the apparel factory, enabled their children to complete upper-secondary education and perhaps their grandchildren to attend college and plan a longer-horizon, better-paid work life. Thus, many of the benefits of apparel employment are intergenerational (box 5.1).

WHICH WAY FORWARD?

How can apparel exporting countries maximize women's opportunities to transition from jobs to careers, albeit indirectly? This chapter looks at what countries, development institutions, and other stakeholders can do to reenergize and speed up the "quiet revolution" in LMICs, depending on how far along they are in the transition. It makes four policy recommendations—all of which apply to our seven sample countries to varying degrees—with a focus on designing policies that target specific types of apparel workers (table 5.1).

BOX 5.1 Apparel: Investing in Women in the Years to Come

Gains from apparel industry employment benefit future generations of females. Compared with 48 percent of children of agricultural workers who focus solely on studying, 73 percent of children whose mothers are employed in the textile and apparel industry pursue education without simultaneously working (Kotikula, Pournik, and Robertson 2015). Moreover, only 9 percent of children of apparel workers do not pursue education, compared with 25 percent of children of agricultural workers.

The case countries' increasing FLFP rates among married women and their increasing shares of married women among apparel employees (chapter 2) suggest that family incomes have likely risen because of dual income households—a key driver of increased education. Higher family income, in turn, may reduce the need for young women to enter the workforce to support their families before marriage and instead encourage them to further their education—or, in other words, to pursue a career.

The intergenerational benefits of apparel jobs portray another reason to expand mid-skill manufacturing industries. Whereas a "job" is not a prerequisite for a "career," if females do not engage in mid-skill industries and occupations, there is not enough demand for every woman to have a career without raising the average income levels of the country's population (that is, gross domestic product [GDP] per capita). When female participation in mid-skill industries is quite limited, that may increase income inequalities within a country and create a greater divide or "missing middle" between low- and high-income households. However, when opportunities for women expand in mid-skill industries, current mothers might not be working in what we call a career, but their daughters will have an increased chance of pursuing a career path.

TABLE 5.1 Policy Recommendations to Increase FLFP and Women's Transition from Jobs to Careers in Seven Middle-Income Countries

Policy recommendation	Implementation considerations	Countries[a]
Increase participation of female production workers in export-oriented apparel manufacturing and related industries	Implement programs to attract and retain female workers in export-oriented manufacturing industries	Bangladesh; Egypt, Arab Rep.; Pakistan; Turkey
Increase the number of female supervisors, and upgrade jobs within apparel to manufacturing-related services	Implement internships and skill-specific training programs to upskill female production workers and include more women in mid-skill occupations	Sri Lanka, Turkey, Vietnam
	Focus programs on supplying graduates who are employable and aligned with industrial policy development	Egypt, Arab Rep.; Sri Lanka; Turkey

(Table continues next page)

TABLE 5.1 Policy Recommendations to Increase FLFP and Women's Transition from Jobs to Careers in Seven Middle-Income Countries *(continued)*

Policy recommendation	Implementation considerations	Countries[a]
Increase access to education to promote female participation in careers	Increase upper-secondary enrollment and entry points to the industry	Bangladesh, Cambodia, Pakistan
	Reduce information gaps on available career paths	All
Break glass ceilings	Reform legal barriers that reduce women's access to and permanence in employment opportunities	Bangladesh; Egypt, Arab Rep.; Pakistan; Sri Lanka
	Promote inclusive workplace practices	All
	Engage foreign support and involvement	All

Source: World Bank.
Note: FLFP = female labor force participation.
a. Policies can be addressed by all seven countries studied in this report; however, some are more relevant to specific countries based on our results.

The overall message is that these countries should use the apparel industry as a launching platform to overcome the fixed costs of introducing more women into the labor market. But for this strategy to work, they must implement complementary policies that tackle the barriers that hinder women in their pursuit of long-term labor force participation and better-paid occupations.

Increase Participation of Female Production Workers in Export-Oriented Apparel Manufacturing and Related Industries

Among manufacturing industries, apparel provides one of the few opportunities for females with lower-secondary education or less to enter the workforce. The women are hired to work on the production line (as sewing machine operators and other assembly-related positions), an occupation that covers 70–80 percent of all apparel workers. Their skills are considered low in industry, but evidence from Southeast Asia and some Latin American countries suggests that acquiring the baseline skills for assembly-line manufacturing helps workers to move from apparel to electronics, medical devices, and automotive production when the time to upgrade between industries arrives in the country (Bamber and Frederick 2018; Bamber et al. 2019).

What is worrisome is that even though apparel has long been a female-intensive industry, our report shows that in many LMICs, women are underrepresented, meaning that the female share of apparel employment is below the world average (48 percent in 2015). This applies to most of our case countries. In Bangladesh, Egypt, Pakistan, Sri Lanka, and Turkey, the female share of total apparel employment is equal to or below 50 percent. These countries still have room to expand apparel employment for female production workers.

IMPLEMENT PROGRAMS TO ATTRACT AND RETAIN MORE FEMALE WORKERS

To boost the share of women in export-oriented apparel and other female-intensive manufacturing industries (such as food or textile manufacturing), policy makers must step up efforts to attract and retain more female workers, as Jordan has done. Since 2010, the Jordanian government has supported the creation of satellite units to encourage employment of locals (ILO and IFC 2018a). The satellite factory program aims to increase Jordanian labor force participation in apparel by building factories and providing resources for training in rural areas. The objective is to provide training and employment opportunities for the unemployed—especially women in governorates with high rates of unemployment and poverty—and attract investments to remote areas and poor communities. Importantly, whereas men dominate supervisor positions in migrant-operated factories in qualified industrial zones, satellite factories are predominately supervised by women (ILO and IFC 2018b).

Steps can also be taken to ease mobility and safety concerns. For example, in Pakistan, the distance females must travel to work is a challenge for increasing female employment in apparel factories (Frederick and Daly 2019). In Egypt, women face mobility constraints, particularly in more conservative areas, stemming from norms about how far women can travel without a chaperone and fear of harassment (Kabeer 2013). One promising measure for reducing harassment is to reserve spaces for women on public transportation, as evidence in Mexico suggests (Aguilar, Gutiérrez, and Soto 2019). Another is providing alternative means of transportation (such as bicycles)—a policy intervention in India that increased girls' enrollment in secondary schools (Muralidharan and Prakash 2017).

Countries with comparatively high education levels, such as Egypt or Turkey, might face a different set of challenges to increasing the share of female manufacturing workers. One is that workers will probably be unwilling to accept the low wages offered to production workers in apparel and related industries. However, apparel can also provide some room to expand production and employment opportunities in rural areas, although doing so would create challenges to exporting related to higher lead times and intricate chain logistics. These challenges would have to be weighed. This rural strategy would be more feasible to implement in countries where distances are shorter (as in Sri Lanka) or in countries with multiple apparel and manufacturing clusters (like Vietnam) that enable rural areas to be better connected.

Increase the Number of Female Supervisors and Upgrade Apparel Jobs to Manufacturing-Related Services

A good starting point to support women's transition to longer-horizon working trajectories is to increase the number of women in supervisory positions—and in apparel, the most realistic way to advance is to become a line leader or production supervisor. These workers also fall into the production category, but they need to have secondary or technical education and account for only a small percentage of all apparel workers. Note that, in apparel, workers are split between production (75–90 percent) and knowledge-intensive, high-skill services (10–25 percent). Within production, 70–80 percent work on the production line, and 5–10 percent are supervisors.

Although tasks performed in food processing, furniture production, electronic assembly, or medical supplies manufacturing are different from those in apparel manufacturing, the skills associated with supervisory work are less industry-specific and can enhance opportunities for job mobility across industries. In other words, promotions within the apparel industry will not only increase the earnings and benefits for working women in apparel but also increase their prospects of remaining in the labor market. For example, if such women interrupt their work lives to attend to childcare responsibilities, they can return to the labor market through either apparel or other manufacturing industries.

IMPLEMENT INTERNSHIPS AND SKILL-SPECIFIC TRAINING PROGRAMS

One way for women to move up to the supervisory level is through skill-specific training programs. Training ensures that workers have the necessary skills for the position, increases female participation and confidence in their abilities, and exposes men to females in leadership positions, which can also help to change male perceptions that females are less capable.

These programs should target female workers and account for the barriers they face, such as the cost of the program, lack of gender-specific facilities, and travel. To address cost concerns, the government can subsidize employers directly to incentivize them to hire and train women. For example, Saudi Arabia's Support Women's Jobs in Factories program subsidizes women's salaries and training for up to six months while they receive training in computer, English, managerial, and behavioral skills (Kronfol, Nichols, and Tran 2019). Further, locating training institutes near factories in industrial areas can minimize the number and scale of transportation options that need to be developed.

In Bangladesh, a free six-week training program was offered to 80 apparel factories to promote women to supervisory roles. Before the training, both genders perceived women to be less capable than men across all skill areas needed to be a supervisor. Females also rated themselves as being weaker than existing supervisors across all areas, whereas male participants did not. After the training and after the women worked on the line as supervisors, the performance gender gap completely closed and male operators exposed to the female trainees improved their view of females as supervisors (Macchiavello et al. 2020).

Development and implementation of such programs can benefit from collaboration with experienced foreign or multinational organizations. In Bangladesh, the Gender Equality and Returns (GEAR) initiative of the Better Work program—a collaboration between the International Labour Organization (ILO) and the World Bank Group's International Finance Corporation (IFC)—has made significant strides in advancing women's economic potential and improving access to better jobs and opportunities. GEAR is scaling up to train 700 female operators to promote career-progression opportunities for women in the ready-made garment sector. In the first phase, GEAR trained 144 female workers, of whom 58 are now in supervisory roles. GEAR-promoted female supervisors also saw a 39 percent average increase in salary, and lines led by GEAR-trained females saw an average increase of 5 percent in efficiency. The program also offers a three-day Supervisor Skills Training program (ILO and IFC 2019).

FOCUS PROGRAMS ON SUPPLYING EMPLOYABLE GRADUATES

Programs to upskill female production workers that are aligned with the evolving needs of the manufacturing industries will not only help include more women in mid-skill occupations but also support a long-run industrial upgrading strategy. Increasing education or training will not raise the number of jobs and careers available for women if labor demand is insufficient to absorb the newly educated women. Shortages and gaps between curriculum and industry are common barriers across LMICs. Workers and training programs for supervisors are often scarce in the apparel industry (Quang et al. 2020).

Vocational and short-term training can be particularly effective for filling industry skill gaps when employers and training providers work together. In Indonesia, women who attended junior vocational school instead of junior regular school were more likely to join the labor force at the end of their studies (ADB 2015). Investing in training by funding the development of relevant programs and providing benefits to factories to train workers is a key opportunity to upskill workers and increase female participation in mid-skill positions. Countries should form industry and skills councils, develop national skills development strategies, and use these programs to support female inclusion and permanence in the labor force.

When educational programs and industry priorities are aligned, greater opportunities for employment emerge. Industry-relevant skills training in emerging sectors has been shown to support the development of such industries and support female employment within them. In Nigeria, a World Bank project that provided information and communication technology (ICT) training to female university graduates increased by almost 30 percent their likelihood of working in the ICT industry after graduating (Croke, Goldstein, and Holla 2018).

Where do our case countries fit in? As income and education rise in each one, a policy that considers training in industry can also take place in services. In Sri Lanka and Turkey, thanks to their relatively high income and education levels, there is room to expand domestic professional services. In both, more than one out of every three working women have at least upper-secondary education, making these countries good candidates to support higher-skill service industries for women pursuing higher educational attainment for careers. These women may particularly benefit from specialized training in specific professional service industries that have higher labor demand and require industry-specific skills.

In Sri Lanka, Turkey, and Vietnam, a stronger footprint across manufacturing sectors—combined with sufficient average education levels and training—creates an opportunity to further expand women's opportunities in manufacturing-related services, such as in the wholesale, logistics, and distribution stages of the supply chain. Wholesale firms are also top employers of clerks, an occupation that plays an important role in facilitating the jobs-to-careers transition. In Egypt, a bigger move into services may also be relevant, although its income per capita suggests that such a shift may be limited to urban areas.

Increase Access to Education to Promote Female Participation in Careers

Expanding education matters for all countries because it is an enabler for women to stay in the labor market—the primary characteristic of a career. In industry, although careers are related but not limited to HSOs, other career paths are also feasible considering on-the-job experience and permanence in the labor market. Whether countries succeed in fostering more-advanced sectors with mid-skill occupations (like clerks or supervisors), HSOs (like managers, professionals, or technicians), or both, will depend on higher education levels and industrial upskilling or diversification programs.

INCREASE UPPER-SECONDARY ENROLLMENT AND INDUSTRY ENTRY POINTS

Differences in educational attainment between men and women are among the reasons why females represent a lower share of higher-skill positions in apparel factories in LMICs (ILO and IFC 2018a). Among our country cases, this applies to Bangladesh, Cambodia, and Pakistan, where education levels are still quite low and where a very small share of the female workforce has at least an upper-secondary education—a level that is typically necessary to meet the basic requirements for clerical and supervisory roles or for managerial and professional jobs. In Cambodia and Pakistan, limited primary education is also a major issue because a large share of women still have not completed any formal education. In Bangladesh, despite significant improvements in the number of females enrolled in primary education, only 23 percent of Bangladeshi women have completed lower-secondary education.

In Bangladesh, Cambodia, and Pakistan, another issue is the education gender gap at the upper-secondary and higher levels. Stipend programs for girls' enrollment in primary, secondary, and upper-secondary schools can be an effective solution to increase female enrollment and achieve better gender balance, as proven in Bangladesh (Rahman and Islam 2013). A similar program could be created in Cambodia and Pakistan as well and extended to the upper-secondary levels.

In countries where relatively few females have tertiary education, programs are needed that provide scholarships and stipends to young females to stay in school to pursue careers in the apparel industry. Female apparel-factory workers are often from rural households that depend on the daughter's wages to support the family. Education and training institutions should provide information on opportunities in the apparel industry and factories. Many apparel companies or external organizations can offer scholarship opportunities to the children of apparel workers to pursue advanced education in exchange for returning to the factory for a set number of years. Communication channels between education and training institutes and industry are also needed so that individuals who have completed relevant courses can be connected with potential employers (JICA 2017).

REDUCE GAPS IN INFORMATION ABOUT AVAILABLE CAREER PATHS

It is also vital that programs aimed at keeping women in school communicate the potential earnings of different careers. A wider understanding of the economic returns captured by high school and university graduates can encourage a greater investment in education (Jensen 2010). For example, information that breaks down occupational characteristics such as average hours, education, and salary can help job seekers make informed decisions.

This report provides evidence of the latter, including that upper-secondary education is highly rewarded in the labor market—by wage premiums in Pakistan of almost 90 percent and in Vietnam of almost 50 percent. Information on the potential earnings from a given career path should also be readily available to parents so they can make the necessary human capital investments. The reality is that even if the financial means exist, decisions are often made with limited knowledge about the job market or educational opportunities.

Although most occupations in apparel manufacturing are production workers, about 15 percent of the workforce are high-skilled. Unlike supervisors, these workers are rarely promoted from the factory floor. For example, in Sri Lanka, female line managers stated that a lack of a higher education required for top-level positions was a barrier to career advancement (Kuruppuarachchi and Surangi 2020). Management positions typically require degrees in textile engineering, quality, or production management; a master's in business administration; or a diploma or a certificate along with experience in technical design. But these courses tend to be less popular among females than stitching and fashion design courses (JICA 2017), making a case for actively promoting them.

In all our case countries, there are opportunities to increase female participation in HSOs. Nearly all careers in Bangladesh, Egypt, Pakistan, and Turkey are held by men; the shares of men and women are equal in Sri Lanka; and women in careers outnumber men in Cambodia and Vietnam (see chapter 3). The number of HSOs available in apparel varies by firm and country and depends on the firm's business model. Egypt, Sri Lanka, and Turkey have the most potential, given current gender ratios and the availability of women with at least upper-secondary education. What is needed now is to raise female awareness of these programs and career paths and to incentivize and enable females to choose apparel careers and educational programs—as is being done in two innovative programs in the United States and Bangladesh (box 5.2).

BOX 5.2 North Carolina and Bangladesh: Programs That Spotlight Apparel Careers

North Carolina Textile Foundation

Industry leaders created the North Carolina Textile Foundation in 1942 as a nonprofit charitable and educational corporation to aid and promote all types of textile education and research at North Carolina State University (Wilson College of Textiles, n.d.). It administers more than 100 scholarships each year at the Wilson College of Textiles, including 10 full scholarships to incoming students (full tuition, stipend to study abroad, leadership development, and networking opportunities). A similar foundation and scholarship program could be created in apparel exporting countries to recruit talented young females to enter textile degree programs.

The College of Textiles also offers the Summer Textile Exploration Program (STEP) to rising high school seniors—a model that apparel exporters could use to raise awareness and interest in textile careers among upper-secondary students. Both programs also offer an opportunity to highlight female leadership in the industry by including female instructors.

Pathways for Promise

The Pathways for Promise initiative of the Asian University for Women (AUW) in Chittagong, Bangladesh, aims to boost the number of women in leadership positions and

(Box continues next page)

BOX 5.2 North Carolina and Bangladesh: Programs That Spotlight Apparel Careers *(continued)*

offers exposure to female leadership. It provides full scholarships for female workers from disadvantaged backgrounds to earn bachelor's degrees and provides a year of coursework for women without adequate secondary education to prepare for entry into university studies (Karim 2020).

The program started in 2016 and graduated its first class in December 2020, of whom four were Bangladeshi garment workers. The women also received a monthly stipend equivalent to their monthly wages during their studies to offset the loss of wages from not working in a garment job. Without this stipend, they could not have left the workforce for five years, because their families relied on the income (Karim 2020).

The AUW also fills a big educational gap by providing a learning environment that is tailored to females and free of charge. Females from 18 countries across Asia and the Middle East attend the university to pursue degrees in a range of subjects, and 85 percent of the students are on scholarship.

Although individual preferences play an important role in the job-versus-career decision, gender stereotypes and social norms also have significant effects. Gender stereotypes often portray an image of occupations that are suitable for women (Schomer and Hammond 2020). But these social norms may limit expectations—and planning and investment in education—along with possibly conveying inaccurate information about the availability, earnings, and skills needed for different occupations, especially in "male-dominated" fields. It is also vital to ensure that vocational guidance counselors do not perpetuate gender-based stereotypes, as has occurred in Vietnam, where training instructors advised women against pursuing traditionally male careers (Buchhave et al. 2020).

Further, women tend to have smaller professional formal or informal networks than men, resulting in less information about the needs and opportunities of employers and career pathways as well as fewer referrals to apparel firms that are hiring. Portals that allow firms to share job postings outside their networks and create organizations or groups that help women to network are potential solutions to increase females' awareness of job and educational opportunities.

Break Glass Ceilings

Lack of skills and awareness of opportunities can hinder female labor participation. Expanding education, upskilling occupations, and upgrading or expanding apparel and manufacturing industries can certainly pave the way for women to enter and stay in the labor market.

However, individuals are highly influenced by the laws and social norms surrounding them, and it is possible that women lack the right incentives to join the labor market because of cultural norms. For example, women might choose not to continue their education or to work because of the asymmetric household responsibilities assigned by traditional gender roles. Women might also be passed over for promotion or unfairly dismissed from work as a result of gender discrimination. For women to pursue career paths—either through long-term investments in education or through job experience and permanence—policy makers have a responsibility to define a gender-equal structure of work in terms of labor market and family policies.

REFORM LEGAL BARRIERS THAT REDUCE WOMEN'S EMPLOYMENT OPPORTUNITIES

Vast legal constraints to equal employment must be addressed across occupations. Indeed, most of our case countries do not have laws to guarantee equal pay or equal access to certain occupations—and persistent gender wage gaps may reflect the impact of lacking such measures. Further, all our country cases except Cambodia either have laws that prohibit women from working in certain industries (ranging from manufacturing or mining to services) or lack antidiscrimination laws that would protect women in the workplace. Many countries impose legal restrictions on women's entry, permanence, and mobility in the labor market (table 5.2).

Women, like men, should be given the choice to decide whether a job is appropriate, regardless of gender or parental status. When a country's laws limit women's ability to equally participate in the labor market, they broadly signal that country's perception of gender equality and norms.

TABLE 5.2 **Summary of Laws Limiting Gender-Based Employment Discrimination in Seven Middle-Income Countries, 2020**

Country	Equal remuneration by law	Dismissing pregnant women is prohibited	Discrimination in employment based on gender is prohibited	Women can do the same night work as men	No mobility restrictions for women	Women can work in the same industrial jobs as men
Bangladesh	X	X	X	✓	✓	X
Cambodia	X	✓	✓	✓	✓	✓
Egypt, Arab Rep.	X	✓	✓	X	X	X
Pakistan	X	X	✓	X	X	X
Sri Lanka	X	✓	X	X	✓	X
Turkey	✓	✓	✓	✓	✓	X
Vietnam	✓	✓	✓	✓	✓	X

Source: Elaboration from the World Bank's Women, Business and the Law 2020 database.
Note: A checkmark designates the existence of the specified legal provision, and an X the lack of it.

Working schedules are also limiting in some countries, and there are no safeguards for job permanence for pregnant women. In Sri Lanka, laws prohibit women from working more than 9 hours per day or 48 hours in a week.[1] Egyptian and Pakistani women could not work night shifts until recently, when such restrictions were lifted, but the reformed law imposes costs on employers (such as following certain security measures or obliging them to provide safe transportation during night shifts).

It is also important to identify barriers that inhibit female employment that may not be covered as part of legal requirements and to enforce sanctions for noncompliance. For example, a review of advertisements for top managers and supervisors in Vietnam found that 65 percent specified a male gender requirement (Chang, Rynhart, and Huynh 2016). Hiring solely based on gender might even be considered nondiscriminatory in some regulatory frameworks.

Moreover, governments must ensure that policies do not reinforce gender norms. For instance, maternity leave labels women as the primary caregiver and can direct women into jobs that offer time away from work and discourage employers from hiring women because of maternity leave costs. In our country cases, maternity leave ranges from 84 to 180 days, which means prolonged detachment from the workforce. If a woman has multiple children, this can result in detachment from the workforce for one or two years. Time away from work is necessary for a woman to have a child, and laws are necessary to protect a woman's job while she is away. However, women may not want to take the full allotted amount of time away from work or may prefer to fulfill the same number of tasks in a shorter time or to work a reduced schedule (Das and Kotikula 2019).

Several alternative options exist. For instance, childbirth benefits can be separated into time away from work and a remuneration package to cover childbirth-related expenses. Providing time off to men and women is another option that signals equal roles for men and women regarding childcare responsiblities. Shifting the cost of maternity and paternity benefits from employers to social security systems spares employers from bearing a cost that applies to only one gender. Among our country cases, only Turkey and Vietnam cover the cost of leave after childbirth (and only for mothers).

Although the presence or absence of laws is not the same as enforcement (and a more in-depth analysis is warranted), there is a general alignment between FLFP and gender equality laws. Cambodia, Turkey, and Vietnam tend to have the fewest restrictions on women's employment, whereas Bangladesh, Egypt, Pakistan, and Sri Lanka have the most. Thus, there is a pressing need for policy makers to take steps to remove these obstacles.

Governments have a role in coordinating far-reaching reforms that address multiple problems and engage different stakeholders. Such efforts can include reforming family laws, combating workplace harassment, banning discrimination in hiring and wages, and even strengthening trade policy. Not all policies addressing gender inequality in the labor market must deal with economic incentives or reforming laws. Trade reforms can have gendered effects that benefit certain female-dominated industries such as apparel.

For example, Indonesia's tariff reductions resulted in the expansion of female-dominated industries, which in turn reduced employment segregation (Das and Kotikula 2019).

PROMOTE INCLUSIVE WORKPLACE PRACTICES

Workplace practices ranging from workspace configuration to interaction styles can either facilitate or deter women's entry, stay, and advancements in their work. Thus, it is important to promote those practices that make industries and occupations welcoming to women.

Apparel factories are clustered in similar geographic areas or industrial zones, which offers an opportunity to create targeted programs. Given that few factories provide childcare facilities to workers or allowances for external childcare, governments could increase access to childcare facilities in geographic areas with high concentrations of female workers. In these areas, governments would also ideally ensure that there are sufficient secondary and tertiary schools and affordable housing opportunities to enable families to increase savings, which would in turn support the intergenerational pathway to careers.

In addition, governments can adopt reforms to address gender equity, whether in the apparel industry or the general labor market. For example, past reforms to address sexism at work in the Middle East and North Africa—a region supported by the work of national specialized councils to develop and support these reforms—made it one of the regions that has registered the most advancement on this issue, although much remains to be done (World Bank 2020).

Further, companies may need to make female employment a strategic priority and even shift to a female-dominated workforce to provide an environment that is acceptable to women without adding excessive costs. For example, men and women may prefer to work in separate areas of the factory; require separate restroom facilities and prayer rooms; and need benefits such as transportation, maternity leave, or childcare, which add extra costs to employers (JICA 2017).

Similarly, companies may need to address workplace harassment, which will require clear mechanisms (including predetermined consequences for the perpetrators and protection for whistleblowers). Harassment and fear of harassment are major workplace barriers for women throughout the economy (Das and Kotikula 2019). For example, harassment is associated with low job satisfaction, low productivity, absenteeism, and withdrawal. Further, fear of harassment can discourage women from joining male-dominated industries or joining the labor market altogether.

ENGAGE FOREIGN SUPPORT AND INVOLVEMENT

The countries with low FLFP are also the ones with the highest levels of sexism (as discussed in chapter 3). In these countries, most firms are domestic rather than foreign owned, and research suggests that foreign-owned firms tend to employ more women (World Bank and WTO 2020). These findings suggest that a way to help overcome the obstacles posed by social barriers would be to increase the involvement of foreign firms and organizations—particularly from countries whose cultural norms are less sexist and in industries that tend to be more female intensive. The results might be difficult to quantify, but if countries are unaccustomed to women in the workforce, familiarizing them with female workers might begin to overcome that important barrier.

Among our country cases, Cambodia and Vietnam have the highest shares of foreign direct investment (FDI) in the apparel industry and the highest FLFP rates. In Cambodia, foreign firms also provide more formal employment and higher manufacturing wages than domestic firms (Helble and Takeda 2020). And in China, foreign manufacturing affiliates from countries with more gender-equal cultures (according to the United Nations Development Programme's Gender Inequality Index) employ proportionally more women, appoint more female managers, and generate cultural spillovers: the domestic firms' female labor share increases with the prevalence of foreign affiliates in the same city (Tang and Zhang 2021).

However, in countries with foreign-owned firms and liberal expat labor policies, the government must first encourage skill transfer to nationals and then enable women to pursue HSOs, given that a large FDI presence can also lead to shortcomings. In Cambodia, the dominance of foreign-owned firms has meant that few decisions are made locally, thus significantly reducing opportunities for industrial upgrading of jobs for women. In fact, it has the lowest share of HSOs in apparel among our sample countries. Whereas most production workers are female, the few HSOs that do exist are filled mostly by male foreign expats (ILO and IFC 2018b).

Multinational lead firms are increasingly supporting programs to support gender equality—from education to leadership training and life skills. Apparel-specific examples include Nike (The Girl Effect, Adolescent Girls Initiative), Gap Inc., and H&M. For example, Gap and the Better Work program collaborated to create the Workplace Cooperation program, now the Better Work Academy (Pike 2020). Foreign multinationals are often the first to employ female workers in untraditional positions such as service sector workers.

International institutions can partner with the private sector to encourage progress in making gender equity a priority. In apparel, the Better Work program of the ILO and IFC is a prime example of such an organization. Better Work is an initiative to improve working conditions in garment factories and promote private sector competitiveness in global supply chains. Its activities include advisory services, tailored training, a dynamic information management system, and a practical workplace assessment tool for measuring compliance with international labor standards (ILO and IFC 2018b).

Conclusion

This report's four policy recommendations seek to increase the probability that women will enter the labor market and that apparel exporting countries will foster environments that support female career development. Industrial alignment and diversification, education expansion and skill training, and combating conservative norms have intertwined synergies. More jobs or careers in an industry will not secure positions for women if their human capital is too low or if cultural barriers limit their hiring. Nor can educated women increase their labor participation if their skills are not aligned with available occupations or if childcare responsibilities reduce their available working time.

These sets of recommendations will need a decisive commitment from governments to be enacted. However, no recommendation alone will suffice to achieve the transition from jobs to careers. To achieve the goal of bringing more women into higher-skill, longer-horizon, better-paid, and more life-fulfilling occupations, national programs should consider their simultaneous implementation. Fortunately, today, thanks to vast empirical evidence on successful policies, the "quiet revolution" of women's advancement from jobs to careers need not take the 100 years that it took in the United States.

Note

1. Sri Lanka, Factories Ordinance (No. 45 of 1942), Part VII, Sec. 67. https://www.ilo.org/dyn/natlex/docs/ELECTRONIC/47666/88132/F1807109239/LKA47666.pdf.

References

ADB (Asian Development Bank). 2015. *Women in the Workforce: An Unmet Potential in Asia and the Pacific*. Manila: ADB.

Aguilar, A., E. Gutiérrez, and P. Soto. 2019. "Benefits and Unintended Consequences of Gender Segregation in Public Transportation: Evidence from Mexico City's Subway System." *Economic Development and Cultural Change* 69 (4): 1379–410.

Bamber, P., J. Daly, S. Frederick, and G. Gereffi. 2019. "The Philippines: A Sequential Approach to Upgrading in Manufacturing Global Value Chains." In *Development with Global Value Chains: Upgrading and Innovation in Asia*, edited by D. Nathan, M. Tewari, and S. Sarkar, 107–31. Cambridge: Cambridge University Press. doi:10.1017/9781316221730.005.

Bamber, P., and S. Frederick. 2018. "Central America in Manufacturing Global Value Chains (GVCs): Apparel, Medical Devices and Wire Harnesses." Report for the Inter-American Development Bank, Duke Global Value Chains Center, Durham, NC.

Buchhave, H., W. Cunningham, G. Tam Nguyen, and N. Weimann-Sandig. 2020. "Perceptions of Gender Disparities in Vietnam's Labor Market." Study, World Bank, Washington, DC.

Chang, J.-H., G. Rynhart, and P. Huynh. 2016. "ASEAN in Transformation: Perspectives of Enterprises and Students on Future Work." Working Paper No. 11, Bureau for Employers' Activities, International Labor Organization, Geneva.

Croke, K., M. Goldstein, and A. Holla. 2018. "Can Job Training Decrease Women's Self- Defeating Biases? Experimental Evidence from Nigeria." Policy Brief Issue No. 28, Gender Innovation Lab, World Bank, Washington, DC.

Das, S., and A. Kotikula. 2019. "Gender-Based Employment Segregation: Understanding Causes and Policy Interventions." Jobs Working Paper, Issue No. 26, World Bank, Washington, DC.

Frederick, S., and J. Daly. 2019. "Pakistan in the Apparel Global Value Chain." Research report for the World Bank, Duke Global Value Chains Center, Durham, NC.

Goldin, C. 1984. "The Historical Evolution of Female Earnings Functions and Occupations." *Explorations in Economic History* 21 (1): 1–27.

Goldin, C. 2006. "The Quiet Revolution That Transformed Women's Employment, Education, and Family." *American Economic Review* 96 (2): 1–21.

Helble, M., and A. Takeda. 2020. "Do Women Benefit from FDI? FDI and Labor Market Outcomes in Cambodia." Working Paper No. 1093, Asian Development Bank Institute, Tokyo.

ILO and IFC (International Labour Organization and International Finance Corporation of the World Bank Group). 2018a. "Better Work Annual Report 2018: An Industry and Compliance Review. Jordan." Geneva: ILO.

ILO and IFC (International Labour Organization and International Finance Corporation of the World Bank Group). 2018b. *BetterWork Global Gender Strategy 2018–2022*. Geneva: ILO.

ILO and IFC (International Labour Organization and International Finance Corporation of the World Bank Group). 2019. "Bangladesh Factories Set for More Female Supervisors." Report on the Gender Equality and Returns (GEAR) initiative, Better Work website, March 13. https://betterwork.org/2019/03/14/bangladesh-factories-set-for-more-female-supervisors/.

Jensen, R. 2010. "The (Perceived) Returns to Education and the Demand for Schooling." *Quarterly Journal of Economics* 125 (2): 515–48.

JICA (Japan International Cooperation Agency). 2017. "Social and Gender Survey Report." Report of 2016–17 survey by the JICA Project for Skills Development and Market Diversification (PSDMD) of Garment Industry in Pakistan, Lahore.

Kabeer, N. 2013. *Paid Work, Women's Empowerment and Inclusive Growth: Transforming the Structures of Constraint*. New York: UN Entity for Gender Equality and the Empowerment of Women (UN Women).

Karim, N. 2020. "Garment Workers to Graduates: Bangladeshi Women Aim to Shake Up Textile Sector." Reuters, July 26. https://www.reuters.com/article/us-bangladesh-workers-education-trfn/garment-workers-to-graduates-bangladeshi-women-aim-to-shake-up-textile-sector-idUSKCN24S002.

Kotikula, A., M. Pournik, and R. Robertson. 2015. "Interwoven: How the Better Work Program Improves Job and Life Quality in the Apparel Sector." Report No. 99729, World Bank, Washington, DC.

Kronfol, H., A. Nichols, and T. T. Tran. 2019) "Women at Work: How Can Investment Incentives Be Used to Enhance Economic Opportunities for Women?" Policy Research Working Paper 8935, World Bank, Washington, DC.

Kuruppuarachchi, K. A. P. S. T., and H. A. K. N. S. Surangi. 2020. "The Glass Ceiling and Women Career Advancement: A Study Based on Ready-Made Garment Industry in Sri Lanka." *Kelaniya Journal of Management* 8 (2): 18–39.

Macchiavello, R., A. Menzel, A. Rabbani, and C. Woodruff. 2020. "Challenges of Change: An Experiment Promoting Women to Managerial Roles in the Bangladeshi Garment Sector." Working Paper 27606, National Bureau of Economic Research, Cambridge, MA. doi:10.3386/w27606.

Muralidharan, K., and N. Prakash. 2017. "Cycling to School: Increasing Secondary School Enrollment for Girls in India." *American Economic Journal: Applied Economics* 9 (3): 321–50.

Pike, K. 2020. "Impacts on the Shop Floor: An Evaluation of the Better Work – Gap Inc. Program on Workplace Cooperation." Better Work Discussion Paper No. 40, International Labour Organization, Geneva.

Quang, T. T., N. Pimpa, J. Burgess, and B. Halvorsen. 2020. "Skills Development in the Vietnamese Garment Industry: The Engagement of the Vocational Education Institutions and Industry." *International Journal of Entrepreneurship* 24 (2): 1–10.

Rahman, R., and R. Islam. 2013. "Female Labour Force Participation in Bangladesh: Trends, Drivers and Barriers." Asia-Pacific Working Paper Series, International Labour Organization, Geneva.

Schomer, I., and A. Hammond. 2020. "Stepping Up Women's STEM Careers in Infrastructure: An Overview of Promising Approaches." Energy Sector Management Assistance Program (ESMAP) Paper, Report No. 150758, World Bank, Washington, DC.

Tang, H., and Y. Zhang. 2021. "Do Multinationals Transfer Culture? Evidence on Female Employment in China." *Journal of International Economics* 133: 103518.

Wilson College of Textiles. 2021. "Wilson College Giving." North Carolina State University. https://textiles.ncsu.edu/giving/nc-textile-foundation.

World Bank. 2020. *Women, Business and the Law 2020.* 6th ed. Washington, DC: World Bank.

World Bank and WTO (World Trade Organization). 2020. *Women and Trade: The Role of Trade in Promoting Gender Equality*. Washington, DC: World Bank.

APPENDIX A

Data, Methodology, and Supplementary Tables

Methodology and Data Description

The basis for describing economic activities throughout this volume is the International Standard Industrial Classification of All Economic Activities (ISIC) system. The ISIC system is composed of divisions identified by a single letter, and 2- to 4-digit codes to provide increasing levels of detail (UN DESA 2008). It can be used to group economic activities into the three broad sectors: agriculture, manufacturing, and services (table A.1). This report uses the term "industry" to refer to a 2-digit ISIC code. Occupations are defined using the International Standard Classification of Occupations (ISCO), composed of 10 major groups (ILO 2012).[1]

TABLE A.1 ISIC Industry Classifications Used in This Report, by Broad Sector

Sector	Industry, ISIC Rev. 3.1	Industry, ISIC Rev. 4
Agriculture (including forestry, fishing, and mining)[a]	Sections A–C: codes 01–14	Sections A–B: codes 01–09
Manufacturing	Section D: codes 15–37	Section C: codes 10–33
Services	Sections E–Q: codes 40–99	Sections D–U: codes 35–99

Sources: UN DESA 2002, 2008.
Note: Broad sectors are defined under the International Standard Industrial Classification of All Economic Activities (ISIC) system, which groups economic activities under agriculture, manufacturing, and services. ISIC Rev. 3.1 and ISIC Rev. 4 divisions and codes designate industries as classified in UN DESA (2002) and UN DESA (2008), respectively.
a. Mining is not included in the definition of agriculture in the Mincerian equations calculated for regressions in the empirical analysis of gender wage gaps (chapter 2, annex 2A).

Although the terms "industry" and "global value chain" (GVC) are often used synonymously, they have different meanings, particularly when using data based on industrial classification systems. GVCs are composed of a series of activities that span multiple industries and economic sectors. For example, the apparel GVC spans all three sectors: agriculture, manufacturing, and services. "Inputs" come from agriculture (natural fibers such as cotton and wool). "Components" are part of the textile manufacturing industry, and "assembly" is part of the apparel manufacturing industry. Distribution, design, and branding are services carried out by wholesalers, retailers, and myriad other service sectors (Frederick 2019). In many manufacturing GVCs, downstream segments tend to be more labor intensive and upstream segments are more capital intensive.

To analyze labor market outcomes across industries and occupations, we use micro-level labor force survey (LFS) data (details in table A.2). The estimated statistics are generally consistent with those reported by the International Labour Organization or the World Bank. LFS data are linked to standardized classifications of industries and occupations. Some countries use the international systems (ISIC and ISCO) directly, while others use national systems that correlate to the international systems. These classification systems change over time, and time series analysis requires harmonization. Whenever possible, our analysis uses the version of ISIC and ISCO used in the original survey or as provided by the statistics agency to minimize harmonization impacts. We always use the national currency reported.

Education Analysis Issues and Methodology

LFS data on education were converted to number of years and then standardized, to the extent possible, across countries. This enabled us to report education data based on number of years or by shares in education level groups. The available number of education levels varies significantly by country (from 7 to 25 options in the LFS); to standardize them, we had to determine the range of options available across countries and calculate to accommodate countries with fewer options (table A.9).[2] Education groups are based on completion of education in that group; any reported values that fall below completion were moved to fewer years of education to facilitate harmonization across countries.

Like data in the previous chapters, education data were reviewed to determine accuracy and alignment with other reports using the same underlying data sources. Years of data determined to be unreliable are not used. In Bangladesh, for example, the education standardization was possible only for the last two rounds of the LFS for which we have data (2013 and 2016), but only the 2013 results are aligned with previous reports. We convert unstated, blank, or "don't know" answers to missing values. In Bangladesh's 2016 LFS, the latter issue accounts for 22 percent of total observations.

Supplementary Tables

TABLE A.2 **Labor Force Survey Sources and Correlating ISIC and ISCO Data Versions, by Case Country**

Country	Survey name, provider	LFS data years	ISIC version, years	ISCO version, years	ISIC3.1 years	ISIC4 years
Bangladesh	LFS, Bangladesh Bureau of Statistics	2005, 2010, 2013, 2016	ISIC4, 2010–16	ISCO-08, 2013–16[a]	2005	2010–16
Cambodia	Cambodia Socio-Economic Survey (CSES), National Institute of Statistics	2007–09, 2011–14	ISIC4, 2007–14	ISCO-08, 2009–14	2004–08	2009–14
Egypt, Arab Rep.[b]	Economic Research Forum, Central Agency for Public Mobilization and Statistics (CAPMAS)	2009–15	ISIC4, 2009–17	ISCO-88, all	n.a.	2009–17
Pakistan	LFS, Pakistan Bureau of Statistics (PBS)	2008–09, 2010–15	ISIC4, 2013–15	ISCO-08, 2013–15	2008–12	2013–15
Sri Lanka[c]	LFS, Department of Census and Statistics	2007–08, 2011–15	ISIC3.1, all	ISCO-08, all	All	n.a.
Turkey[d]	LFS, Turkish Statistical Institute (TURKSTAT)	2011–13	ISIC4, 2011–13	ISCO-08, 2012–13	n.a.	2012–13
Vietnam[e]	LFS, General Statistics Office (GSO)	2007, 2009–13, 2015	ISIC4, 2007–15	Unknown (ISCO-88)	n.a.	2009–15

Source: World Bank.
Note: ISIC3.1 and ISIC4 refer to the *International Standard Industrial Classification of All Economic Activities (ISIC)* Rev. 3.1 and Rev. 4, respectively (UN DESA 2002, 2008). ISCO-08 and ISCO-88 refer respectively to the 2008 and 1988 versions of the *International Standard Classification of Occupations* (ILO 1990, 2012). LFS = labor force survey; n.a. = not applicable.
a. For the 2005 data year, occupations are based on an earlier version of ISCO (ISCO-88), which was problematic for harmonization with recent systems, so analysis begins with 2010.
b. Data were received from CAPMAS in ISIC4 and ISCO-88 (4-digit level). Any conversions between versions were performed by CAMPAS before receiving the data. Data years 2005–08 are excluded because of discrepancies in employment data.
c. Data year 2005 is omitted because data collection halted that year in response to the effects on Sri Lanka of the 2004 Indian Ocean earthquake and tsunami.
d. Surveys for 2001–08 cover only broad sectors (1-digit level) so cannot be used. The 2009 and 2010 surveys are unusable because the age variable contains values from 1 to 14, and the 2014–17 surveys are not used because of problems in the weight factor variable.
e. Data for 2008 are omitted because wages are not available, and we do not have data for 2014. The ISCO occupation data change between 2008 and 2009.

TABLE A.3 Informal Employment, by Broad Sector and Selected Industries, in Case Countries

Share of informal employment in total employment (%)

Sector and industry	ISIC4/ISIC3.1 industry codes[a]	Bangladesh, 2016	Egypt, Arab Rep., 2015	Pakistan, 2015	Sri Lanka, 2015	Vietnam, 2015	Turkey, 2013
Overall	n.a.	87	63	–	78	81	37
Agriculture sector	1–9/1–14	99	96	–	96	99	82
Manufacturing sector	10--33/15–37	71	52	63	76	52	20
Food manufacturing	10/15	78	48	61	83	73	22
Textiles	13/17	80	34	51	78	53	32
Apparel	14/18	56	60	80	64	46	32
Leather	15/19	77	76	68	77	15	33
Services sector	34+/40+	83	51	74	68	72	23
Retail	47/52	96	85	98	93	94	31
Food/beverage services	56/55	97	80	93	87	97	37
Public administration	84/75	9	2	0	9	22	5
Education	85/80	32	7	16	31	15	3
Human health services	86/85	46	12	33	29	20	2
Other personal services	96/93	97	89	98	97	98	52
Activities of households	97/95	96	95	97	98	100	84
Computers/electronics	26/30, 32, 33	36	20	18	73	13	5
Financial services	64/65	13	7	0	32	15	1
Agriculture	1–9/1–14	100	96	99	89	99	–
Non-agriculture	10–90/15–99	91	47	71	62	57	–
Total	1–99/1–99	95	60	83	70	76	–

Source: Labor force survey data.

Note: Employment data include both genders. Color-coded rows designate the three employment groups defined in chapter 3 as follows: orange shading for agriculture and informal domestic service industries, blue shading for light manufacturing and retail and food/beverage services, and green shading for skilled professional service industries. The bottom three rows of data are from International Labour Organization ILOSTAT data, "Statistics on the informal economy," (1997–2020); ILO data for Bangladesh represent 2017. Turkey is excluded from the ILO data set. Pakistan does not collect data on informality for agricultural industries; thus, an overall estimate is not presented. Cambodia is not listed due to lacking informality data. n.a. = not applicable; — = not available.

a. ISIC industry codes are from *International Standard Industrial Classification of All Economic Activities (ISIC) Rev. 4* (ISIC4) except for Sri Lanka, which uses ISIC Rev. 3.1 codes.

TABLE A.4 **Average Monthly Wages in Local Currency, by Industry, in Case Countries**

Industry	ISIC4/ISIC3.1 code[a]	Bangladesh, 2016 (Tk)	Cambodia, 2014 (CR)	Egypt, Arab Rep., 2015 (LE)	Pakistan, 2015 (PRs)[b]	Sri Lanka, 2015 (SL Rs)	Turkey, 2013 (TRY)	Vietnam, 2015 (D)
Crop/animal production	01/01	7,579	222,586	2,311	5,828	12,213	368	1,224
Food manufacturing	10/15	10,456	258,045	2,438	9,364	21,130	804	2,702
Textiles	13/17	10,251	223,213	2,514	10,357	18,617	743	2,891
Apparel	14/18	11,853	327,513	1,999	9,565	19,262	733	2,848
Leather	15/19	10,504	338,805	2,193	9,152	17,771	730	3,214
Retail	47/52	10,329	429,994	2,031	7,020	21,045	768	2,947
Food/beverage services	56/55	10,942	274,665	2,216	8,123	23,941	727	2,634
Public administration	84/75	22,711	366,678	3,076	18,169	34,319	1,786	3,352
Education	85/80	18,868	391,264	2,730	17,311	31,807	1,531	3,683
Human health services	86/85	20,939	505,370	2,497	17,218	39,174	1,607	3,633
Other personal services	96/93	9,414	243,552	1,993	5,839	17,008	582	2,657
Activities of households	97/95	7,692	–	1,651	5,320	13,935	472	1,965
Computers/electronics	26/30	17,801	1,305,978	4,159	18,277	–	1,355	3,619
Financial services	64/65	32,840	629,687	4,406	28,730	37,050	1,757	5,146
Minimum wage (years)	n.a.	5,300 (2013–17)	323,000[c] (2013–20)	1,200 (2014–18)	13,000 (2015)	12,500 (2016–20)	1,022 (2013)	3,100 (2015)
Female average	n.a.	11,112	316,033	2,017	10,426	21,531	978	1,869
Male average	n.a.	12,123	387,053	2,425	13,321	25,348	1,064	2,881

Sources: Labor force survey and International Labour Organization data.
Note: Wage data include both genders. Wages in local currency. Minimum wage data, from International Labour Organization ILOSTAT, "Statistics on wages" (2010–2020), refer to the minimum monthly earnings of all employees as of December 31 of each year. In cases where a national minimum wage is not mandated, the minimum wage in place in the capital or major city is used. In some cases, an average of multiple regional minimum wages is used. In countries where the minimum wage is set at the sectoral level or occupational level, the minimum wage for manufacturing or unskilled workers is generally applied. — = not available.
a. ISIC industry codes are from *International Standard Industrial Classification of All Economic Activities (ISIC) Rev. 4* (ISIC4) except for Sri Lanka, which uses ISIC Rev. 3.1 codes.
b. Pakistan data cover the private sector only.
c. Cambodia minimum wage is for garment employees only.

TABLE A.5 Average Monthly Wages in the Apparel Industry, by Gender, and the Gender Wage Gap in Case Countries

Country, gender	Average monthly wages, apparel		Change, first to last year (%)	Years of data	Female-male wage gap, first and last year	Average monthly wages, all industries, for last data year
	First year	Last year				
Bangladesh, female (Tk)[a]	5,996	10,084	68	2010–16	1.1 to 1.3 apparel 1.1 to 1.1 overall	11,112
Bangladesh, male (Tk)[a]	6,680	13,354	100			12,123
Cambodia, female (CR)	212,938	323,300	52	2009–14	1.2 to 1.1 apparel 1.2 to 1.2 overall	316,033
Cambodia, male (CR)	248,028	340,784	37			387,053
Egypt, Arab Rep., female (LE)	1,463	1,643	12	2009–15	1.2 to 1.3 apparel 1.1 to 1.1 overall	2,017
Egypt, Arab Rep., male (LE)	1,701	2,208	30			2,425
Pakistan, female (PRs)	1,898	6,908	264	2008–15	3.9 to 1.4 apparel 1.4 to 1.3 overall	10,426
Pakistan, male (PRs)	7,372	9,702	32			13,321
Sri Lanka, female (SL Rs)	8,686	16,929	95	2008–15	1.6 to 1.5 apparel 1.2 to 1.2 overall	21,531
Sri Lanka, male (SL Rs)	14,045	24,642	75			25,348
Turkey, female (TRY)	615	662	8	2011–13	1.3 to 1.2 apparel 1.1 to 1.1 overall	978
Turkey, male (TRY)	784	793	1			1,064
Vietnam, female (D)	1,548	2,707	75	2007–15	1.4 to 1.3 apparel 1.4 to 1.5 overall	1,869
Vietnam, male (D)	2,228	3,403	53			2,881

Source: Labor force survey data.

Note: All wages are in local currencies. All countries based on *International Standard Industrial Classification of All Economic Activities (ISIC) Rev. 4* (ISIC4) classifications except for Sri Lanka, which uses ISIC Rev. 3.1 codes.

a. According to the World Bank's Bangladesh Jobs Diagnostic (World Bank 2017, 48–9), average monthly wages in the garment sector increased from Tk 6,500 to Tk 9,200 (2010 and 2016), and monthly wages in nongarment manufacturing sector increased from Tk 7,200 to Tk 9,000. The 2010 Jobs Diagnostic data for the garment sector are like ours; the 2016 data are lower (but likely represent the full year, whereas ours do not). The Jobs Diagnostic results also show that wages increased more for apparel manufacturing than for nonapparel; however apparel wages were initially lower.

TABLE A.6 **Average Monthly Wages for Females and Both Genders, Manufacturing and All Industries, by Case Country**

Industry	Bangladesh, 2016 (Tk)[a]	Cambodia, 2014 (CR)	Egypt, Arab Rep., 2015 (LE)	Pakistan, 2015 (PRs)	Sri Lanka, 2015 (SL Rs)	Turkey, 2013 (TRY)	Vietnam, 2015 (D)
Manufacturing, both genders	12,399	584,189	1,785	14,035	20,802	1,969	5,231
Overall, both genders	12,915	625,347	1,829	15,559	24,139	2,211	5,127
Manufacturing, female	10,981	555,633	1,285	5,822	16,282	1,674	4,927
Overall, female	12,106	553,236	1,690	10,255	21,769	2,187	4,917
Average minimum wage (years)	5,300 (2013–17)	323,000 (2013–20)	1,200 (2014–18)	13,000 (2015)	12,500 (2016–20)	1,022 (2013)	3,100 (2015)

Source: International Labour Organization (ILO) minimum wage (1980–2020) and monthly wage from labor force survey (LFS) data.
Note: All wages are in local currencies. Based on *International Standard Industrial Classification of All Economic Activities (ISIC) Rev. 4* (ISIC4) across countries; manufacturing represents ISIC4 Division C. ILO and LFS data are for same years, except for Turkey (ILO is 2014 and LFS is 2013).
a. Bangladesh labor force survey 2016 data is for only half the year.

TABLE A.7 Occupational Shares of Apparel Manufacturing Employment, by Case Country

Share of total apparel employment (%)

			Occupational category			
Country	Industry and Occupation Classification Codes	Year	Managers, professionals, technicians (codes 1–3)	Clerks, service (codes 4–5)	Craft and plant (codes 7–8)	Elementary (code 9)
Bangladesh	ISIC4, ISCO-08	2016	9	4	85	2
Cambodia	ISIC4, ISCO-08	2014	1	1	98	1
Egypt, Arab Rep.	ISIC4, ISCO-88	2015	13	3	81	3
Pakistan	ISIC4, ISCO-08	2015	4	1	92	3
Sri Lanka	ISIC3.1, ISCO-08	2015	11	4	76	9
Turkey	ISIC4, ISCO-08	2013	7	5	68	19
Vietnam	ISIC4, ISCO-88	2015	4	4	89	3

Source: Labor force survey data.
Note: Data represent both male and female employment. Skilled agriculture is not included because it makes up less than 1 percent of the apparel workforce. ISCO-08 = *International Standard Classification of Occupations, ISCO-08* (ILO 2012); ISCO-88 = *International Standard Classification of Occupations (ISCO-88), 1988 Edition* (ILO 1990); ISIC4 = *International Standard Industrial Classification of All Economic Activities Rev. 4* (UN DESA 2008); ISIC3.1 = ISIC Rev. 3.1 (UN DESA 2002).

TABLE A.8 Education Levels of Apparel Industry Employees, by Case Country

Share of total apparel employees (%)

Country (year)	No formal education	Primary	Lower secondary	Upper secondary	Tertiary
Bangladesh (2013)	10	36	33	16	6
Cambodia (2014)	27	42	23	7	1
Egypt, Arab Rep. (2015)	30	12	10	40	8
Pakistan (2015)	32	23	36	7	3
Sri Lanka (2015)	0	3	57	39	1
Turkey (2013)	12	42	29	13	4
Vietnam (2015)	3	17	42	31	6

Source: Labor force survey data.
Note: Data cover both men and women and refer only to completed education levels.

TABLE A.9 **Details of Education Level Data Used for Standardized Analysis, by Case Country**

Education level	Grades (range)	Years of education (range)	Years of education	Approx. ages (years)	Bangladesh	Cambodia	Egypt, Arab Rep.	Pakistan	Sri Lanka	Turkey	Vietnam
Do not know, missing values, and "other" group (converted to missing values)	n.a.	n.a.	Omit	n.a.	Do not know (code 98)	Do not know (code 98), Other (code 21)	Missing values (none for 2009–15)	n.a.	Missing values (minimal)	n.a.	Missing values (minimal; 0.1% in 2015)
No formal education completed or less than primary	None–Grade 4	0–5	0	0–10	No class passed (codes 00 and 99), Class 1, 2, 3, 4	No class completed (code 0), preschool or nursery, primary classes 1–5	None, illiterate, read only, read and write, literacy classes or certificate, never attended school	No formal education or currently not enrolled, nursery, KG	No schooling	Less than six years; Literate but not completed any education	Never attended school, not completed primary
Completed primary (and < lower secondary completed)	Grades 5–7	6–8	5	11–13	PSC, Class 6, 7	Completed primary (year 6), Completed years 7–8 (6)	Primary (6)	Primary (8)	Passed Grade 0–4 or Years 1–5	Primary	Primary
Completed lower secondary or middle school (and < upper secondary completed)	Grades 8–11	9–11	9	14–17	JSC, Class 9, 10 (10)	Completed years 9–11, Lower ed. certificate or diploma, Tech. or voc. presecondary diploma or certificate	Preparatory	Middle, Matric (final exams 9th or 10th grade) (both 10)	Passed Grade 5–7 or Years 6–8 (8), Passed 9.5 (11)	Secondary	Lower secondary, primary vocational training

(Table continues next page)

TABLE A.9 **Details of Education Level Data Used for Standardized Analysis, by Case Country *(Continued)***

Education level	Grades (range)	Years of education (range)	Years of education	Approx. ages (years)	Bangladesh	Cambodia	Egypt, Arab Rep.	Pakistan	Sri Lanka	Turkey	Vietnam
Completed upper secondary or high school (and < tertiary completed)	Grade 12–partial university	12–13	12	18–22	SSC, HSC, diploma	Class 12 complete without certificate, Higher education certificate, technical or vocational postsecondary diploma or certificate, College or university undergraduate (no degree)	Academic secondary, professional or vocational secondary (12), Postsecondary or equivalent (14)	Intermediate	GCE(O/L) or NCGE, GCE(A/L) or HNCE (13)	High school, Vocational or technical high school (11)	Upper secondary, secondary vocational, secondary professional
Completed tertiary or college and postgraduate	> 12	14–17	16	22–24	Bachelors	Bachelors	University (16)	Graduation in engineering, medicine, computers, agriculture, other subjects	Degree	Higher-education graduate (15)	Vocational college, college
		18–21	18	24+	Masters	Masters	Postgraduate	MA, MSc, or MPhil	Postgraduate degree	–	University and above
		22+	22	26+	PhD	PhD	–	PhD	–	–	–

Source: Labor force survey data.
Note: GCE(A/L) = General Certificate of Education Advanced Level; GCE(O/L) = General Certificate of Education Ordinary Level; HNCE = Higher National Certificate of Education; HSC = higher secondary certificate; JSC = junior school certificate; KG = kindergarten; NCGE = National Certificate in General Education Examination; PSC = primary school certificate; SSC = secondary school certificate; — = data not available for that category.

Notes

1. ISCO codes are not comparable at the 1-digit (major group) level between ISCO-88 (adopted in 1988) and ISCO-08 (adopted in 2008), and therefore results over time are not comparable without harmonizing systems at the 2- to 4-digit levels.
2. Reports from Scholaro Inc.'s online education database were used as a reference to determine the education level options by country and the equivalence of years of education between education systems.

References

Frederick, S. 2019. "Apparel Skills Mapping and Functional Upgrading in Cambodia: Jobs Diagnostic." Unpublished manuscript, World Bank, Washington, DC.

ILO (International Labour Organization). 1990. *International Standard Classification of Occupations (ISCO-88), 1988 Edition*. Geneva: ILO.

ILO (International Labour Organization). 2012. *International Standard Classification of Occupations, ISCO-08, Volume I: Structure, Group Definitions and Correspondence Tables*. Geneva: ILO.

UN DESA (United Nations Department of Economic and Social Affairs). 2002. *International Standard Industrial Classification of All Economic Activities (ISIC), Rev. 3.1*. New York: United Nations.

UN DESA (United Nations Department of Economic and Social Affairs). 2008. *International Standard Industrial Classification of All Economic Activities (ISIC), Rev. 4*. New York: United Nations.

World Bank. 2017. "Bangladesh Jobs Diagnostic." World Bank, Washington, DC. https://openknowledge.worldbank.org/handle/10986/28498.

ECO-AUDIT

Environmental Benefits Statement

The World Bank Group is committed to reducing its environmental footprint. In support of this commitment, we leverage electronic publishing options and print-on-demand technology, which is located in regional hubs worldwide. Together, these initiatives enable print runs to be lowered and shipping distances decreased, resulting in reduced paper consumption, chemical use, greenhouse gas emissions, and waste.

We follow the recommended standards for paper use set by the Green Press Initiative. The majority of our books are printed on Forest Stewardship Council (FSC)–certified paper, with nearly all containing 50–100 percent recycled content. The recycled fiber in our book paper is either unbleached or bleached using totally chlorine-free (TCF), processed chlorine–free (PCF), or enhanced elemental chlorine–free (EECF) processes.

More information about the Bank's environmental philosophy can be found at http://www.worldbank.org/corporateresponsibility.